Philosophy in the Twentieth Century

PHILOSOPHY
in the
TWENTIETH
CENTURY

A.J. Ayer

VINTAGE BOOKS
A Division of Random House
New York

First Vintage Books Edition, January 1984
Copyright © 1982 by A. J. Ayer
All rights reserved under International and Pan-American
Copyright Conventions. Published in the United States by
Random House, Inc., New York, and simultaneously in Canada by
Random House of Canada Limited, Toronto. Originally published
in the United States by Random House, Inc. and in
Great Britain by Weidenfeld & Nicolson Ltd. in 1982.

Library of Congress Cataloging in Publication Data
Ayer, A. J. (Alfred Jules), 1910–
Philosophy in the twentieth century.
Includes bibliographical references and index.
1. Philosophy, Modern—20th century.
I. Title.
B804.A818 1984   190'.9'04   83-47822
ISBN 0-394-71655-8

Manufactured in the United States of America

987654

To Vanessa

Contents

Preface

This contribution to the history of philosophy was originally conceived as a sequel to Bertrand Russell's *A History of Western Philosophy*. It fulfils this intention to the extent that it also confines itself to the West, that, apart from a revaluation of William James and a considerably expanded treatment of what Russell called Logical Analysis, including a chapter devoted to Russell himself, it takes up the story at the point where he left off, and that rather than mention a whole host of philosophers who have made some contribution to the subject, and devote a few lines to each, it deals with the work of a relatively small number of outstanding philosophers at some depth. There is, however, one area in which I have deliberately failed to follow Russell's example. It seemed to me that his excursions into social and political history did not throw much light upon the views of the philosophers with which he sought to associate them and I did not believe that I could improve on his performance. I have, therefore, been content to give a few biographical details about the philosophers on whom I concentrate and in certain cases to refer to the ways in which they influenced one another.

It will be seen that the greater part of the book is devoted to the representatives of two main schools for which I have a personal predilection, the American pragmatists, ranging from William James and C. I. Lewis in the earlier part of this century to my near contemporaries Nelson Goodman and W. V. Quine, and what is loosely called the analytic movement, covering philosophers as diverse as Bertrand Russell and G. E. Moore, Ludwig Wittgenstein, Rudolf Carnap and other members of the Vienna Circle, C. D. Broad, Gilbert Ryle, J. L. Austin, the Americans Donald Davidson and Hilary Putnam, the Australian D. M. Armstrong, and, among my more recent colleagues at Oxford, Peter Strawson and Michael Dummett. I am not sure that Broad would have been pleased to find himself in this company, but if we consider the distinction that he drew between critical and speculative philosophy, his own work fell on the critical side. I have not ignored speculative philosophy, or metaphysics, and have chosen R. G. Collingwood as the metaphysician whose views I could most sympathetically expound.

To diminish what might appear to be a bias in favour of Anglo-Saxon thought, I have included a chapter on Phenomenology and Existentialism. Here I have concentrated mainly on the work of Maurice Merleau-Ponty, whom I regard as the best representative of this philosophical trend. If I have said nothing about Neo-Marxism, it is not because I fail to find any merit in the writings of such philosophers as George Lukács and Lucien Goldmann but because I did not think that I could improve on Leszek Kolakowski's treatment of these authors in the third volume of his *Main Currents of Marxism*. To have attempted to tackle structuralism would have meant too much of a diversion into literary criticism and anthropology.

Considerations of space, and my own inclinations, have limited my exposition of moral philosophy to the first half of this century. While paying tribute to the extraordinary progress that the subject of formal logic has made during the last hundred years, I have not entered into mathematical technicalities. This is not to say that I have fought shy of the philosophy of logic. On the contrary, one of the themes which emerges from my story is the shift of emphasis which is mirrored in the titles of two of Russell's books from *Our Knowledge of the External World* to *An Inquiry into Meaning and Truth*.

In writing about Russell, Moore, James, Ryle, the Vienna Circle, and also about essentialism, I have drawn rather freely on previously published work of my own. If these echoes disturb any of my readers, I can only ask for their forgiveness. My thanks, as so often before, are due to Mrs Guida Crowley for typing my almost illegible manuscript and otherwise helping me in preparing the book for the press. I am indebted also to Mrs Rosanne Richardson for her retyping of the chapter on Bertrand Russell, which I chose to revise.

A. J. AYER
51 York Street, London W.1
December 1981

Philosophy in the Twentieth Century

I   Philosophical Inheritance

One of the difficulties that faces the historian of philosophy is that his subject is not at all clearly demarcated for him. Not only has the prevalent view of its relation to other subjects, and especially to the natural sciences, been liable to frequent changes in the course of time, but at any given period there may be very wide differences in the aims and methods of those who are deemed to be engaged in its pursuit. This would not be a very serious matter if it came to no more than the fact that the word 'philosophy' was used rather loosely. If the different sorts of enquiry to which it was applied could be effectively distinguished, we could attach different labels to them, and leave to the lexicographers the drudgery of deciding whether the whole set of labels was to be grouped under the heading of 'philosophy' or whether some different grouping, which gave a narrower sense to the term, was more advisable. Unfortunately, the position is not so simple. We do, indeed, distinguish different branches of philosophy, such as logic, the theory of knowledge, the philosophy of mind, the philosophy of language, ethics and political theory, but the conflicting views of the aims and methods of philosophy operate within these branches themselves, even to the point where it is disputed whether some alleged branch of the subject, such as metaphysics, is a genuine pursuit at all, and here the differences are seldom, if ever, so straightforward as a disagreement about the correct or most fruitful application of a word. They are traceable rather to different conceptions of the world and of man's position in it.

It is because these differences are so persistent that philosophy is exposed to the charge, which is frequently brought against it, especially by natural scientists, that it fails to exhibit any progress. Problems which were raised by Plato and Aristotle in the fourth century BC are still discussed, and the work of all the intervening centuries has brought us no nearer to finding a solution of them which even a majority of contemporary philosophers would accept. I believe this charge to be unjust, even though the appearances are in its favour. What must be conceded is that if there is any progress in philosophy it does not take the linear form which characterizes the progress of a natural science. The historian of physics can show how the Ptolemaic system of astronomy was supplanted in the fifteenth century by the heliocentric system of Copernicus, how the Copernican system led to the development a century later of the theories of Kepler and Galileo, how these theories were improved and incorporated in Newton's classical mechanics, how Newton's principles came into conflict in the nineteenth century with the electromagnetic theory of Clerk Maxwell, himself building on the discoveries of Faraday, and how the conflict was resolved in Einstein's theories of relativity. The speculations, say, of Kepler may still be profitably studied in their historical context, but they do not still stand as rivals to the theories of Einstein. Like the instruments of technology, the theories of physics work for a time and are then superseded. The transition is not always smooth, but however revolutionary the new theory may be, however much, like the quantum theory, it breaks with established concepts, once it has proved its value as a tool of explanation and prediction, it wins general acceptance.

It is otherwise with philosophy. The historian of philosophy can, indeed, trace the influence of one philosopher upon another, especially within the confines of what is represented as a particular 'school'. He can show, for example, how Berkeley reacted against Locke and in what ways Hume followed and repudiated both of them. He can go even further and establish the connections between members of different schools. He can show the extent to which Descartes, the seventeenth-century founder of modern western philosophy, still makes use of mediaeval concepts. He can show how Kant was inspired by what he saw as the need for refuting Hume, and what Hegel in his turn owed to Kant. There is, however, no question of one of these philosophers superseding another, except in the sense that his work may enjoy a period of greater popularity. One can still maintain, without forfeiting one's claim to competence in philosophy, that Hume was right and Kant wrong on the point at issue between them, that Locke came nearer to the truth than either Berkeley or Hume, that as against Kant it was Hegel who took the wrong turning. One can still be a Platonist while fully understanding

Aristotle's criticism of Plato, and without being ignorant of all the positions that different philosophers have taken in the centuries that have passed since Plato lived.

In what then can the progress in philosophy consist? To find an answer, we must, I think, look not to the contributions which have been made to the subject by a series of eminent persons, but rather to the evolution of a set of perennial problems. Chief among them perhaps is the problem of objectivity, appearing sometimes as a source of division between realists and idealists, sometimes as the issue between absolute and relativistic theories of truth. The fundamental question is whether, and to what degree, it is possible for us to describe things as they really are, independently of their relation to ourselves: and here, if a relativistic position is taken, it has to be decided whether the frame of reference is supplied by human beings in general, by one or other society, by a society at different stages of its development, or simply by oneself. The division between realists and idealists also has many facets, comprising as it does a number of conflicting views concerning the constitution of mind and matter and their mutual relation, this question calling in its turn for an enquiry into the character and scope of human knowledge.

The assessment of our capacity for knowledge not only provides a principal point of entry for the philosophical sceptic, recurrently posing a challenge, which stimulates theory by calling for a fresh response, but also sets the stage for another deep division of philosophers into rationalists and empiricists. Here again the dispute takes different forms, according as the lines between reason and experience are more or less sharply drawn, but overall it is the mark of an empiricist that he looks to sense-perception, if not as the sole legitimate source of any true belief about the 'external' world, then at least as a final court of appeal which any acceptable theory must satisfy. The stumbling-block for anyone who holds a position of this sort is the development of the 'pure' sciences of logic and mathematics, which seem to possess a security which sensory observation could not bestow on them. One way of dealing with it has been to deny them this security by making the difference between them and the propositions of the natural sciences at most a difference of degree, so that they too are open to revision in the light of further experience. Another has been to grant them their security but to treat it as a gift that we bestow upon them. On this view, they do no more

3

than spell out the consequences of the meanings that we attach to logical or numerical signs. They are useful as tools of inference, but not descriptions of reality. A compromise put forward by Immanuel Kant, at least with regard to mathematics, is that its propositions owe their necessity to their stemming from our ordering of the world in space and time, which is a pre-condition of its being accessible to our understanding. This makes them descriptive not of reality as it is in itself but of the outcome of the way in which we are bound to process it, or rather of our contribution to this outcome. Whether this special form of relativism, which is peculiar to Kant and his followers, should be accepted is again a matter for dispute.

While empiricists concur in giving the leading part to sense-perception in their theories of knowledge, they do not all take the same view of what sense-perception is. The most common opinion, which John Locke, officially regarded as the founder of modern empiricism, inherited from the rationalist René Descartes, has been that the immediate objects of sight or touch or any other of our senses are what they both called 'ideas', conceived by them and by most, though not all, of those who have adopted a similar starting-point as mental entities which have no existence apart from the particular sensations in which they figure. For the most part, those who have held a position of this sort have treated the physical objects, which we are ordinarily said to see or touch, as mediate objects of perception. They are represented as being known to us only by inference as the causes of our sensations. This raises the problem how the inference can be justified and allows also for disagreement concerning the nature of these objects. How far do they resemble their sensory effects? Other philosophers, also claiming to be empiricists, have opposed the introduction of anything like 'ideas' as the immediate data of sense, on the ground that it artificially imprisons us in private worlds, and have conceived of physical objects as directly perceptible. In their case, the question has arisen whether they are doing justice to the scientific evidence, which anyhow creates a problem for all theories of perception. They need to explain how the particles, or other objects, which answer to the concepts of contemporary physics, are related to the physical objects of everyday discourse, which are credited with perceptible qualities by common sense.

For rationalists, mathematics tends to serve as a paradigm, not only because of the certainty which is claimed for it, but above all because of its employment of deductive reasoning. The rationalist typically holds that men are endowed with a faculty of intellectual intuition. Truth is ascribed to the propositions which this faculty authenticates and to everything that follows logically from them. The ideal is to discover the fewest possible number of self-evident premisses, which deductively yield a complete description of reality. When rationalism is blended with idealism, as in the case of Hegel and his followers, reality is identified with a coherent system of judgements rather than with anything outside the system to which its constituents might be supposed to refer. In some cases, such as that of Descartes, the deductive or would-be deductive method is used to vindicate the theories of contemporary science. In others, these theories are condemned as failing to satisfy the demands of reason. Thus, the neo-Hegelians Bradley and McTaggart were not afraid to maintain that neither space nor time nor matter were ultimately real. The drawing of so sharp a distinction between appearance and reality has, indeed, been a relatively uncommon feature of western philosophy, but even more circumspect rationalists, like Leibniz and Spinoza, who saw their systems as according with the science of their day, gave accounts of the world which were greatly at variance with the beliefs of common sense. One reason for this is that the tendency of common sense has been to take the evidence of sense-perception at its face value, whereas in all rationalist systems sense-perception is downgraded. An outstanding example is provided by Plato, who advanced the view that the mutable objects of everyday acceptance owed the inferior degree of reality that he was willing to accord them only to their participation in a timeless system of abstract forms, by which the standard of reality was set.

That abstract entities are real, let alone that they serve as a model for the assessment of reality, has not been an uncontested thesis. It figures in yet another area of constant philosophical dispute. This dispute has several facets, of which the most prominent has been what is technically known as the problem of universals. The simplest definition of a universal is that it is either a quality or a relation, and the problem of the status of qualities and relations is bound up with the conflicting views that have been taken both of their connection with one another and of their connection with the particular things, if any, which they characterize. The extreme antithesis to Plato's theory of forms is the 'nominalist' view that there is nothing more to things having a common quality than our choosing to apply the same

5

label to them. In the interval, we find the view of Aristotle that universals are real, though not independently of the things in which they inhere; the 'conceptualist' theory, which found some favour in the Middle Ages, that concepts are mental but things naturally fall under them; the theory, held by Leibniz, which tries to resolve relations into qualities, and its converse, the more moderate form of nominalism, in which common qualities are replaced by special relations of similarity, which sort out objects into sets, united in each case by their resemblance to some particular exemplar.

It may seem strange that Berkeley, who upheld nominalism in this form, also maintained that things were bundles of qualities. This was because he could discover no sense in the notion of material substance: a rejection which other empiricists have extended to any sort of substance, conceived, after Locke's fashion, as 'an unknown somewhat', supporting some collection of properties. Among philosophers who have found the need to distinguish particular concrete objects from their properties, there has been disagreement over the questions whether or not these particulars can be numerically different, while sharing all the same general properties, whether the possession of any or all of their properties is necessary for their being what they are, whether we are bound to conceive of some of them at least as persisting through time, or whether they can be 'reduced' to a series of events. Nor is it only the notion of substance that has been put in question. Properties too have been considered suspect, and it has been suggested that they give way to classes which would then be the only abstract entities that we should countenance. This suggestion has, however, been opposed in its turn, on the ground that the admission of classes violates the 'nominalistic' principle that no two entities can have the same basic content. If, for example, I am allowed to distinguish myself from the unit class of which I am the only member, and this class from the class of classes in which it shares membership with the null-class, which has no members at all, I can multiply entities to any extent I please. One way of countering this logical extravagance has been to deny the existence of anything but individuals. It might be thought that this was yet another condemnation of abstract entities, but that turns out not to be so. In this form of nominalism an individual need not be something that can be sufficiently distinguished from other things of its kind by its spatio-temporal location, which is what is required of a concrete particular.

An abstract entity, like a colour, is counted as an individual if it functions as a single element in various composite wholes. All nominalists agree in accepting William of Ockham's famous principle, familiarly known as Ockham's razor, that entities are not to be needlessly multiplied. If this still allows them to differ over the question what entities are needed, it is mainly because they are at odds, not only with the rationalists but also with one another, in their responses to the deeper question what constitutes the need.

Attempts have been made to dispose of the Platonic view of universals by ascribing it to what is said to be the obvious error of construing general terms as names. Whatever the force of this argument, it does bring out the point that there is a close connection between the different views taken of the relative status of particulars and universals and different interpretations of our use of singular and general terms. For instance, the rejection of common qualities in favour of relations of similarity is an obvious offshoot of the thesis that we come to understand general terms through a process of abstraction which leads us to select the different ways in which things resemble one another. Another example is the manifest parallel between the thesis that things are bundles of qualities and the belief that singular terms can be transmuted into predicates. More generally, the reality attributed to abstract entities has been considered by some as essential, and by others as fatal, to the development of an adequate theory of meaning. The question is how a series of sounds, or written marks, succeed in functioning as signs of something other than themselves. Clearly, it is not merely a matter of their physical constitution. The mere fact that a written mark has such and such a size and shape cannot account for its being a singular or general term. It is not the acoustic qualities of a series of noises that alone make them form an indicative sentence, the utterance maybe of a truth or falsehood. If sounds and inscriptions assume the character of words and sentences, it is because they are so interpreted. But in what does this interpretation consist? A simple answer to this question is that it consists in our being induced by them to focus our attention upon one or other of a range of abstract entities. So the concatenation of the letters 'r', 'e' and 'd' in that order becomes an inscription of the English word 'red' by presenting an English speaker with the concept of redness. The same office is performed for a French speaker by the sequence of letters 'r', 'o', 'u', 'g' and 'e'.

7

Similarly, the English sentence 'All is lost save honour' and the French sentence 'Tout est perdu fors l'honneur' are supposed to acquire meaning, and in this case the same meaning, because they are both understood to 'express' the proposition that all is lost except honour. Such concepts and propositions are supposed to exist objectively, whether or not they are ever brought to anyone's attention. Neither does it matter to their existence whether the concepts actually apply to anything, or whether the propositions are true or false.

This theory is more nakedly exposed to an objection of the same order as that which the advocates of a common-sense treatment of perception brought against the 'theory of ideas'. It can be argued that the interposition of abstract entities between our utterances and the actual things we want to talk about constitutes a barrier rather than a bridge. Neither does our being treated to such statements as that sentences mean propositions serve to provide us with any explanation of meaning: it is as if we wanted to know about nutrition and were told no more than that what we eat is food. A causal approach, in which signs are treated as stimuli, appears more fruitful; but the attempts which have been made so far to relate the meaning of signs to the occasions of their utterance and the associated behaviour of their interpreters have come a long way short of fulfilling their promise. It may be that we have to take some semantic notion such as that of 'truth' or 'reference' as primitive, but even on this favourable basis the construction of a satisfactory theory of meaning has yet to be achieved.

Similar divisions are found in the sphere of moral philosophy. Here too the claim has been made that we can know by intuition that actions of such and such a type are absolutely right or wrong, or that such and such states of affairs are intrinsically good or evil. Those who maintain a position of this type may differ in their opinion of the relations that moral terms like 'right' and 'good', 'duty' and 'obligation' bear to one another, but they agree in taking at least one of them to apply to a property that its possessors really have, independently of their effects upon us or our attitudes towards them. Such properties are held to be 'non-natural', in the sense that although they may be supervenient upon the physical and mental properties of their possessors, they do not themselves fall into either class.

Some philosophers who have refused to allow that the truth of moral propositions can be known by intuition have adopted the view that moral qualities are the objects of what they have called a moral sense. This is more than a nominal dispute, since those who believe in a moral sense would dismiss non-natural qualities as mythical. Their view of moral qualities is rather that they are analogous to colours, when these are treated not as intrinsic properties of physical objects but merely as 'ideas' which we receive from these objects through our physical senses. The truth of moral propositions is accordingly made to depend upon our responses to the situations to which they refer; whether it be the responses of the speaker himself, or those of the normal members of the society to which he belongs. There is, indeed, an extension of this approach which denies any truth-value to moral statements, except in so far as they are merely descriptions of the workings of accepted codes. Beyond this, they merely express the speaker's valuations, possibly with the intention that others will thereby be induced to share them.

These are not the only forms that a naturalistic theory of ethics may take. There has been a long tradition of identifying good with pleasure and evil with pain, and philosophers who have followed this tradition have sometimes maintained that it is right to seek most pleasure for oneself, more often that one should try to maximize utility, in the sense of bringing about 'the greatest happiness of the greatest number'. A view of this kind may also be taken by those who construe happiness in terms of the satisfaction of desire, without making the assumption that what is desired is only the achievement of pleasure or the avoidance of pain. There is, too, the question whether the criterion of utility, in this sense, is to be applied to the circumstances of each particular action, or whether it is sufficient that the action fall under some rule the observance of which is generally beneficial.

The conflict between rationalists and empiricists extends even to political theory. The issue here is whether one believes in such things as natural rights, or natural justice, or whether one finds a conventional basis for every form of political obligation in the view which the members of a given society take of their several or collective interests.

We have seen that rationalism and idealism do not always go together. When they do, as in the case of Hegel and his followers, they tend to be associated with monism, the conception of reality which lays stress on its unity. The opposition of monism and pluralism, which

9

again has many different aspects, is the third of the principal divisions in philosophy. In its extreme form monism sees it as a matter of logic that everything is unified. It is in this spirit that metaphysicians, since the time of Parmenides, who was born in the sixth century BC, have denied the reality of change and motion. In some cases their position has rested on the assumption that all relations are internal to their terms, in the sense that they help to constitute the identity of the things which they relate. Since any two things are somehow related, if only spatio-temporally, this has the startling consequence that we cannot refer to anything without referring to everything; for in saying that any one object exists, we shall be implicitly affirming the existence of all the others. Some metaphysicians, who have shrunk from drawing this conclusion, have adopted the hardly less ridiculous alternative that we never do succeed in referring adequately to anything, with the consequence, which they do not shrink from accepting, that nothing that we say about the world is ever altogether true.

The extreme form of pluralism is the assumption that all relations are external, with the consequence that the existence of any one object is logically independent of the existence of any other. A difficulty here is that logical independence is a function of the way in which the objects in question are described. An author's relation to his works is external, in the sense that he might have existed without writing them, but it is internalized by the description of him as their author. The position of the extreme pluralist, therefore, needs to be more carefully formulated. He must be understood to hold both that a great, perhaps infinite, number of things exist and that each of them is self-contained, in the sense that it is possible to find a way of describing its properties which is complete, to the extent that there is none of them that could not be added to the list, and also such that one never comes upon a relational property the possession of which is essential to the thing's identity. So stated, this is a very strong condition. It may have to be weakened a little to allow the pluralist's objects to occupy positions in space and time, for this will then be a facet of their identity, and their inclusion in a spatio-temporal system may be seen as a derogation from their independence. It will, however, be mitigated by the fact of its always being contingent that they occupy the spatio-temporal positions that they do. Even if it be necessary in the case of any given object x that there be some other objects which are spatio-temporally related to it, there will be no particular objects y and z to which it is necessarily so related.

If the elements of a system of this kind are observable, and there is also a method for deciding with respect to each of the properties whether a given element possesses it or not, then all the propositions which are descriptive of the system can be tested independently of one another. This is not, in general, true of scientific theories because of the relatively loose manner in which these theories are adjusted to the observational data by which they are sustained. The result is that when they run, or appear to run, foul of observation, there is never only a single way in which harmony can be restored. If the perceptual evidence is accepted, some part of the theory will have to be modified or sacrificed, but we have a liberal choice as to what changes we make. This point is sometimes made by saying that the propositions of a scientific theory face the verdict of experience, not individually but as a whole. Some philosophers take this 'holism' further, to the point of saying that every accredited observation puts the whole corpus of our beliefs at risk, but this is surely an exaggeration. Admittedly we cannot say in advance how far our enquiries will carry us: a chemical discovery may lead us to revise our ascriptions of works of art; a fresh piece of historical evidence may re-activate a medical hypothesis which had been too readily discarded. Nevertheless, the success of scientific experiments depends on our being able to treat small numbers of our beliefs as isolated from the rest. We should have no hope of lighting on particular causes and effects unless we could reduce the field of possible candidates to a manageable compass. We may never be quite sure that we have not overlooked some relevant factor, but if everything were relevant, nothing could ever be ascertained. Even at the height of an epidemic a doctor can, and indeed must, treat one patient at a time; nor would his practice be likely to be improved by an excursion into the politics of the early Roman Empire.

This is not to reject the monistic view that everything can ultimately be explained in terms of the laws that govern the behaviour of homogeneous particles. It is at most to insist that even if this were true, the application of these laws to particular cases would depend upon a limited number of particular circumstances. Whether any such view is to be accounted true is not a purely philosophical question. It comes within the province of the philosophy of science to decide what is to pass for the 'reduction' of one special science to another, of biology to chemistry, for example, or of chemistry to physics: but once the requirements are set, the question whether they can be fulfilled is a matter for scientific discovery. Again, once the conditions for homogeneity are fixed, the question whether they are satisfied belongs to physics. That the 'ultimate' particles of matter are homogeneous, in any unforced sense of this term, is not something that can be taken for granted in advance of physical theory and experiment.

Neither is the concept of matter itself unproblematic, any more than the concept of mind. These concepts are intertwined with those of publicity and privacy, but they do not run exactly parallel. For instance, shadows and reflections and mirages are public, but one might hesitate to call them material: thoughts are mental, but it is not immediately obvious that they are incapable of being shared. Some philosophers have maintained that thoughts are also physical. Their view has been that all events are physical, but that a few of them also answer to mental descriptions. Others have followed a monistic approach of the opposite kind. They have argued that the things which pass for physical objects are nothing but classes of sensations, whether actual or possible. Others again have held that both mind and matter are constructible out of 'neutral' elements of experience, the differences lying only in the difference of relations among these common elements.

Among the divergent views of this question, there is the view, held by Spinoza, that thought and physical extension are modes of a single substance, the view, held by Descartes and others, that there are both mental and physical substances, the view, held by Berkeley, that there are only mental substances, and the view, held by Hobbes and others, that there are only material substances but that some of these material substances have irreducibly mental properties. Among philosophers who have felt obliged to dispense with the concept of substance, replacing it with that of the co-currence of properties, the questions have again arisen whether these properties are uniquely mental, or uniquely physical, whether some are both mental and physical, or whether the properties are of these two distinct kinds, which are mutually irreducible, in the sense that members of the one class are neither logically nor physically identifiable with those of the other. This leaves open the question of their causal relationship, and here it has been held, alternatively, that they interact, that physical properties are causally dependent on mental properties, in the sense that they depend for their existence on being known, that mental properties are causally dependent on the physical state of the person who 'owns' them, however this person may be thought to be constituted, that mental properties have only mental effects, and that mental properties are causally inoperative, as being the effects of physical properties, but not themselves the causes of anything. This last view is held by those who believe that the physical world is a closed system; that everything that happens can be accounted for in physical terms, if it can be accounted for at all; but that there are mental occurrences, which are not themselves physical, though there may be physical explanations for them.

Finally, pluralism may take the form of denying that there is a single world, which is waiting there to be captured, with a greater or lesser degree of truth, by our narratives, our scientific theories or even our artistic representations. There are as many worlds as we are able to construct by the use of different systems of concepts, different standards of measurement, different forms of expression and exemplification. Our account of any one such world may be more or less accurate, our representations more or less acceptable, but when two rival systems come into conflict there may be no way of adjudicating between them. In that case there may be no sense in asking which is right. The strength of such a view is the truism that we cannot envisage a world of any sort, independently of some method of depicting it; its weakness is that it blurs the distinction between fact and fancy. For all the attractions of pluralism, we do not want to be driven into admitting that 'anything goes'.

I embarked on this review of philosophical standpoints with the avowed intention of showing that there can be progress in philosophy. It may, however, appear that I have achieved just the opposite. If so many conflicting theories remain in the field, each with its partisans, what issues can be said to have been even provisionally resolved? And if none of the issues has been resolved, in what can the progress be supposed to consist? I can answer this objection only by saying that the progress consists not in the disappearance of any of the age-old problems, nor in the increasing dominance of one or other of the conflicting sects, but in a change in the fashion in which the problems are posed, and in an increasing measure of agreement concerning the character of their solution. As in a guessing game, the players have not yet found the answers, but they have narrowed the area in which they can reside. I shall try to explain this in greater detail by making a number of specific points.

(1) An outstanding feature of twentieth-century philosophy, of whatever sort, has been the growth of its self-consciousness. Philosophers have been more seriously concerned with the purpose of their activity and the proper method of conducting it. This has been due mainly to two causes: first, the conspicuous progress made in the natural and, to a lesser extent, the social sciences, and, secondly, the detachment of philosophy from science which took place in the nineteenth century, partly through the sciences' insistence on their own autonomy and partly through the involvement of philosophy in the romantic movement. Though Kant, writing at the close of the eighteenth century, was able to talk of philosophy as the queen of the sciences, the restoration of this sovereignty has been neither conceded nor seriously claimed. In this connection it is interesting to note that there is a present tendency for formal logic to detach itself from the main body of philosophy, just for the reason that it is the one branch of the subject that has made continuous progress throughout the century in a scientific fashion, and consequently lays claim to scientific mastery of its own concerns.

(2) This is not to deny that there is scope for a philosophy of logic, just as there is scope for a philosophy of physics, a philosophy of history, a philosophy of law, or a philosophy of art. What has been recognized is that philosophy is not competitive with any of these subjects, though it may seek to bring illumination to them. The philosopher of art does not supply recipes for writing poems or for painting pictures: he does discuss the nature of symbolism, the sense, if any, in which a poem or a picture may lay claim to truth; he may try to supply criteria for the evaluation of a work of art. Similarly, the philosopher of physics does not engage in physical speculations: there are no new planets, or particles, that sweep into his ken. He may try to put a sharper edge on certain physical concepts, such as that of probability or the fulfilment of a function, but principally his is a task of interpretation. He examines the relation of physical theories to their evidence, the differences in their structure, the ways they evolve out of one another, their pretensions to objectivity, their compatibility with the assumptions of common sense.

(3)   The implication is that philosophy takes its subject-matter from elsewhere, whether it be from one or other of the arts or sciences, or the pre- and semi-scientific beliefs and discourse of everyday life. Its standpoint is critical and explanatory. One of the discoveries which has been made is that it lacks the capital for setting up in business on its own.

(4)   This does not preclude the elaboration of a world-view, though philosophical system-building has gone almost wholly out of fashion. It does, however, require that the world-view incorporate the deliverances of science and possibly also of the arts. What has been discarded is the idea that one can proceed deductively from allegedly self-evident first principles and arrive by pure reflection at a picture of the world, which has an independent claim to validity. Even those pluralists who talk of our making worlds are bound to admit that what we describe or express or exemplify is not entirely subject to our fancies. There are limits to what it will tolerate. If we have always to look through some pair of spectacles, not all of which yield the same results, we still have to look *through* them. Merely to wear them is not enough.

(5)   The common belief that 'it is the business of the philosopher to tell men how they ought to live', although it has the authority of Plato, is based upon a fallacy. The mistake is that of supposing that morality is a subject like geology, or art-history, in which there are degrees of expertise, so that just as one can look to an art-historian, in virtue of his training, to determine whether some picture is a forgery, one can look to a philosopher to determine whether some action is wrong. The philosopher has no such training, not because of any defect in his education but because there is no such thing as an authoritative guide to moral judgement, of which he could have acquired the mastery. So far as the conduct of life is concerned, he has no professional advantage over anyone else. The realization of this fact has tended in this century to lead moral philosophers to treat their subject as one of what is technically called the second order. Instead of trying to lay down moral maxims, they have concerned themselves rather with the definition of moral terms, the demarcation of judgements of value, the question whether, and if so how, they should be differentiated from statements of fact. More recently, without its being denied that these questions are important, there has been a tendency to ignore the ruling that moral philosophy should be

restricted to them. Even though he can claim no special expertise, there is no reason why a moral philosopher should not advance, let us say, a novel theory of justice, if he thinks it worthy of general acceptance. There is equally no reason why he should not apply his intelligence to the solution of concrete moral problems such as the question when, if ever, men have the right to kill. Whether those who embark on such topics should be said to be engaging in philosophy is a verbal question of very little interest. What counts is the breadth and soundness of their arguments.

(6)   A good example of the way in which a problem gains a sharper outline through long discussion is that of the stubborn question of the freedom of the will. The idea of there being a straightforward conflict between the thesis that all natural events, and consequently all human actions, are causally determined, and the thesis that men as moral agents elude the grasp of causal necessity, has proved to be deceptively simple. It conceals many knots that need to be untangled. In the first place, the thesis of determinism turns out to be empty, if it amounts to no more than the claim that every natural event can be brought under some generalization or other. It acquires content only when the laws which are supposed to reign in a given area are actually specified. Secondly, there is no call for any talk of necessity, unless it is simply a way of saying that the event in question fits into a causal pattern. The suggestion that it is therefore fated to occur is wantonly misleading. In fact, it has not yet been shown that human behaviour is subject to law, in the sense required, but the possibility that it will be found to be so cannot be ruled out. Let us suppose, for the sake of the argument, that the science of physiology advances to the point where it can provide explanations for all human behaviour. It would not follow from this that men's actions could not also be explained in terms of their desires and beliefs, any more than from the fact that the moves of a chess-playing machine may be explained in terms of its programming and construction it follows that they cannot also be explained in terms of their function in the game. In short, if it were proved that men's actions were causally determined, it would not impair their claim to be rational agents. But would it then follow that their wills were free? Again, this is not a clear issue. If the question is whether they were able to do what they had chosen, the answer is plainly that they very often would be. But this is not sufficient for the misguided theists who profess to find in God's gift of free will to men a

ground for relieving him of the responsibility for all the evils in the world which they suppose him to have created. They require not only that men be often free to do what they have chosen, but also that their choices themselves be free. But what are we to understand by this? That sometimes men's choices are causally inexplicable? That they do not always have reasons for choosing as they do? The first of these propositions must be held to be doubtful; the second may well be true. But even if they are both true, what is that to the purpose? Do we really want to conclude that men are responsible agents just to the extent that their actions are inexplicable? Our theist may protest that this is a travesty of his position. He wants to credit men with the power of self-determination. But what is this supposed to be? If it does not mean that men sometimes act spontaneously, or in other words that it is sometimes a matter of chance that they act as they do, it does not mean anything at all. But what sort of responsibility is it that is conferred only by chance? One can only conclude that the 'theological' concept of free will is utterly confused.

It is interesting to speculate whether this confusion extends to the concept of free will which is built into our everyday legal and moral judgements and also into the affective attitudes of pride or shame, gratitude or resentment, reverence or indignation, which the moral judgements sustain. I am strongly inclined to think that it does, and therefore that our moral and legal judgements should be disinfected of it. At the same time I doubt if it is in my power to give up such attitudes as I have mentioned in favour of a strictly scientific approach to myself and my fellow men, and I doubt if I should wish to, even if it were in my power. I think, therefore, that there is a case for retaining a muddled concept of free will, just in so far as the myths which it engenders are salutary.

(7)   It has recently been proclaimed as a discovery that philosophy studies human thought and that the clue to the study of human thought lies in the analysis of the use of language. The first of these propositions is too general to be of much interest, even when we discount the fact that there are ways of studying human thought, such as appear in the records of psychological experiments, which are not philosophical, though there is no reason why a philosopher, who is concerned, for example, with the mechanism of perception, should not draw upon their results. The second proposition also needs to be made more precise. The study of language has many facets and not all

of them have any obvious bearing on philosophy. It is not clear, for example, what philosophical moral is in general to be drawn from comparative philology, or from the tracing of etymologies, though here again there may be something philosophically suggestive in the different meanings given in different languages, or at different periods in the same language, to words such as we commonly translate as 'substance' or 'cause'. Nevertheless, it is true that many of the traditional problems of philosophy have revealed themselves as being closely connected with questions of language: the problem of self-identity, for example, with the analysis of the use of proper names and other singular terms, the problem of universals with the explanation of the use of general terms, the problem of truth with an account of the assertion of indicative sentences. There is also the point that analysing the use of words can be a way of revealing the nature of what the words designate. For instance, if we can specify the conditions under which the sentence form 'x remembers y' is satisfied, we have answered the question what memory is.

(8)   For my own part, I think that if one were looking for a single phrase to capture the stage to which philosophy has progressed, 'the study of evidence' would be a better choice than 'the study of language'. The study of evidence includes the study of language, since in order to discover what support propositions of one type bestow on those of another we need to know what is meant by the sentences by which the propositions are respectively expressed. Indeed, the two operations go together. Similarly, the enquiry into the nature of something such as memory through an analysis of the sentences in which words like 'remembering' occur can equally well be represented as a study of the grounds for the acceptance of memory-claims. But the study of evidence goes further, inasmuch as it does not limit us, as 'the study of language' appears to do, to elucidating the content of our beliefs, but also raises the question of our warrant for holding them; and this is surely a philosophical question when it is conceived in sufficiently general terms. Finally, we can give 'the study of evidence' a broad enough interpretation to make it cover two questions which have returned into the forefront of philosophical interest. What are we justified in taking there to be? and How far is what there is of our own making?

II The Revolt from Hegel

At the turn of the century idealism was dominant, mostly in forms inspired by the philosophy of Hegel. It is true that Marx and Engels had set out to 'turn Hegel on his head', retaining his dialectic while converting his idealism into materialism, but their views had made little impact on the philosophical world and among their disciples only the Russian Plekhanov, whose *Essays in the History of Materialism* appeared in 1896, had produced original work of any importance. A counter-acting force in Germany had been the school of Franz Brentano (1838–1916), whose leading disciple Alexius von Meinong had advocated an extreme form of Platonic realism, but the Phenomenology into which this movement was developed by Edmund Husserl (1859–1938),[1] though owing less to Hegel than to a one-sided view of Descartes, acquired an increasingly idealistic tinge. In the United States, the leading Hegelian, Josiah Royce, was confronted at Harvard and perhaps outmatched by the Platonist George Santayana and the Pragmatist William James. Indeed, William James, of whose work I shall be writing at length, was one of the main architects of the downfall of Hegelianism. His hostility to Hegel was not shared by the founder of Pragmatism, Charles Sanders Peirce, but much of Peirce's work remained unpublished in his lifetime, and his place as one of the outstanding nineteenth-century philosophers was not accorded to him until the second quarter of this century. In this he resembled the great German logician Gottlob Frege (1848–1925), whose writings on the philosophy of language and the foundations of mathematics were indeed published from the 1870s onwards, but not generally appreciated at their full value until very nearly the present day.

[1] See Chapter VII.

In England, the leading Hegelian was F. H. Bradley (1846–1924), whose devotion to the Absolute exceeded that of his master in that it led him to deny the reality of matter, space and time. Bradley and his disciple Harold Joachim were outnumbered at Oxford by the disciples of the professor of logic, J. Cook Wilson (1849–1915), an Aristotelian scholar who upheld a form of common-sense realism, but the work of the two Hegelians retains the greater interest. In particular, Joachim's book *The Nature of Truth*, which was published in 1906, contains the most concise and powerful statement of one important aspect of the Hegelian position. It is primarily an attack on the correspondence theory of truth, in favour of a coherence theory, on the ground that we cannot extract from the system of judgements which constitutes reality any opposing sets of terms between which the relation of correspondence could be supposed to hold. Since Joachim admits that we can never formulate the complete system of judgements which would be required for total coherence, as he interprets it, his book ends on a sceptical note.

The University of Cambridge also fostered a distinguished Hegelian in the person of J. Ellis McTaggart (1866–1925). Relying on more rigorous argument than Bradley, and making more of an effort to save the appearances, McTaggart nevertheless came to much the same negative conclusions. His major work, *The Nature of Existence*, was not published until 1921, but already in the 1890s he was exercising a considerable influence on the Cambridge school of philosophy. Among the younger men whom he imbued with his doctrine were Bertrand Russell and G. E. Moore. After a fairly short time they both reacted against him. Since their rejection of Hegelianism, especially in the case of Bertrand Russell, had a decisive bearing on the subsequent development of philosophy not only in England but in parts of Europe and throughout the English-speaking world, a history of twentieth-century philosophy may well begin with an account of their philosophical careers.

Bertrand Russell

Bertrand Russell was born in 1872 and died in 1970, some two months short of his ninety-eighth birthday. On both sides, his family belonged to the English Whig aristocracy, and he was a grandson of Lord John Russell, the famous Liberal statesman, who was three times Prime Minister, introduced the first Reform Bill of Parliament in 1832, and was later created the first Earl Russell. Bertrand Russell himself became the third Earl Russell on the death of his elder brother Frank in 1931. Both his parents having died before he was four years old, he was brought up by his paternal grandmother and privately educated. He won a mathematical exhibition to Trinity College, Cambridge, in 1890, switched to philosophy in his third year there and took his degree in 1894. He was a Fellow of Trinity from 1895 to 1901 and again, though mainly non-resident, from 1944 onwards, and a lecturer in philosophy there from 1910 to 1916 and from 1944 to 1949. Otherwise he held few academic appointments, though he was Visiting Professor at the University of Peking in 1920 to 1921, at the University of Harvard in 1914 and again in 1940, and occasionally for short periods at other American and British universities.

One reason for this was that his interests extended in many directions outside philosophy. He was a fluent and prolific writer, and of the more than sixty books that he published only about a score are strictly philosophical. In the tradition of his family, he maintained a life-long interest in politics, and his first published work, which appeared in 1896, was a book on German Social Democracy. Before he became a peer he stood three times unsuccessfully for Parliament, twice in the Labour interest and once in 1907 as a candidate of the National Union of Women's Suffrage Societies. He was four times married and thrice divorced. His politics cost him two prison sentences, one of six months in 1918 for libelling the American army, and in 1961, when he was eighty-nine years old, a week in the prison hospital for incitement to civil disobedience, in support of the Campaign for Nuclear Disarmament. It was his active campaigning against England's participation in the First World War that prevented the renewal of his lectureship at Trinity in 1916. He was not, however, always a pacifist. He was in favour of armed resistance to Hitler, and for a short period after the Second World War believed that Russia should at least be threatened with the employment against her of the atom bomb. Though he was always radical in his political views, he was consistently hostile to Communism after he visited the Soviet Union and met its leaders in 1919. Nevertheless, towards the end of his life he came to think that the triumph of Communism would be a lesser evil than the effects of an all-out nuclear war.

Another of Russell's abiding interests was in education, on which he also wrote extensively; and principally for the benefit of his two elder children by his second wife, Dora Black, he joined her in founding and running a primary school in the 1930s. It was his progressive views on education and on morals, as expressed in his more popular works, that led in 1940 to his being judicially pronounced unfit to hold a Chair of Philosophy at the City College of New York. The action was brought against the city by a parent at the instigation of some of the local clergy, and Russell himself was not allowed to be a party to it. From his adolescence onwards he was opposed to any form of theism and especially to Christianity, as is shown in his book *Why I am not a Christian*. He was a most effective polemicist, a lucid popularizer of both physical and social science, and a powerful advocate of the liberal causes in which he believed. If some of his more popular works, such as *Marriage and Morals*, for which he won a Nobel Prize, seem dated, it is largely because of the change in the moral climate which they themselves did much to bring about. We shall, however, be concerned here only with his philosophy, in a narrower sense of the term.

His Approach to Philosophy

As he relates in his autobiography, Russell was led to take an interest in philosophy by his desire to find some good reason for believing in the truth of mathematics. When his brother first introduced him, at the age of eleven, to Euclidean geometry, he objected to being required to take the axioms on trust. He agreed to do so only in deference to his brother, who made it a condition of their going any further, but he did not give up his belief that the propositions of geometry, and indeed those of any other branch of mathematics, needed some ulterior justification. For a time he was attracted to the view of his lay godfather, John Stuart Mill, that mathematical propositions are empirical generalizations, which are inductively justified by the number and variety of the observations that conform to them, but this conflicted with the belief, which Russell was unwilling to give up, that the true propositions of pure mathematics are not just contingently but necessarily true.

The solution on which he hit, under the prevailing assumption that all mathematics could be reduced to propositions about the natural numbers, was the reduction of these propositions in their turn to the propositions of a system of formal logic. This enterprise, which he did not yet know had been attempted by Frege thirty years before, required, first, the discovery of a method of defining the natural numbers in purely logical terms, and, secondly, the development of a system of logic which would be sufficiently rich for the propositions of arithmetic to be deducible from it. He attempted the first of these tasks in his book *The Principles of Mathematics*, which was published in 1903, and the second, in collaboration with his former mathematical tutor Alfred North Whitehead, in the three monumental volumes of *Principia Mathematica*, which appeared between 1910 and 1913. A more popular account of this enterprise is given in Russell's *Introduction to Mathematical Philosophy*, which he wrote while he was in prison in 1918, and published in the following year.

What Russell and Whitehead achieved, in accordance with their conception of number as essentially applicable to classes, was both to give a purely logical account of what it is for a class to have a particular number and, by a method of correlating the members of classes, to capture the notion of cardinal number in a general definition. But what, one may ask, is the purpose of this exercise, other than as a display of elegance and economy? The answer is that Russell regarded such economy as a safeguard of truth. As he put it in his collection of essays, *Mysticism and Logic*, which appeared in 1916: 'Two equally numerous collections appear to have something in common: this something is supposed to be their cardinal number. But so long as the cardinal number is inferred from the collections, not constructed in terms of them, its existence must remain in doubt, unless in view of a metaphysical postulate *ad hoc*. By defining the cardinal number of a given collection as the class of all equally numerous collections, we avoid the necessity of the metaphysical postulate, and thereby remove a needless doubt from the philosophy of arithmetic.'[1]

Unfortunately this explanation leaves one puzzled. The 'needless doubt' is the doubt whether there really are such things as numbers, but what sort of a doubt is this? In what would the discovery that there are no numbers consist? How would it be made? There seems

[1] *Mysticism and Logic*, p. 56.

no possible way of its being made except by its being shown that numbers are not reducible to classes, or to numerals, or to anything else. But if this could be shown, would we then be obliged to give up arithmetic or regard it as a play of our fancy? I should not mind saying that it was a play of our fancy, just in the sense that its propositions were not descriptive of the world, but did no more than express rules of inference in accordance with a system of counting that we had chosen to adopt. But not all mathematicians would agree with this. And how should I argue with one who took a realistic view?

Anyhow, Russell avoids this trouble, if his methods succeed in reducing numbers to classes, provided that he is not equally puzzled about the existence of classes; and at that stage he was not. His earliest philosophical books, *An Essay on the Foundation of Geometry*, which came out in 1897, and *A Critical Exposition of the Philosophy of Leibniz*, which came out in 1900, were written from a Kantian point of view, but by the time he published *The Principles of Mathematics* he had been converted by Moore to an extreme form of Platonic realism. Anything that could be mentioned was then said by him to be a term; any term could be the logical subject of a proposition; and anything that could be the logical subject of a proposition, including non-existent entities like unicorns, or even logically impossible entities, like the greatest prime number, was credited with being, in some sense. Subsequently, Russell came to think that such an extreme tolerance of the multiplication of entities showed, as he put it, 'a failure of that feeling for reality which ought to be preserved even in the most abstract studies'. 'Logic,' he continued, 'must no more admit a unicorn than zoology can; for logic is concerned with the real world just as truly as zoology, though with its more abstract and general features.'[1] This seems to suggest some retention of logical realism, but in fact Russell went so far in the other direction as to deny the reality of classes, substituting for them the equivalent of properties, possibly at some cost to his mathematical programme. Not only that but he also abandoned the view that every nominative expression stands for a term which is somehow possessed of being. His reasons for the change are to be found in his famous theory of descriptions, which he himself regarded as

[1] *Introduction to Mathematical Philosophy*, p. 169.

one of his two major contributions to philosophy, the other being his theory of types.

The Theory of Descriptions and the Theory of Types

The problems which led Russell to formulate his theory of descriptions were connected with his assumption that the meaning of a name is to be identified with the object which the name denotes. The question whether a sign is a name is thereby linked with the question whether there is an object for which it stands. We have seen that at one time Russell was very generous with the provision of such objects, but that he was restrained by the growth of his 'feeling for reality'.

There were also special difficulties arising from this profusion of names. For example, if denoting phrases like 'The author of *Waverley*' function as names, and if the meaning of a name is equated with its bearer, it will follow that what is meant by saying that Scott was the author of *Waverley* is simply that Scott was Scott. But, as Russell pointed out, it is clear that when the Prince Regent wanted to know whether Scott was the author of *Waverley*, he was not expressing an interest in the law of identity. Again, if the phrase 'The present king of France' names an object, and if what is said about an object must be either true or false, one or other of the two propositions 'The present king of France is bald' and 'The present king of France is not bald' must be true. Yet if one were to enumerate all the things that are bald and all the things that are not bald, one would not find the present king of France on either list. Russell remarked, characteristically, that 'Hegelians, who love a synthesis, will probably conclude that he wears a wig'.[1] On this view, there is a difficulty even over saying that there is no such person as the present king of France, since it would appear that the 'object' must have some form of being for the denial of its existence to be intelligible. The problem, in Russell's words, is 'How can a non-entity be a subject of a proposition?'[2]

In view of Russell's assumption that a name has no meaning unless it denotes an object, these difficulties all arise from the further assumption that denoting phrases like 'The author of *Waverley*' and

[1] *Logic and Knowledge*, p. 48.
[2] ibid.

'The present king of France' function as names; and it is this further assumption that Russell chooses to sacrifice. His theory of descriptions is designed to show that expressions which take the form of definite or indefinite descriptions are not used as names, so that it is not necessary for them to denote anything in order for them to make their contributions to the meaning of the sentences into which they enter. Russell characterized these expressions as 'incomplete symbols', by which he meant both that their contribution to meaning did not consist in denotation, and that they were susceptible of analysis. The theory of descriptions was intended to show how these two conditions are satisfied.

The way in which this is shown is very simple. It depends on the assumption that in all cases in which a predicate is attributed to a subject, or two or more subjects are said to stand in some relation, that is to say, in all cases except those in which the existence of a subject is simply asserted or denied, the use of a description carries the covert assertion that there exists an object which answers to it. The procedure is then simply to make this covert assertion explicit. The elimination of descriptive phrases, their representation as incomplete symbols, is achieved by expanding them into existential statements and construing these existential statements as asserting that something, or in the case of definite descriptive phrases just one thing, has the property which is contained in the description. So, in the simplest version of the theory, which is set out in *Principia Mathematica*, a sentence like 'Scott was the author of *Waverley*' is expanded into 'There is an x, such that x wrote *Waverley*, such that for all y, if y wrote *Waverley*, y is identical with x, and such that x is identical with Scott'. Similarly, 'The present king of France is bald' becomes 'There is an x, such that x now reigns over France, such that, for all y, if y now reigns over France, y is identical with x, and such that x is bald'. The question how a non-entity can be the subject of a proposition is circumvented by changing the subject. The would-be denoting phrase is transformed into an existential statement which in the case of the present king of France happens to be false.

It is easy to see that this procedure can be applied not only to expressions which have the grammatical form of descriptive phrases but to any nominative sign which carries some connotation. The connotation of the sign is taken away from it and turned into a predicate with an indefinite subject; when a subject for the predicate is found, the same treatment is applied, so that the original predicate is augmented by another, and so the process continues until one gets to the point where the subject of all these predicates is either referred to indefinitely by the expression 'there is an x such that', standing for what is technically known as the existential quantifier, or named by a sign which has no connotation at all. The name fulfils the function of holding the predicates together, but beyond that it serves purely as a demonstrative. In his more popular expositions of the theory, Russell often wrote as if he took ordinary proper names like 'Scott' really to be names, as he understood the term, but since he held, in my view rightly, that such proper names are ordinarily given some connotation, even though it may vary on different occasions of their use, his more consistent view was that they are implicit descriptions. Like ordinary descriptions, they can be used significantly, even though the objects to which they purport to refer do not exist. On the other hand, it is a necessary condition for anything to be what Russell calls a logically proper name that its significant use guarantees the existence of the object which it is intended to denote. Since the only signs which satisfy this condition, in Russell's view, are those that refer to present sensory or introspective data, he here makes his logic interlock with his theory of knowledge.

This theory of descriptions was at first greeted as 'a paradigm of philosophy'.[1] Subsequently, it was criticized as failing to give an accurate account of the way in which descriptive phrases are actually used. It was suggested that such phrases are normally understood not as covertly asserting but rather as pre-supposing the existence of the object to which they are intended to refer, so that what we should say, in the case where the reference fails, is not that the propositions which the descriptive phrases help to express are false, but that they lack any truth value.[2] This practice could, indeed, be followed, but it has the apparent disadvantage of severing the assertion of a proposition from the assertion of its truth, since if 'p' has no truth-value, 'it is true that p' is false. Another point which has been made is that more often than not the sentences in which we employ a descriptive phrase to pick out some object are not amenable to Russell's treatment as they stand. When we say 'The baby is crying' or 'The kettle is boiling' we do not mean to imply that there is only

---

[1] For example by F. P. Ramsey in *The Foundations of Mathematics*, p. 263.
[2] cf. P. F. Strawson, 'On Referring' in *Mind* (1950), reprinted in *Logico-Linguistic Papers*.

one baby or only one kettle in the universe. We leave it to the context to show which particular object of this or that kind we are referring to. But if we have to insert into a sentence of this sort some predicate which the object in question satisfies, the mere fact that there may be several different predicates which meet this condition makes it at least very doubtful whether the proposition expressed by the sentence at which we arrive as the result of the analysis will be logically equivalent to the one which was expressed by the sentence with which we began.

This objection would be serious if the theory of descriptions were designed, as Russell may himself have intended, to provide exact translations of the sentences on which it operates. But in fact, whether Russell was fully aware of it or not, what the theory supplies is not a rule of translation but a technique of paraphrase. Its method is to make explicit the information which is implicitly contained in the use of denotative expressions, whether they be proper names or descriptive phrases, or is left to be picked up from the context. If, as Russell later came to think,[1] the function of holding predicates together can be performed by a relation of compresence, it leads to the conclusion that denotative expressions or singular terms, as they are now usually called, are dispensable, except perhaps as demonstrative signs.

Because it does lead to this conclusion, it does not matter that the theory was designed to meet a spurious problem, the problem arising out of Russell's false assumption that the meaning of a name is identical with the object which it denotes. A name refers to its bearer, if it has one, but its meaning is not identical with its bearer: there are many things true of the bearer, that it has such and such a life-span, for example, or that it occupies such and such a spatio-temporal position, which it would be nonsensical to ascribe to the meaning of a name. Neither is it necessary to the use and understanding of a name, in any ordinary sense of the term, that it should succeed in its reference. The meaning of the sentence 'King Arthur fought the Saxons', advanced as a historical assertion, remains the same whether King Arthur really existed or not. It was Russell's insistence that the use of names should guarantee the existence of their objects which obliged him to confine their reference to what he called 'ego-centric particulars' and in the end to treat them as demonstra-

[1] See his *An Inquiry into Meaning and Truth* (1940).

tives, like the words 'this' and 'here' and 'now', which, in their ordinary construal, are not names at all.

Even so, these demonstratives come into the class of singular terms, and it is hard to decide whether they too are eliminable. The question is whether language can be entirely freed from the context of its utterance. Clearly the sentence 'I am now writing these words on the terrace of my house in Provence' is not equivalent to any set of sentences to the effect that such and such words are written by a man answering to such and such a unique description on the morning of July 29, 1979, at a place answering to such and such spatial co-ordinates. But does the paraphrase convey the same information? If not, what does it leave out? One is inclined to say that it does not tell us that *I* am the person answering to the given description, that *today* is July 29, 1979, that *this* is the place picked out by the co-ordinates. The reference of the demonstratives could be pinned down by further descriptions, but still one might feel that something essential had been left out. The answer then would have to be that what was left out could only be shown, not described, with the implication that language cannot be freed from its dependence on context. Yet a recording angel, writing a history of the world, which included the fact of my writing these words, would not need to employ any such demonstratives. Perhaps the moral is that we, taking part as we do in the history of the world, and speaking from our position inside it, cannot assume the standpoint of the recording angel. Or rather, we can assume his standpoint but have to return to our places in order to interpret the utterances which we issue from it.

An important historical effect of the theory of descriptions was to give currency to the distinction between the grammatical form of a sentence and what Russell called its logical form. This distinction suffered from the failure of Russell and his followers to explain at all clearly what they took logical form to be. Russell himself often spoke as if facts had a logical form which sentences could copy; the logical form which underlay the grammatical form of an indicative sentence was then identified with the logical form of the actual or possible fact which would verify what the sentence expressed. This would be all very well, if we had any means of determining the logical forms of facts other than through the grammatical forms of the sentences which are used to state them. What happens, in practice, is that we decide, on other grounds, which forms of sentences convey this information most perspicuously, and that these are not always the grammatical forms in which the sentences are originally cast. The general point which emerges is that sentences which appear to have the same grammatical structure may be transformable in very different ways.

A similar influence has been exerted by Russell's theory of types. This theory was devised to deal with an antinomy, discovered by Russell, which held up the progress of *Principia Mathematica* and led Frege to say, when Russell communicated it to him, that the foundations of mathematics had crumbled. The antinomy arises out of the natural assumption that to every property there correspond the two classes of those objects that possess the property and those that lack it. But now consider the property, applicable to classes, of not belonging to itself. At first sight this seems a genuine property. For example, the class of countable objects is itself countable; the class of men is not itself a man. But what of the class of classes which are not members of themselves? If it is a member of itself, it is not; and if it is not, it is.

Russell's solution of this paradox depends on the principle that the meaning of what he calls a propositional function, that is to say a predicative expression with an indefinite subject, is not specified until one specifies the range of objects which are candidates for satisfying it. From this it follows that these candidates cannot meaningfully include anything which is defined in terms of the function itself. The result is that propositional functions, and correspondingly propositions, are arranged in a hierarchy. Objects which are candidates for satisfying functions of the same order are said to constitute a type, and the rule is that what can be said, truly or falsely, about objects of one type cannot meaningfully be said about objects of a different type. Consequently, to say of the class of classes which are not members of themselves that it either is, or is not, a member of itself is neither true nor false, but meaningless.

Russell applies the same principle to the solution of other logical antinomies and also to that of semantic antinomies like the paradox of the liar, in which a proposition is made to say of itself that it is false, with the result that if it is true, it is false, and if it is false, it is true. The theory of types eliminates the paradox by ruling that a proposition of which truth or falsehood is predicated must be of a lower order than the proposition by which the predication is made. Consequently, a proposition cannot meaningfully predicate truth or falsehood of itself.

The theory of types achieves its purpose, but in a somewhat arbitrary fashion and perhaps at too great a cost. For instance, it led to a difficulty within mathematics which Russell could solve only by introducing a special principle that hardly passes muster as a logical truth. Moreover, it is in general by no means obvious that we can never speak significantly in the same way about objects of different types. We can, for example, count objects at different levels, yet we do not think that numerical expressions have a different meaning according as they are applied to classes which differ in the type of their membership. Russell's answer was that in such a case the expressions do have a different meaning. Expressions which seem to be applicable to objects of different types were said by him to be systematically ambiguous. It was because the ambiguity is systematic that it escaped our notice. The fact is, however, that were it not for the theory of types, we should have no reason in these cases to suppose that there was any ambiguity.

The fashion nowadays is to give a separate treatment to the semantic and the logical paradoxes and to try to dispose of the logical paradoxes by some other method than the theory of types. For instance, there are those who hold that the class-paradox can be avoided by depriving it of its subject; they maintain that there just is no class of classes which are not members of themselves. This solution would be more satisfactory if we had any clear criterion for deciding what constitutes a genuine class.

Whatever its status within logic, the theory of types has had a very strong secondary influence. We shall find that much subsequent philosophy has been stimulated by the suggestion that sentences to which there is no obvious objection on the score of grammar or vocabulary may nevertheless be meaningless.

His Theories of Knowledge and of What There Is

After his Platonic period, Russell came and remained very close to the tradition of classical British empiricism, as exemplified in their different ways by Locke, Berkeley, Hume and John Stuart Mill. Like them, he believed in starting with the entities of whose existence and properties we can be the most nearly certain, which he identified with the immediate data of our inner and outer senses. In *The Problems of Philosophy*, published in 1912, where he emphasized his celebrated distinction between knowledge by acquaintance and knowledge by description, he counted among the objects of acquaintance one's self, one's current mental states and acts, the sense-data which were the objects of one's sensory acts, and some of the objects of memory. By 1921, however, when he published *The Analysis of Mind*, he had come to think of the self as dissoluble into a series of experiences and he no longer believed in the existence of acts of sensing of which he had previously taken sense-data to be the objects. He therefore rejected the term 'sense-datum' and instead spoke of percepts as the objects that are immediately given in sense-perception. Since he had also abandoned the view that memory brings us into direct relation with the past, the only particulars that remained as possible objects of acquaintance were one's current feelings, images and percepts. As opposed to feelings and images, Russell never held that either sense-data or percepts were necessarily private to their percipient or momentary in their duration but, on causal grounds, he held that they were so in fact.

Whatever view he took of the character of the immediate data of perception, Russell consistently maintained that physical objects, unless they are somehow reducible to percepts, are not directly perceived. Here again he followed the classical empiricist tradition in relying on the so-called argument from illusion. In *The Problems of Philosophy* he concentrated mainly on the fact that the apparent properties of physical objects vary under different conditions, which he interpreted as showing that none of them can be identified with the real properties of the objects concerned; but in his later writings, such as *The Analysis of Matter*, which appeared in 1927, he laid greater stress on the causal dependence of these appearances upon the environment and upon the character of our nervous systems. Thus he appealed to the fact that light takes time to travel in order to show that we must be mistaken in thinking that we see the sun as it now is; at best, we can be seeing it in the state in which it was several minutes ago. But his main argument went deeper. He maintained that in view of the known dependence upon the environment and upon our nervous systems of the perceptible properties, such as size and shape and colour, which were attributed to physical objects, we have no good reason to believe that the objects possess these properties in the literal way in which they are thought to do so by common sense. If the attitude of common sense is represented by naive realism, the theory that we directly perceive physical objects much as they really are, then Russell's opinion of common sense was that it conflicted with science: and in such a context he thought science ought to be given the verdict. 'Science,' he said, 'is at no moment quite right, but it is seldom quite wrong and has, as a rule, a better chance of being right than the theories of the unscientific. It is, therefore, rational to accept it hypothetically.'[1] As for naive realism, Russell goes so far as to suggest that it can be logically disproved. As he put it in *An Inquiry into Meaning and Truth*,[2] with a pithiness for which Einstein expressed his admiration: 'Naive realism leads to physics, and physics, if true, shows that naive realism is false. Therefore naive realism, if true, is false; therefore it is false.'

Whether such arguments do prove that we directly perceive any such things as percepts, as opposed to physical objects, is open to doubt. The fact that a thing such as a curtain may appear a different colour to different observers, or to the same observer under different conditions, does indeed show that our selection of one colour as the real colour of the curtain is to some extent arbitrary, but it hardly seems to warrant the conclusion that what each of us sees is not the curtain but something else. The fact that light from a distant star may take years to reach us does refute the naive assumption that we see the star in its contemporary state, but again does not seem sufficient to prove that we see some contemporary object which is not the star. The general causal argument is, indeed, more powerful. If we make it a necessary condition for a property to be intrinsic to an object that it can be adequately defined without reference to the effects of the object upon an observer, then I think that a good case can be made for saying that physical objects are not intrinsically coloured, though whether this entitles us to say that they are not 'really' coloured will still be debatable. Even so, it does not obviously follow that the colour which we attribute to a physical object is a property of something else, a sense-datum or a percept. If we are going to draw any such conclusion from Russell's arguments we shall have to make two further assumptions: first, that when we perceive a physical object otherwise than as it really is, there is something we can be said

[1] *My Philosophical Development*, p. 17.
[2] p. 15.

to perceive directly, which really has the properties that the physical object only appears to us to have; and secondly, that what we perceive, in this sense, is the same, whether the perception of the physical object is veridical or delusive. Russell took these assumptions for granted, but they are not generally thought to be self-evident; indeed, most contemporary philosophers reject them. My own view is that Russell could have obtained what he wanted merely by insisting on a point which he does make, that our ordinary perceptual judgements embody inferences, in the sense that they go beyond any mere descriptions of the contents of the experiences on which they are based. 'Percepts' could then be equated with the contents of these experiences. It is, however, important that they should not be introduced as private entities. At this stage the question of privacy or publicity does not arise.

If we can grant Russell so much as this, the next question to be considered is whether our primitive data are, as he puts it, 'signs of the existence of something else, which we can call the physical object'.[1] The answer which he gives in *The Problems of Philosophy* is that we have a good, if not conclusive, reason for thinking that they are. The reason is that the postulation of physical objects as external causes of sense-data accounts for the character of the data in a way that no other hypothesis can. Russell did not then think that we could discover anything about the intrinsic properties of physical objects, but he did think it reasonable to infer that they are spatio-temporally ordered in a way that corresponds to the ordering of sense-data.

This postulation of physical objects as unobserved causes violated Russell's maxim that wherever possible logical constructions are to be substituted for inferred entities,[2] and in his book *Our Knowledge of the External World as a Field for Scientific Method in Philosophy*, which was published in 1914, and in two essays, written in 1914 and 1915, which were reprinted in his *Mysticism and Logic*, he sought to exhibit physical objects as logical constructions. It was for this purpose that he introduced the concept of a 'sensibile', with the explanation that sensibilia were possibly unsensed objects of 'the same metaphysical and physical status as sense-data', and that of a 'perspective', which was understood in such a way that two particu-

---

[1] *The Problems of Philosophy*, p. 20.
[2] Namely 'Sense-data and Physics' in *Mysticism and Logic*, p. 155. See also 'Logical Atomism' in *Logic and Knowledge*, p. 326.

lars, whether sense-data or sensibilia, were said to belong to the same perspective if and only if they occurred simultaneously in the same private space.

The theory which Russell developed with these concepts owes something to Leibniz's monadology. He treated each perspective as a point in what he called 'perspective space', which, being a three-dimensional arrangement of three-dimensional perspectives, was itself a space of six dimensions. The physical objects which were situated in perspective-space were identified with the classes of their actual and possible appearances. To illustrate how these appearances were sorted, Russell used the example of a penny which figures in a number of different perspectives. All the perspectives, in which the appearances of the penny are of exactly the same shape, are to be collected and put on a straight line in the order of their size. In this way we obtain a number of different series, in each of which a limit will be reached at the point 'where (as we say) the penny is so near the eye that if it were any nearer it could not be seen'.[1] If we now imagine all these series to be prolonged, so as to form lines of perspectives continuing 'beyond' the penny, the perspective in which all the lines meet can be defined as 'the place where the penny is'.[2]

This is a very ingenious theory, but I think that it fails on the count of circularity. The difficulty is that if the physical object is to be constructed out of its appearances, it cannot itself be used to collect them. The different appearances of the penny, in Russell's example, have first to be associated purely on the basis of their qualities. But since different pennies may look very much alike, and since they may also be perceived against very similar backgrounds, the only way in which we can make sure of associating just those sensibilia that belong to the same penny is by situating them in wider contexts. We have to take account of perspectives which are adjacent to those in which they occur. But then we are faced with the difficulty that perspectives which contain only sensibilia as opposed to sense-data are not actually perceived; and there seems to be no way of determining when two unperceived perspectives are adjacent without already assuming the perspective-space which we are trying to construct.

[1] *Mysticism and Logic*, p. 162.
[2] ibid.

Another serious difficulty is that the method by which Russell ordered the elements of his series does not serve its purpose. He relied on the assumption that the apparent size of an object varies continuously with the distance, and its apparent shape with the angle, from which the object is viewed. But the psychological principle of constancy makes this empirically false. The assumption might be upheld, if apparent shapes and sizes were determined physiologically, but to do this would again be to bring in physical objects before we had constructed them.

Some of these difficulties arise from Russell's mistaken assumption that his sensory elements are located in private spaces. Instead of his complicated ordering of perspectives, he could, if he had started with neutral data, have obtained his sensibilia merely by projecting spatial and temporal relations beyond the sense-fields in which they are originally given. Even so, there seems to be no unobjectionable way in which he could have arrived at a theory which permitted the transformation of propositions referring to physical objects into propositions which referred only to percepts. I believe that the most that can be achieved in this direction is to show how a primary system of percepts can be developed and how this can serve as a theoretical basis for our belief in the physical world of common sense.

Russell carried this reductionism to its furthest point in *The Analysis of Mind*. Largely following William James, he there maintained that both mind and matter were logical constructions out of primitive elements which were themselves neither mental nor physical. Mind and matter were differentiated by the fact that certain elements such as images and feelings entered only into the constitution of minds, and also by the operation of different causal laws. Thus the same percepts, when correlated according to the laws of physics, constituted physical objects and, when correlated according to the laws of psychology, helped to constitute minds. In their mental aspect, these elements engaged among other things in what Russell called 'mnemic causation', a kind of action at a distance by which empirical data produced subsequent memory images. On the view, which he then held, that causation is just invariable sequence, there is no theoretical objection to such action at a distance, but it is inconsistent with the principle, which Russell later adopted, in his book *Human Knowledge: Its Scope and Limits*, published in 1948, that events which enter into causal chains are spatio-temporally

continuous. He persisted in holding that minds are logical constructions, but never seriously tried to solve the problem of showing what
relations have to hold between different elements for them to be
constituents of the same mind.

It would appear too that Russell's materials are too sparse to furnish
an adequate account of all mental concepts. Consider, for example,
the concept of belief and its relation to truth. In his Platonic period
Russell was content to say that belief was a special mental attitude
directed towards a proposition, and that propositions were just true or
false in the same simple way as roses are red or white. Having rightly
rejected this theory, if only on the ground that it makes it unintelligible
why one should prefer true to false beliefs, Russell adopted the view
that when one makes a judgement one's mind stands in a multiple
relation to the various terms with which one's judgement is concerned.
This relation has a 'sense' in that it orders the terms in a certain fashion.
When I judge that A loves B and when I judge that B loves A, the terms on
which my judgement operates are the same in either case, but in the
first case the relation of loving is before my mind 'as proceeding from A
to B' and in the second case as proceeding from B to A. My judgement is
true if the terms in question really are related in the sense in which they
are judged to be, and false if they are not.[1]

Apart from the difficulty of extending it to propositions of a more
complex sort, the weakness of this theory is that by taking the singular
terms on which a judgement operates to be actual individuals, it makes
no provision for the cases in which one believes something to be true of
a subject under one description but not under another. If I judge that
the author of *Coningsby* was a romantic writer, I am understood to be
judging that Disraeli was a romantic writer, even though I think of
Disraeli only as a statesman and have no idea that he also wrote novels.
This difficulty may be overcome by taking the constituents of the
judgements to be the 'intentional objects' which the relevant
descriptions pick out, but the status of 'intentional objects' is dubious,
and we are anyhow left no wiser about the nature of judgement or
belief.

In *The Analysis of Mind* Russell says of the content of a belief that it
'may consist of words only, or of images only, or a mixture of the two,
or of either or both together with one or more sensations'.[2] He had

---

[1] See 'On the Nature of Truth' in *Philosophical Essays* and *The Problems of Philosophy*, pp.
124 ff.
[2] p. 236.

37

previously held that when the belief consisted of images it was made true by the resemblance of the images to some fact, but this was clearly a mistake. The existence of a physical resemblance between two sets of objects can never in itself be sufficient to make one a representative of the other. There has to be a convention according to which one party to the relation is interpreted as signifying that there exists something which resembles it in certain respects. But then this is only one among many possible conventions: there is no special virtue in resemblance. In *The Analysis of Mind* Russell speaks more vaguely of beliefs being made true or false by pointing to facts or away from them, and ends by admitting that it is not sufficient to list images or sensations or feelings as the contents of a belief. 'It is necessary that there should be a specific relation between them of the sort expressed by saying that the content is what is believed.'[1] We are not, however, told what this relation is. Later, in *An Inquiry into Meaning and Truth*, Russell shows some predilection for a behavioural theory of belief and some inclination to regard a belief as true when it can be verified, but neither theory is worked out in detail.

By the time he published his 'Portraits from Memory' in 1958, Russell had apparently given up the view that images and feelings are intrinsically mental, since he there maintained that 'An event is not rendered either mental or material by any intrinsic quality but only by its causal relations'. He also asserted that what are called mental events are identical with physical states of the brain, but exactly how he came to this conclusion is not made clear.

It is, however, consistent with his reversion, from the time he published *The Analysis of Matter* onwards, to his earlier view that physical objects are known to us only by description, as the external causes of our percepts, with the consequence that we can make only conjectural inferences about their intrinsic properties. One obvious difficulty with any theory of this kind is to see how we can be justified in believing that any such external objects exist at all. We may, indeed, be entitled to postulate unobservable entities, so long as the theories into which they enter have consequences which can be empirically tested, but it seems to me that a more serious problem is created when all physical objects are treated as inferred entities and located, as Russell locates them, in an inferred space of their own, to which we have no perceptual access. Not only is it not clear to me

[1] *The Analysis of Mind*, p. 250.

what justification there could be for believing in the existence of such a space, but I am not sure that I even find the idea of it intelligible.

A further objection is that the causal account of perception on which Russell relies itself seems to require that physical objects be located in perceptual space. When my seeing the table in front of me is explained in terms of the passage of light-rays from the table to my eye, the assumption is surely that the table is there where I see it. Admittedly, we sometimes distinguish between the place where a physical object appears to be and the place where it really is, but the calculations which lead us to make such distinctions are themselves based on the assumption that other objects are where they appear to be. It is only because we start by equating the physical position of the things around us with the positions ascribed, on the basis of observation, to something of the order of Russell's sensibilia that our more sophisticated methods of locating more distant objects can lead to verifiable results.

This does not mean that we are driven back to naive realism. Even if we discard Russell's distinction between physical and perceptual space, we can still regard physical objects as really possessing only those structural properties that physicists ascribe to them. We are not even debarred from regarding percepts as being private to their percipients. If we can develop the common-sense conception of the physical world as a theoretical system with respect to a neutral basis of sensory qualities, we can allow the system to 'take over' the elements out of which it grew. The physical object is set against the percepts from which it was abstracted and made causally responsible for them. The relatively constant perceptual qualities which are attributed to it come to be contrasted with the fluctuating impressions which different observers have of it, and the impressions assigned to the observers. At a still more sophisticated level we can replace the common-sense physical object by the scientific skeleton on which the causal processes of perception are taken to depend. So by a fusion of Russell's theories we may perhaps arrive at the truth.

Though his writings on moral questions were extremely influential, Russell was never greatly interested in moral theory. In his early days he was content to follow Moore in taking a realistic view of 'good', as the fundamental ethical term, and in regarding right actions as those that were productive of the best consequences. His only original contribution was his insistence that free will, so far from being inconsistent with determinism, actually requires it. Later, in his book *Human Society in Ethics and Politics*, which was published in 1954, he took a view akin to Hume's, saying in one passage that 'An occurrence is "good" when it satisfies desire'[1] and in another that 'Effects which lead to approval are defined as "good" and those leading to disapproval as "bad".'[2] In politics his standpoint was mainly utilitarian, but he seems to have attached an independent value to freedom and to justice, and to have grown increasingly distrustful of the powers of the state. In his two most serious contributions to political theory, the books *Principles of Social Reconstruction* and *Roads to Freedom*, which were published respectively in 1916 and 1918, he advocated a form of Guild Socialism, a system which provided, among other things, for workers' control of industry. Later, as we have seen, he was more concerned with international affairs. It pleased him to be compared to Voltaire and, like Voltaire, he brought wit, lucidity and passion to his attacks on superstition, public folly, hypocrisy and injustice. He was, however, by far Voltaire's superior as a technical philosopher.

G. E. Moore

George Edward Moore was born in 1873 and died in 1958. The son of a retired doctor, he was educated as a day-boy at Dulwich College, and entered Trinity College, Cambridge, with a classical scholarship in 1892. Having passed through 'an intense religious phase' at the age of eleven to thirteen, he never thereafter saw any good reason to believe in the existence of a God. He expected to become a teacher of the classics but was persuaded by Russell, with whom he became friends in his second year at Cambridge, to turn his attention to philosophy. Russell said of him that 'for some years he fulfilled my ideal of genius'. In 1898 he was elected to a prize-fellowship at Trinity which he held until 1904. In 1903 he published his first book, *Principia Ethica*, which had a very profound influence on such persons as Lytton Strachey, Clive Bell, Leonard Woolf and other members of the 'Bloomsbury' coterie. He had private means which

[1] p. 55.
[2] p. 116.

enabled him to continue working at philosophy in London and in Edinburgh, without holding any official position, until 1911, when he was appointed a University lecturer at Cambridge. In 1925 he succeeded James Ward as Professor of Philosophy at Cambridge and again became a Fellow of Trinity. He held the Chair until his retirement in 1939. He married in 1916 and had two sons. During the war he lectured at various universities in the United States. He was editor of *Mind* from 1921 to 1947.

Apart from *Principia Ethica*, the only books which Moore published in his lifetime were a small book on *Ethics*, for the Home University Library, which appeared in 1912, a collection of articles called *Philosophical Studies*, which came out in 1922, and *Some Main Problems of Philosophy* which, although not published until 1953, was, with a few minor verbal alterations, a reproduction of two series of lectures which Moore delivered at Morley College, a working men's college in London, in the years 1910–11. Another collection of articles, called *Philosophical Papers*, was in proof at the time of Moore's death and was published in 1959. Moore left to his executors a series of notebooks, ranging in date from 1913 to 1953, in which he had entered brief reflections on a fairly wide range of philosophical problems. These notes were edited by Casimir Lewy and published in 1962 under the title of *The Commonplace Book of G. E. Moore*. Lewy also edited some of Moore's lecture notes for courses given in the academic years 1925–6, 1928–9 and 1933–4, and published them in 1965 under the title of *Lectures in Philosophy*. There is also interesting material in Moore's reply to his critics in the volume entitled *The Philosophy of G. E. Moore* which Dr Schilpp edited and published in 1942.

Moore had a strong and attractive personality and he influenced the philosophers of his time as much by his teaching as by his comparatively slender stock of published writings. This may be one reason why his works have had a much stronger influence in England than elsewhere.

'Principia Ethica'
The principal theses of *Principia Ethica* are that the primary business of ethics is to enquire into the extensions of the properties 'good' and 'bad'; that 'good' is a simple unanalysable non-natural quality; that

philosophers who have identified good with pleasure, or progress in evolution, or any other natural property, have committed what Moore calls 'the naturalistic fallacy'; that a similar fallacy has been committed by those philosophers who have identified good with some metaphysical entity, or in general attempted to derive ethics from metaphysics; that egoism is irrational, since it cannot be the case that each person's interests are the sole good; that a right action is, by definition, the one among all possible actions in the circumstances that would have the best effects; that since the effects extend indefinitely into the future we never know what actions are right; that there is, however, a probability that we act rightly when we follow generally accepted rules; that the good or evil of a whole is organic, in the sense that it is not necessarily equal to the sum of the good, or evil, of its parts; and that the best organic wholes, the greatest intrinsic goods, are the enjoyment of beautiful objects and the love for one's friends when their mental and physical qualities merit it.

Moore offers no proof that these are the greatest goods, and indeed it is fundamental to his position that there can be no proof. These are matters only for intuition. If someone has a different intuition he may well be wrong, but he cannot be shown to be wrong so long as he sticks to his guns. It may, however, be possible to show that he has confused the proposition he thinks he is intuiting with a different proposition which he would reject, if the confusion were pointed out to him, and it may also be possible to show that he has arrived at his intuition through the acceptance of some false proposition and that he would abandon the proposition he claims to intuit if he were persuaded that this other proposition was false. Moore believed, for example, that this would apply to most philosophers who had held that pleasure was the sole good. He thought that with the notable exception of Henry Sidgwick (1838–1900), they had nearly all committed the naturalistic fallacy of identifying good with pleasure, and that once they had been persuaded to understand that this was a fallacy, few if any of them, when obliged to consult their intuition, would continue to hold that only pleasure was good.

But is the naturalistic fallacy a fallacy at all? It may be a mistake to identify good with pleasure, but is it clear that every attempt to treat good as anything other than a simple unanalysable quality must be mistaken? At the outset, Moore complicated the question by taking the unusual view that a definition 'states what are the parts which invariably compose a certain whole'[1] and then failing to explain in what sense a quality can have parts; but his main reason for holding that what is meant by the word 'good' cannot be identified with what is meant by any other expression is that the result of such an identification must be either trivial or false. Thus he remarks that one philosopher 'will affirm that good is pleasure, another perhaps that good is that which is desired',[2] and then if one contradicts the other, substituting his own definition of good, what he will be saying is that pleasure is not what is desired: and what has that, asks Moore, to do with ethics? Moore does not notice that if each party to the discussion substitutes his own definition of good, there will be no disagreement at all, since each will then be saying that pleasure is not what is desired. This might have made him think that something was amiss with his argument, but he might have taken it as showing just how muddled these philosophers were. In any event he refuses to allow that the dispute is a verbal one about the meaning of the word 'good'. For, he argues, moral philosophers are 'anxious to persuade us that what we call good is what we really ought to do'. And how absurd it would be to say 'You are to do this, because most people use a certain word to denote conduct such as this'.[3] Besides, if the word 'good' did stand, say, for pleasure, then in saying that pleasure was good, one would simply be saying that pleasure is pleasure. And surely this is not what is intended by someone who says that pleasure is good.

What Moore strangely failed to see, at the time, was that this argument can be brought against any definition whatsoever. A favourite example of his own of a successful definition was the proposition that brothers are male siblings. But if the word 'brother' does stand for male sibling, then in saying that brothers are male siblings one is simply saying that brothers are brothers, and surely this is not the information that the definition was meant to convey. When it was pointed out to him, Moore recognized the difficulty as what he called the Paradox of Analysis. I do not know that it has yet been solved. Moore's position, as reported by his literary executor, Casimir Lewy, was that 'It was essential to hold that to be a brother *is* to be a male sibling and that the proposition "To be a brother is to be

[1] *Principia Ethica*, p. 9.
[2] ibid., p. 12.
[3] ibid., p. 12.

a male sibling" is *not* identical with the proposition "To be a male sibling is to be a male sibling" '.[1] Perhaps what he meant by saying that these are different propositions is what Frege would have meant by saying that the expressions 'brother' and 'male sibling' have different senses but the same reference, but this is hardly more than a restatement of the problem. It does not explain what the definition accomplishes.

I am not sure that I can dispose of the paradox, but two points seem clear to me. The first is that the proposition that to be a brother is to be a male sibling is not itself a proposition about the meaning of English words. The proof of this is that the proposition could equally well be expressed in another language, when it would be obvious that no English words were being mentioned. But the second point is that even though the proposition is not about words, it is only the verbal information that it incidentally provides which saves it from being trivial. To say that to be a brother is to be a male sibling is not to *say* anything about the use of the English word 'brother' or any other word; but what one learns from the statement is a fact about the correct use of the English word 'brother' or the French word 'frère', or the corresponding word in whatever the language is in which the proposition is being expressed. The proposition is *not* linguistic and what it asserts *is* trivial, but the point of expressing it in a non-trivial way is to convey linguistic information.

The upshot of this discussion is that, so far as his general argument about definition goes, Moore's naturalistic fallacy is a mare's nest. He has, however, a further argument which bears specifically upon the attempt to define 'good'. The argument is, in his own words, that 'Whatever definition be offered, it may always be asked, with significance, of the complex so defined, whether it is itself good'.[2] He takes as an example of a plausible definition the suggestion that 'To be good may mean to be that which we desire to desire'. But now let A be something that we think good. Then we can significantly ask 'Is it good to desire to desire A?' But evidently, Moore argues, this is not equivalent to asking 'Do we desire to desire to desire to desire A?'[3] Consequently, the suggested definition must be incorrect, and a similar argument could be used against other definitions of this type.

---

[1] G. E. Moore, *Essays in Retrospect*, p. 302.
[2] *Principia Ethica*, p. 15.
[3] ibid., p. 16.

On the other hand, this argument does not have the same force against attempts to define 'good' in other ethical terms. Suppose, for example, that someone defines 'good' as 'worthy to be desired for its own sake'. Then the fact that we can ask whether what is worthy to be desired for its own sake is good proves no more than that we can query the correctness of the definition. At the worst we shall revive the paradox of analysis. And what this suggests is that if there is a 'naturalistic fallacy', it consists in defining 'good' in such a way as not to carry the implication that what is good is something to be sought or done. It is, in short, to ignore its normative aspect. If this is so, then Moore's argument merely echoes Hume's saying that 'ought' is not derivable from 'is'. It starts with the premiss that 'good' is a normative word and draws the valid conclusion that it must be a mistake to try to give it any purely descriptive meaning. Ironically, on this view, Moore himself was guilty of an extension of the naturalistic fallacy when, having satisfied himself that 'good' could not stand for any natural quality, he inferred that it stood for a non-natural one. Apart from the obscurity of the notion of a non-natural quality, the proper conclusion of his argument should have been that 'good', not being a descriptive term, did not stand for any quality at all.

This conclusion is less startling than it sounds. It is consistent with allowing ethical terms like 'good' to have a descriptive meaning in the very frequent cases in which they are used under the pre-supposition of the mutual acceptance of some moral code. In these cases, what is being asserted is that some motive, or action, or other state of affairs of which the term is predicated complies with the code, or with some element of it. Moore, however, as his examples show, is concerned with the case in which no such pre-supposition is being made, the case where the ethical term is used to set a standard rather than measure the accord with one already set; and it is in *this* usage that a term like 'good' is not descriptive but only normative; exhortatory or commendatory.

Where Moore is at his best is on the critical side. He shows very neatly that Hume's point extends to metaphysics, in that you cannot conjure normative statements out of descriptive statements merely by making your descriptive statements more fantastic, or passing them off as other worldly, and he makes the telling point against Kant that if the good will really were the only thing good in itself, it should not matter to Kant, in the way it does, whether those who display the good will are or are not rewarded with happiness. Moore is persuasive also when he argues that once they were freed of the psychological error of supposing that only pleasure can be desired, not many people would wish to maintain that pleasure was the sole good. He is, however, unfair to Mill when he treats his whole argument as vitiated by the simple mistake of misconstruing the word 'desirable', taking it to mean 'able to be desired' rather than 'worthy to be desired'. Possibly, Mill did make this mistake, but it would not vitiate his argument. If 'ought' implies 'can', and only pleasure could be desired, then it would follow that only pleasure should be desired. What would not follow was that all forms of pleasure were equally desirable. It would still be possible to establish a hierarchy of pleasures, which is what, in fact, Mill actually does, though it usually brings down on him a charge of inconsistency. But there is nothing inconsistent in the argument: only pleasures can and therefore should be desired; some forms of pleasure are morally superior to others; therefore these should be indulged in. All that is required is a criterion of inferiority, and this Mill supplies. Pleasure A is superior to pleasure B if it is preferred by most of those who have sampled them both. Apart from the falsity of his premiss, Mill's only mistake was sometimes to write as if he took pleasure to be not merely a necessary but a uniquely sufficient condition of good.

Moore's attack on egoism is valid on his own premisses. If good were a quality and the right action the one that in the given circumstances produced as much of this quality as possible, any talk of 'my good' or 'your good' would be irrelevant. It would be our common duty to bring about as much good as possible, no matter who was to profit by it. On the other hand, if talk of good is construed as a declaration of policy, and right actions taken to be those that bring the policy to fruition, there is no reason why one should not favour the policy that each man should look after his own interests. One might judge it morally inferior to the policy of paying at least some attention to the general interest, but that is not the point at issue, which is whether egoism is incoherent.

On the positive side, Moore takes his conclusion that we can never know what actions are right more lightly than I think he should. One might expect him to say that we should do the action which, among the possible alternatives, would most probably have the best consequences in the foreseeable future, or something of that sort, but surprisingly he does not. He is content with the general argument that we shall probably not go far wrong if we abide by the accepted rules. But this argument is very weak. Consider the case of murder. Moore begins by conceding that 'the general disutility of murder can only be proved, provided the majority of the human race will certainly persist in existing'.[1] If 'the existence of human life is on the whole an evil', and men could be persuaded to acknowledge this, one would be doing good by murdering them. Since they will not acknowledge this, even if it is true, the effort to murder them will generally be resisted, and this will produce an atmosphere of turmoil in which the achievement of the highest goals, the enjoyment of beauty, for example, is unlikely to be reached. So Moore sums up by saying that 'apart from the immediate evils which murder generally produces', the grief caused to the victim's friends, for example, if not the loss to the victim himself, 'the fact that, if it were a common practice, the feeling of insecurity, thus caused, would absorb much time, which might be spent to better purpose, is perhaps conclusive against it'.[2] But apart from the whimsicality of this argument, the most that it can prove is that the overt practice of murder is unlikely to have the best result. It has nothing to say against the exceptional, undetected murder, committed for the murderer's own advantage, with a victim whose departure will leave the world none the poorer. On this view, the only fault of Raskolnikov in Dostoyevsky's *Crime and Punishment* is that he was afflicted with an irrational conscience. The point is arguable, but it should be argued.

In general, Moore's rules of conduct pay no attention to the special position of the agent. They take no cognizance of the facet of our moral thinking which is brought to the fore, for example, by Bradley in the chapter 'My Station and Its Duties' of his *Ethical Studies*. When I examine my own actions, I find that I do not in fact believe that I ought to bring about as much good as possible, no matter to whom. I feel that I have special responsibilities, to my family, to my friends, to my colleagues, to my pupils, to my creditors, to those who have done me favours, to those to whom I have made promises, even to the local authorities and the government; and, again, that I have special loyalties both to persons and to organizations: and I consider it right to honour these obligations and to discharge these loyalties, even to

---

[1] *Principia Ethica*, p. 156.
[2] ibid., pp. 156–7.

the detriment of some greater good that I might be doing to persons with whom I have no such ties. I think it possible that a Utilitarian might work out a scheme in which such obligations and loyalties were given their weight, but I doubt if he could make it wholly consistent with his principles, and certainly Moore makes no attempt to do so.

Not only that, but the idea that I am acting, or should be acting, only with a view to maximizing the occasions on which people can enjoy beauty – defined, by the way, in a circular fashion as that of which the admiring contemplation is good in itself[1] – or appreciate one another's good qualities seems extraordinarily remote from the facts. I cannot give a list of all the types of action that I believe to be right, but apart from fulfilling our obligations they would include such things as relieving people's material wants, defending civil liberties, exposing mischievous superstitions, helping to rescue the victims of political persecution; preserving pictures for the Tate Gallery would come on the list, but not in the highest place.

It is not a fatal objection to Moore that his is the morality of a leisured class. No doubt we should all be working to bring about social changes which would make it possible for everyone to take so lofty a view. It is more of an objection that it is the morality of a leisured class of prigs. Among the highest goods, not one physical pleasure is included. Since lust is rated one of the greater evils, the implication is that it is better to contemplate one's lovers' perfections than to enjoy the possession of their bodies. Russell said of Moore's admirers that, whereas Russell and his friends had 'believed in ordered progress by means of politics and free discussion', 'they aimed rather at a life of retirement among fine shades and nice feelings, and conceived of the good as consisting in the passionate mutual admirations of a clique of the elite'.[2] Russell adds that they fathered this doctrine quite unfairly upon Moore. In view of Moore's sincerity, and the nobility of his character, I wish that the unfairness had been greater than it really was.

Moore and Prichard

It is interesting to contrast Moore's ethical views with those of Harold Arthur Prichard, the most talented member of the school of philosophers, mainly drawing its inspiration from J. Cook Wilson, which

---

[1] *Principia Ethica*, p. 201.
[2] *The Autobiography of Bertrand Russell*, I, p. 64.

was the dominant philosophical force at Oxford in the period between the two world wars. Prichard, who was born in 1871, the son of a London solicitor, and died in 1947, was educated at Clifton and at New College, Oxford, to which he came with a mathematical scholarship in 1890. Having obtained first-class honours in Mathematical Moderations he switched to Philosophy and Ancient History and graduated with first-class honours in Literae Humaniores in 1894. After a few months in which he was articled to a solicitor, he returned to Oxford as a Fellow of Hertford College, which he forsook for Trinity College in 1898. He married in the following year, and had two sons and a daughter, his wife eventually becoming an Alderman of the City of Oxford. As a tutorial Fellow of Trinity he put so much effort into his teaching that after twenty-four years his health gave way and he resigned his fellowship in 1924. Three years later he was elected to the Chair of Moral Philosophy at Oxford, which he held until his retirement in 1937. He was opinionated and pugnacious in philosophical discussion, though said to have been a kindly man in private life.

Like his mentor, Cook Wilson, Prichard was reluctant to commit his views to print. The only book that he had published in his lifetime was *Kant's Theory of Knowledge*, which appeared in 1909. During the period of his professorship he made some attempt to write a book on moral philosophy but it was uncompleted at his death. A large portion of it, together with his two most important published articles and a number of unpublished essays and fragments, was edited by the Provost of Oriel, Sir David Ross, himself primarily an Aristotelian scholar but also a moral philosopher of Prichardian temper, and published in 1949 under the title of *Moral Obligation*.

Prichard's book *Kant's Theory of Knowledge* is mainly an attack on Kant for having any theory of knowledge at all. Again like Cook Wilson, Prichard took the view that knowledge is self-certifying. If one knows that something is the case, no question of doubt arises; one can doubt whether some belief which one holds is true, but then *ex hypothesi* this state of belief is not a state of knowledge. Neither is it proper to ask how one knows whatever it may be. Having identified the proposition in question, one directly apprehends its truth.

It seems to me that this conception of knowledge, which can, indeed, be traced back to Plato, is radically mistaken. Except in the rare cases where the truth of some proposition is a logical condition of one's believing it, as in the assumption of one's own existence, and perhaps also those in which the character of an experience that one is undergoing, like a feeling of intense pain or the content of a day-dream, is such as to exclude any doubt of its occurrence, the fact that someone is convinced that something is so is never logically sufficient to entail that it really is so. There is no mental state which, because of its nature, serves as a guarantee of truth. If knowledge has mistakenly been thought to be such a state, it is because of the purely linguistic fact that one cannot correctly speak of knowing what is not true. It may happen that one has to renounce a claim to knowledge, because the proposition of which one supposed oneself to know the truth has turned out to be false, but what follows from this is that one has used the word 'know' in a case where one of the conditions for its application is not satisfied, not that one has been in any error concerning one's state of mind. If fully confident true belief sometimes falls short of being knowledge, it is not because of any difference on the mental side, but because the grounds for the belief in some way fail to come up to the mark. To explore the varied nature of the grounds, and to set the mark accurately, affords plentiful employment for a theory of knowledge.

This is not to say that every proposition stands in need of an endless sequence of proofs. At some stage in an empirical enquiry one comes to records of experience for which one gives no further reason. In pursuing a deductive argument, one just has to see that one step follows from another. But in the second case, and arguably even in the first, one cannot disallow the possibility of error. There is a limit to the precautions that we can or need take; but this point can be granted, without our being driven into the mistake of holding that there is some special cognitive attitude, which has the magical property of being infallible.

Prichard was a realist in the sense that Kant and Hegel were not. He believed that the character and existence of what was known were independent of the knowledge of it. At the same time he was persuaded, largely by Berkeley's argument, that the data of the senses did not exist independently of our perception of them. This disqualified them from being objects of knowledge and, since he also held that knowledge must be direct, he was led to conclude that perception was not at all a source of knowledge. We were, indeed, under the impression that we frequently saw physical objects, which existed independently of our seeing them, but this was an illusion. What really happened, as he put it, was that we constantly mistook colours for bodies. If he did not relapse into scepticism, it was because he thought that a reasonable belief in the existence of bodies could be founded on some causal argument, though the argument was not one that he ever himself developed. He did not explain even how we came by the idea of bodies, though this should have been a problem for him, since he was committed to holding that we never observed an instance of any body, and since he also maintained that we were familiar with universals only through being acquainted with their instances.

The main features of Prichard's moral philosophy are contained in the first important article that he wrote, 'Does Moral Philosophy Rest On A Mistake?', which appeared in *Mind* in 1912. The mistake which he attributed to moral philosophers was similar to that which he attributed to those who sought for a theory of knowledge. It consisted in the attempt to answer an improper question. Just as, in Prichard's view, it was illegitimate to query a state of knowledge, so there could be no question about one's being in a state of a moral obligation. If one was placed in a given situation and reflected upon all the relevant details, one became aware that it was one's duty to act in such and such a fashion, and that was that. By generalizing from such occasions one could arrive at moral principles, which would be valid in most of their instances, but knowledge of one's particular duties came first. In a situation where two such moral principles conflicted, one could know which to follow. It might be thought an objection that not everyone would take the same view of such a case, or indeed of one's duties generally, but Prichard's answer to this was simply that not everyone had attained the same degree of moral enlightenment.

If an act is one's duty and one knows it to be so, the question whether one is justified in doing it does not arise. Plato, Bishop Butler and other moral philosophers have been at great pains to try to show that it is in one's interest to do what is right, but their efforts have been misguided. In the first place it is not true that acting rightly is always in one's interest, if this means that its consequences will always make one happier than those of some other act that one might have done instead; and secondly, if it were true, it would be beside the point, the only justification for doing a right act being that it is right. There might be some use in trying to make it appear that acting rightly was always in one's interest, if men were so constituted that a view to their own interest was their only motive for action, but this is not in fact the case.

Both in this article and in his other writings about moral obligation, Prichard is particularly anxious to dissociate the rightness of an act both from any intrinsic goodness that the act may have and from the goodness of its consequences. Thus, while he agrees with Moore that good is indefinable, he does not accord it the same primacy. He thinks that an act can acquire intrinsic goodness only through the motive from which it is done, whether the motive be a sense of duty or the display of some virtue like generosity or courage. But an act cannot be made right by being done from a sense of duty: if the sense of duty is justified, the act must be right independently. As for other virtuous motives, which come under the heading of desires, Prichard contends first that a moral obligation is always an obligation to perform some activity, which being moved by a desire is not, and secondly that we are not in command of our desires.

This last argument, which rests on the familiar maxim that 'ought' implies 'can', appears to be dubious. The assumption is that we are free to act upon the motives with which we are provided, but not free to provide ourselves with motives. I can see no *a priori* ground for drawing this distinction, nor does it appear to be empirically justified. If our freedom to acquire desires is denied to us on the ground that there are causal explanations for our possession of them, there may just as well be causal explanations for our choosing whether or not to put them into effect. Prichard himself is given to appealing to our ordinary ways of thinking, and in fact when we make moral judgements we are just as ready to praise and blame people for their motives as for their acts. We do not, for example, find it at all strange to say that people ought to be generous, and we do not regard this injunction as restricted to those who have the good fortune to be endowed with generous feelings.

Prichard's main argument against making the rightness of an act depend upon the goodness of its consequences is that it pre-supposes the untenable proposition that what is good ought to exist. The ground on which he holds this proposition to be untenable is that it might well be, for instance in a case where the right action was not done, that the good consequences were not thought to occur, and in that event there would be no view that we could take of them. In his own words, 'We can no more either think or assert of something which we think does not exist that it ought to exist than we can think or assert anything else about it. Of what we think does not exist we can think and assert nothing at all.'[1] By parity of reasoning, an act which is not thought to be done cannot be thought right. Prichard implicitly admits this point when he argues in another context that 'there are no such characteristics of an action as ought-to-be-doneness and ought-not-to-be-doneness'.[2] He consistently takes the property of 'being morally obliged' as primitive and ascribes it to actual persons.

Even so, he is relying on what is surely a very bad argument. It is true that we cannot consistently ascribe the actual possession of properties to what we deny existence, though we can perfectly well say of non-existent things that they would have such and such properties if they did exist. But the obvious conclusion, in the present instance, is that we are not required to regard 'being something that ought to exist' as a property at all. There is no reason, on the face of it, why we should not say of purely hypothetical events that they would have been better than some events which actually occurred, but if exception is taken to conditionals of this form, and a real subject insisted on, we can easily meet the demand by saying that the world would be a better place if it were to exhibit such and such features rather than such and such other features which it actually does exhibit.

A much better argument, on which Prichard lays less stress, is that in many cases it appears, at least at first sight, that the reason why something ought to be done lies in the actual past rather than in the hypothetical future. I ought to fulfil this engagement because I have promised to; you ought to return the money because you have borrowed it; the prisoner ought to be released because he did not commit the crime. This argument need not be fatal to the Utilitarians. They can reply that these duties do not obtain, irrespectively of the consequences of fulfilling them, and that the reason why promise-keeping, the freeing of innocent persons and the like are held to be right is that they generally lead to the best consequences. Nevertheless, I suspect that this answer will not be found to serve for

[1] *Moral Obligation*, p. 93.
[2] ibid., p. 37.

every particular case.

A question which troubled Prichard was whether one was bound to act in accordance with the circumstances of the case, as they really were, or only as one believed them to be. Prichard opts for the second alternative, on the ground that if its rival were true we could never know what our duties were. There must always be this uncertainty, because our duty will, on this view, be to act in such a way as to cause some change or other, and whatever else we may know we cannot, according to Prichard, ever know the truth of any causal proposition about the future. This has as a consequence not only that one never knows what one can do, but also that when one initiates an action one never knows what one is doing. One only finds out subsequently what one has done. One can, however, set oneself to do something, thinking it likely that our volition will have such and such effects and it is in this that one's duty consists, with the addition that one must have begun by considering the circumstances as fully as one could.

It is worth pointing out that from the point of view of the agent this is an unreal problem. One cannot say to him: 'Act in accordance with the circumstances as they really are, and not just as you believe them to be.' How could he possibly obey such an instruction, except by acting in some random fashion in the hope that it would meet the circumstances? If he is to proceed rationally, he must act in accordance with his beliefs. The position is quite different, however, when the question is put retrospectively. For then, even if we do not disagree with the agent on moral grounds, the fact that he was mistaken in his view of the circumstances may well lead us to conclude that his action was wrong. Nor is it a defence that he could not have known, beyond the possibility of error, what action would be right. The principle that 'ought' implies 'can' may be acceptable, insofar as we cannot fairly be held to be obliged to do what is not in our power, but it does not entail that we ought to do only what we know that we can do, especially if the word 'know' is construed so narrowly that our ability to effect any sort of change in the future has to be accounted as something unknowable.

In spite of the defects in his reasoning, there is, I think, a sense in which Prichard's approach to moral philosophy is preferable to Moore's. Moore might be said to offer us something more in the way of guidance, since he is a Utilitarian of a kind, whereas Prichard just leaves us to our intuitions of our duties; but Moore's injunction to perform the action of which the *total* consequences would be better than those of any possible alternatives is not one that one could have any serious confidence in being able to carry out, and he too leaves it to our intuition to decide what is intrinsically good. They agree that moral judgements are objective in the sense that the proposition that some action is right, or some state of affairs good, cannot be analysed in terms of people's feelings or opinions about the action or the state of affairs in question; but while Prichard takes this to be obvious, Moore, in his little book *Ethics*, advances the bad argument that any such subjective analysis would entail that the same action might be both right and wrong, or the same state of affairs both good and bad. The argument is fallacious because it does not carry the subjectivism through. It is true that one and the same action may be approved of by one person and disapproved of by another, but this is not, on a subjectivist view, to say that the same action may be both right and wrong. It entails rather that one cannot characterize an action as right or wrong, except in relation to the person or persons by whom it is being assessed. Where Prichard has the advantage is in his more serious concern with the details of obligation, and with such questions as the relation of act and motive. Moore, especially in *Principia Ethica*, gives the impression of being less interested in the theory of conduct, and more concerned with the definition of his refined Utopia.

The Refutation of Idealism

In the autobiography which he contributed to *The Philosophy of G. E. Moore*, Moore confessed that of all his Cambridge teachers McTaggart had the strongest influence over him. Thus, in his earliest published paper, a contribution to a symposium on time, which appeared in *Mind* in 1897, he is still able to write of the temporal as being inferior in reality to the timeless, and in an article on 'Freedom', which was published in *Mind* in 1898, he went so far as to say that 'The arguments by which Mr Bradley has appeared to prove the unreality of time appear to me perfectly conclusive'. By the following year, however, he had been converted to an extreme form of Platonic Realism. In 'The Nature of Judgement', another article in *Mind*, he maintained not merely that concepts were objectively real, but that they and the propositions which they combined to form were the only things that there really were. His main argument for this extraordinary conclusion was that the concept of existence is subordinate to that of truth, which itself consists in a relation between concepts. Then, since it cannot be the case that an object satisfies a concept unless the proposition that the object exists is true, the satisfaction of a concept itself becomes a matter of its having a certain relation to other concepts. So to say that this is a piece of paper is to say that the concepts which combine to form the concept of 'a piece of paper' are also combining in a specific manner with the concept of 'this' and 'now' and 'existence'. What the combination has to be in order that the proposition should be true is something that cannot be further defined. It is immediately recognizable, like red or the number two. We see now how Russell came to say, in this early period, that propositions are true or false, just as roses are white or red.

Absurd as this doctrine is, the mistake which leads to it is the same as has led many philosophers to adopt a coherence theory of truth. It is the failure to see that the process of verification must consist, at some point, not just in making the judgement that some object exists, which then takes its place alongside other judgements in the struggle for survival, but in actually having some experience. To discover that some predicate is satisfied is not to discover that two concepts cohere but to relate a concept to what one discovers there to be. The experience is not turned into a judgement by its own need to be conceptualized.

This article of Moore's marks his abandonment of idealism, but except for a slighting reference to Bradley contains no attack against it. His famous official rejection of it is found in an article called 'The Refutation of Idealism', which appeared in *Mind* in 1903. In this article Moore takes what he calls 'Modern Idealism' to assert that reality is spiritual, and he takes this, perhaps rather unfairly, to mean that what we believe to be inanimate objects are really animate. Moore does not claim to be able to disprove this proposition, but he thinks that he can show that its advocates have no good reason for accepting it. This is because he thinks that their acceptance of it is based on a belief in a proposition which he claims that he can disprove.

This proposition is the Berkelian *esse est percipi* – to be is to be perceived, where 'being perceived' is taken in the wider sense of 'being experienced'. Moore spends some time discussing what the proponents of the proposition can be understood to mean by it, and decides that they cannot intend it as a proposition about the meaning of words. What they must mean is that *esse* and *percipi* are logically independent but necessarily connected. Again, Moore does not claim to be able to disprove this proposition, but he believes that his adversaries accept it only because they confuse it with the proposition that *esse* and *percipi* are logically connected; and this is the proposition he sets out to refute. His refutation consists in drawing a distinction between an object and one's consciousness of it. If I am having a sensation of the colour blue, my consciousness and the colour must be different things, since the element of consciousness is present also in other instances, such as my sensation of pain, whereas blue is not. Consequently, Moore argues, 'If anyone tells us that the existence of blue is the same thing as the existence of the sensation of blue he makes a mistake and a self-contradictory mistake, for he asserts *either* that blue is the same thing as blue together with consciousness, *or* that it is the same thing as consciousness alone'.[1]

This is not a good argument. Waltzing is not the same thing as dancing, since the tango is also a dance, but it does not follow that one can waltz without dancing the waltz. In the same way, nothing in Moore's reasoning shows that blue and green sense-data, as he would call them, can exist independently of being sensed. Moreover, he mistakes the purport of Berkeley's idealism. Berkeley did not maintain a general connection between 'being' and 'being perceived' but a specific connection, which he treated as analytic, between 'being a sensible quality' and 'being perceived'. If one wishes to refute Berkeley one has to discredit his assumption that the physical objects of common sense are composed of sensible qualities.

Moore is more successful in his attack on one of the main tenets of Hegelian idealism, the proposition that all relations are internal to their terms, or in other words that every relation in which an object stands to any other is necessary to its being the object that it is, from which, in view of the fact that any two things are somehow related, it will follow that the world is a network of necessary connections. Moore suggests that idealists may have reached this absurd conclusion through a failure to distinguish a necessarily true proposition from one that is generally false. The necessarily true proposition is that the possession by an object A of a relational property P logically entails that in the case of any object X, if X has not got P, X is not

[1] 'The Refutation of Idealism' in *Philosophical Studies*, p. 18.

identical with A. The generally false proposition, with which the other is confused, is that if A has P, then in the case of any object x the proposition that x has not got P entails that x is not identical with A. To illustrate the confusion, Moore takes as examples the propositions 'All the books on this shelf are blue', 'My copy of *The Principles of Mathematics* is a book on this shelf' and 'My copy of *The Principles of Mathematics* is blue'. Then it is certainly true that 'All the books on this shelf are blue' logically entails 'If my copy of *The Principles of Mathematics* is a book on this shelf, my copy of *The Principles of Mathematics* is blue'. On the other hand the proposition that 'If all the books on this shelf are blue', then 'My copy of *The Principles of Mathematics* is a book on this shelf' entails 'My copy of *The Principles of Mathematics* is blue' is false if its antecedent is true; for the entailment affirmed in the consequent evidently does not hold by itself.[1]

Moore's argument is sound, and it seems likely that the idealists whom he is criticizing were guilty of the confusion which he attributes to them. Nevertheless, the problem is more complex than he makes it appear, if only because he seems to overlook the fact that there is no once-for-all answer to the question whether the possession of such and such a property is necessary to the identity of a given object. It depends, among other things, upon the way in which the object is described. For instance, we cannot consistently affirm that the one and only person who wrote *Hamlet* did not write *Hamlet*, but it does not at all follow that writing *Hamlet* was necessary to Shakespeare's identity. For the proposition that Shakespeare wrote *Hamlet* is manifestly contingent. No doubt its negation is false, but it is not self-contradictory.

The fact is that no property is internal to an individual, if its being internal implies that one can find no way of referring to the individual which is logically consistent with denying it the property. Moore gives as an example of an internal relation the property which is possessed by a coloured patch, half of which is red and half yellow, of containing the red patch as a part. He argues that if it did not contain that part, it would necessarily be a different whole.[2] But clearly this is no more than a result of the way he has chosen to describe the whole in

[1] 'External Relations' in *Philosophical Studies*, p. 301.
[2] ibid., pp. 287–8.

question. It would not obtain, if he had described the patch initially as one which occupied such and such a spatial position, or as the surface of such and such an object, or in any number of other ways in which it could equally well be identified.

It has, indeed, to be admitted that there is a difference between the cases in which someone makes a false statement, or entertains a counterfactual hypothesis about some particular to which he can properly be taken as referring, and those in which his descriptions are so wide of the mark that the reference should be held to fail. The question is whether there are any settled principles of individuation, by means of which one can discriminate between these cases, and I do not think that there are. So much depends upon the context of the speaker's utterance, the beliefs that he actually holds, even his position in time relatively to his referential target. For instance, living when I am and knowing what I do, I should be inclined to say that anyone who spoke of a philosopher not yet born would necessarily not be referring to Moore; yet a historian writing several hundred years hence need not be held to be missing the reference if he gave a reasonably accurate account of Moore's life and works but made the mistake of locating him in the twenty-first century. No doubt it is necessary for a successful reference that some hold be achieved on the object's actual history, but I do not think that the ascription to it of any particular property or even any disjunction of properties can be regarded as essential.[1]

The Defence of Common Sense

From the time when he delivered the lectures which were eventually published as *Some Main Problems of Philosophy*, Moore's chief philosophical interests were the defence of what he called the common-sense view of the world, and the analysis of the propositions which were comprised in it. In defending the common-sense view of the world, Moore did not commit himself to subscribing to every belief that might be held by a majority of his fellow citizens. For instance, he never thought there was any good reason to believe in the existence of a deity or of an after-life. He was concerned only to uphold three very general propositions, which he thought that nearly everybody took for granted, together with great numbers of particular propositions from which they followed.

[1] cf. my discussion of the use of proper names and essentialism in Chapter IX, below, pp. 265–70.

The first of these general beliefs was 'that there are in the universe enormous numbers of material objects'.[1] Moore did not offer any positive definition of a material object, but he gave as examples, human bodies, animals, plants, mountains, grains of sand, minerals, drops of water, manufactured articles, such as pieces of furniture and machines, the earth, the sun and the stars. All these things were supposed to be located in a single space and time.

The second belief was that men, and perhaps some other animals, have minds, which Moore takes as meaning that they perform what he calls acts of consciousness. Again, he does not try to define acts of consciousness but gives as examples, hearing, seeing, remembering, feeling, thinking and dreaming. Moore attributes to common sense the belief that these acts are located not only in time but in space, their spatial position being that of the bodies of the creatures who are performing them. He thinks that these acts are also believed to be attached to bodies, in the sense of being causally dependent on them. Material objects are among the things on which acts of consciousness are directed, but in the vast majority of cases they are not themselves conscious, and they can exist without there being any consciousness of them.

The third main belief which Moore attributes to common sense is the belief that we really do know that there are material objects and acts of consciousness, and that they have the properties that he has listed. Not only that, but 'We believe that we *know* an immense number of details about particular material objects and acts of consciousness, past, present and future'.[2] It is, indeed, from the truth of these more specific propositions that the truth of the more general propositions follows.

This comes out clearly in an essay called 'A Defence of Common Sense', which first appeared in 1925 in the second series of *Contemporary British Philosophy* and was reprinted in Moore's *Philosophical Papers*. In this essay he begins by giving a long list of propositions, every one of which he claims to know with certainty to be true. These propositions fall into three groups. In outline, the propositions of the first group are that there exists, and has for some time existed, a human body which is his body; that during the time that it has existed, this body has been 'in contact with or not far from

[1] *Some Main Problems of Philosophy*, p. 2.
[2] ibid., p. 12.

the surface of the earth'; that there have existed many other things, 'also having shape and size in three dimensions', from which it has been at various distances and with some of which it has been in contact; that among these things have been other human bodies of which the same propositions are true; that many of these bodies have ceased to exist; that the earth had existed for many years before he was born; and that during many of those years a large number of human bodies had at every moment been alive upon it, and had, in very many cases, ceased to exist before he was born. The second group of propositions consists, in outline, of the propositions that since his birth he has had many different experiences; that he has often perceived his own body, and other things in its environment, including other human bodies; that he has often observed facts about these things, such as the fact, which he is observing as he writes, that a particular mantelpiece is nearer to his body than a particular bookcase; that he is aware of facts which he is not at present observing, such that his body existed on the previous day and was then for some time nearer to the mantelpiece than to the bookcase; that he has had expectations with regard to the future; that he has held many beliefs, both true and false; that he has thought of imaginary things without believing in their reality; that he has had dreams; that he has had feelings of many different kinds; and that many other human beings have had similar experiences. Finally, the third group consists of the single proposition which states with regard to many other human beings, who resemble Moore in that, *mutatis mutandis*, the propositions of his first two classes are also true of them, that each of them has frequently known, with regard to himself and his body, propositions corresponding to those that Moore has listed.[1]

Moore's negative argument in favour of there being material objects is that if the thesis that there are none is true, no philosopher has ever held it; for philosophers are themselves embodied persons. This does not show his opponents' case to be self-contradictory, since it is not logically necessary that there be philosophers, but it is a strong argument *ad homines*. A position which Moore does claim to be self-contradictory is the apparently weaker one of those who argue that we do not know that there are material objects. He finds the contradiction in the use of the word 'we' which he takes as implying

[1] *Philosophical Papers*, pp. 32–5.

the claim to know that the speaker and other persons exist. This argument is questionable, if it is possible to hold, as some philosophers have, that in referring to oneself one is referring to a being who has experiences but is not known to be embodied, though he may be so in fact; for them the use of the word 'we' need be taken to imply no more than that if there are other persons, in this limited sense, the same applies to them.

Moore's only positive argument is very simple. It is set out in a lecture entitled 'Proof of an External World' which was delivered to the British Academy in 1939 and is also reprinted in his *Philosophical Papers*. 'I can,' he then said, 'prove now, for instance, that two human hands exist. How? By holding up my two hands, and saying, as I make a certain gesture with the right hand, "Here is one hand", and adding, as I make a certain gesture with the left, "And here is another". And, if by doing this, I have proved *ipso facto* the existence of external things, you will see that I can also do it now in numbers of other ways: there is no need to multiply examples.'[1] And a little later Moore went on to prove that material objects had existed in the past simply by reminding his audience that he had held up his hands not long before.

Moore did not on this occasion consider the possibility that he might be dreaming, and later, in a lecture on 'Certainty', delivered in 1941 and included in the *Philosophical Papers*, where he addressed himself to this question, he could do no more than suggest, implausibly, that the proposition that he was dreaming might be formally inconsistent with the conjunction of his current sense-experiences and memories. He would have done better to stick to his old style and claim that he knew himself to be awake.

Though Moore himself does not make it explicit, there is an assumption underlying his claims to knowledge. The assumption is that the reasons which we have for holding what he calls our common-sense beliefs are sufficient reasons. In the present circumstances, the evidence of my senses, interpreted in the light of theories which have been vindicated by the whole course of my experiences, puts it beyond doubt that I am seated at a table and using a pen to write upon a sheet of paper. My memory supplies me with conclusive answers to such questions as who I am, what I was doing yesterday, how I came to be here. Admittedly, there is room for error even in

[1] ibid., p. 146.

the case of such modest propositions as these. Our memories do sometimes err with respect to recent events. There are such things as hallucinations. Under the most normal conditions, our judgements of perception may be careless. Yet when such errors do occur, they are easily corrected. I discover that my memory or that my senses have deceived me because the beliefs to which they have led me are not corroborated by my subsequent perceptions, including those that furnish me with the testimony of other people. At this common-sense level our experiences are self-governing. They offer no foothold for philosophy to intervene. As Moore was given to saying, any philosophical argument which was designed to discredit the common-sense view of the world was bound to be less certain, more likely to be defective, than the propositions which it attacked.

But now it is plain that this argument can be generalized. If the propositions of common sense are self-governing, in the way that Moore took them to be, so are the propositions which belong to the formal or the natural sciences, so are those that belong to literary scholarship, to the study of history or of law. In all these cases there are recognized standards of proof and recognized procedures for determining whether these standards have been met. If someone refuses to regard a favourable experiment as confirming a scientific theory, then, unless he has some special reason for mistrusting the experiment, unless he has grounds for suspecting that there has been an error of observation, or that there is some other special reason why the apparent result of the experiment is not to be taken at its face value, he simply has not understood what the theory is. If someone refuses to accept the result of a logical or mathematical demonstration, without having any special reason for thinking that the procedure which was employed in this instance was faulty or inaccurately carried out, he simply does not understand how logic and mathematics work.

This argument has serious consequences for philosophy. For what follows from it is that the truth or falsehood of all these propositions is not even a matter for philosophical discussion. It depends only on the satisfaction of the appropriate criteria: and whether the criteria are satisfied is always a matter of empirical or formal fact. What part, then, was there left for philosophy to play? The answer which Moore accepted in practice, and his followers also in theory, was that it could engage in the activity of analysis. But what activity is this? And what purpose does it serve?

A simple answer to the first of these questions is that a successful analysis of a proposition tells us what we mean by the sentences which we use to express it. Its purpose would then be to represent the proposition in a more illuminating way, to bring out some complexity in it which the previous formulation concealed. The same would apply to the analysis of concepts. But although this answer covers the example of brothers being male siblings, which Moore used to illustrate the 'paradox of analysis', it cannot be quite correct. If it were, philosophy, on this view of its function, would not be significantly different from lexicography; and this is not the case.

That there is a significant difference is made clear by the fact that while Moore does not question the truth of the propositions which enter into the common-sense view of the world, he is very doubtful about their analysis. But if he is to know that a sentence, like the English sentence 'This is a human hand', expresses a true proposition, he must know what it means. And indeed he insists in his essay 'A Defence of Common Sense' that to anyone who commands the language to which they belong the meaning of such sentences is perfectly plain. How then can there be a problem about the analysis of the propositions which they express, especially if, as Moore requires, the proposition which furnishes the analysis is to be equivalent to the proposition analysed?

The answer is that one can understand a sentence perfectly well, and yet be puzzled when it comes to giving an account of the conditions which are necessary and sufficient for the truth of the proposition which it expresses. A good example is that of sentences containing personal pronouns. An English speaker, for instance, has no difficulty in understanding the use of the word 'I' or even in giving an account of its use. It is the pronoun by which a person refers to himself as the subject of his utterance. Yet if the same speaker were asked to give an account of personal identity, he might well be at a loss. Does his being the same person over a period of time consist in the duration of a spiritual substance? Is it a question of the relation of a particular series of experiences, and if so what is that relation? Does it consist in the persistence of a particular body? Does it consist in the attachment to a particular body of a series of experiences, and if so what is the nature of this attachment? Are the experiences themselves physical events? These are difficult and contested questions, and they all need to be answered if we are to give an analysis of propositions expressed by English sentences containing the English word 'I'; sentences, the ordinary meaning of which is easily understood.

Moore himself did not pay much attention to the question of self-identity. The problem of philosophical analysis on which he chiefly concentrated was that of finding the correct analysis of propositions about material objects like 'This is a human hand' or 'That is the sun', and he never found a solution to it. As he said in 'A Defence of Common Sense', the only things about it which ever seemed quite certain to him were, first, that when one knows or judges such a proposition to be true, 'there is always some *sense-datum* about which the proposition in question is a proposition – some sense-datum which is *a* subject (and, in a certain sense, the principal or ultimate subject) of the proposition in question', and secondly 'that, nevertheless, *what* I am knowing or judging to be true about this sense-datum is not (in general) that it is *itself* a hand, or a dog, or the sun, etc. etc. as the case may be'.[1] As for the question what one is then judging, Moore thought that there were three possible theories, one of which he eventually rejected, though he had at times seemed to think it the most attractive of the three. This was the theory that what we are judging, and what we know when we know a proposition of this sort to be true, is that the sense-datum is identical with part of the surface of the material object in question. The second theory was that we know or judge there to be some relation R such that some unique thing, or set of things, which is part of the surface of the material object in question has the relation R to this sense-datum. Most philosophers who have adopted this type of theory have taken R to be some causal relation, but Moore says that the only view of this kind which seems to him to have any plausibility is that 'R is an ultimate and unanalysable relation'.[2] And the third theory was the phenomenalist theory, which Mill summarized by saying that things are permanent possibilities of sensation. On this view, to know, for example, that this is a hand is to know that under the appropriate conditions one would perceive other sense-data which are related to this one in certain specific ways.

But now we see how wide the difference can be between knowing what a sentence means and knowing the analysis of the proposition which it expresses. It is hard to envisage how any mere reflection on the

[1] ibid., p. 54.
[2] ibid., p. 57.

meaning of sentences like 'This is a hand' could lead us to the theories between which Moore hesitates. In the first place, how do sense-data get into the picture?

The answer is that they are the product of a theory. Moore is using the term 'sense-datum', as we have seen that it was used at one stage by Russell, to refer to what is immediately given in experience. Like Russell, Moore agreed with the many philosophers who have held that a perceptual judgement, like the judgement that this is a table, is an inference for which the awareness of some sensory items supplies the premiss. It may be recalled that this is an assumption which is now quite widely rejected, so that many philosophers, so far from sharing Moore's certainty that the ultimate subjects of perceptual judgements are sense-data, deny that there are any such entities at all. My own view, as I have indicated, is that while it is not necessary to have recourse to anything of the order of sense-data, in order to describe the facts, the introduction of a term, which fulfils this function, is legitimate and advantageous. It makes it easier to show how the common-sense view of the physical world operates as a theory with respect to our sense-experiences. This goes, however, only a limited distance towards vindicating Moore's approach.

The reason why it does not go the full distance is, I believe, that Moore set the problem in a way that made it impossible for him to solve it. The assumption from which he started was that a sentence like 'This is a hand' could be expanded in the first instance into 'There is just one hand that stands in the relation R to *this*', and that the 'this' in the second sentence denoted a sense-datum. His problem then was to find the right value for the relation R, or, in other words, to discover exactly what we are saying about a sense-datum when we assert such a proposition as that this is a hand. But if, as would appear to be the case, the function of a demonstrative like the English word 'this' is not to name any object but merely to direct the hearer's attention to the object which the speaker wishes him to identify, the correct answer may be that in asserting a proposition of this kind we are not saying anything at all about a sense-datum. This is not inconsistent with my view that it is possible to construct a physical system on the basis of what I now prefer to call sense-qualia. For, even if I am right on this point, it does not follow that the statements of the physical system can be translated into sensory statements, any more than the statements of theoretical physics can be translated into the physical object statements by which the theory is supported. Neither does it follow that I am referring to a sense-quale, when I am speaking at the physical level, even if the physical object of which I am speaking is finally identified by the use of a demonstrative. It is of course possible to designate a sense-quale and ask how it is related to the physical object to which it corresponds. And then, if one has been able to show in general how standardized percepts, as I call them, are converted into physical objects, the correct answer may just be that it is one of a group of sense-qualia out of which the relevant standardized percept can be abstracted.

If this answer is correct, it vindicates Moore's reluctance to give up the theory that sense-data are sometimes identical with parts of the surfaces of physical objects. This theory is not acceptable as it stands. If, as I maintain, the physical object is an idealization, no sense-quale, or group of sense-qualia, can be identical with any part of it. Nevertheless, it is in the theory's favour that the physical object is an idealization of sense-qualia, and that it is from sense-qualia which we take as typical that the object directly derives its perceptual properties. This is not the sort of analysis that Moore was looking for, but it may be the most that can be achieved from his starting-point.

What then remains of Moore's defence of common sense? Not very much, when we consider that it has nothing to say about the relation of the physical world as we perceive it to the physical world as physicists describe it. We have already seen that this is a serious problem. We have to decide how, if at all, these two apparently disparate views of the world can be reconciled. It might be thought that in upholding common sense Moore was opting for the view that physical objects persist in some such form as we perceive them, but he is not so committed. For one thing, it is not entirely clear that this is the view of common sense, which has become sophisticated in some measure by its understanding or misunderstanding of science; and in any case questions of this sort are left by Moore to the grasp of analysis. And the same would apply to the status of acts of consciousness. But if we have to wait upon analysis, which emerges as theorizing, to discover what the constituents of the common-sense view of the world really are, our certainty of their existence is less of an acquisition than one might at first suppose.

What we still owe to Moore is the reminder that the criteria which govern the truth of our everyday judgements of perception are very frequently satisfied, and, with the grant of the same measure of autonomy to other domains, an assignment to philosophy of what turns out to be a major role of interpretation. Less obviously than Russell, but no less effectively, he gives pre-eminence to the theory of knowledge.

III Pragmatism

William James

William James was born in New York in 1842 and died in 1910. He took a medical degree at Harvard, to which he returned in 1872 as an instructor in physiology. He became a lecturer in psychology there in 1876 and a professor of philosophy in 1880. His major work, *The Principles of Psychology*, appeared in two large volumes in 1890. It uniquely combines a physiological with a philosophical approach to the traditional problems of psychology, and as a general review of the subject has probably not yet been superseded. Philosophically, it foreshadows the development of James's 'Radical Empiricism', which blends with his Pragmatism to make his distinctive contribution to philosophy.

Influenced perhaps by his father, the elder Henry James, who was a disciple of the mystic Swedenborg, William James also maintained an abiding interest in religion. He wrote a number of essays on moral and religious questions and collected them in a book called *The Will to Believe*, which was published in 1897. This was followed by *The Varieties of Religious Experience*, a set of Gifford lectures delivered in Scotland in 1901–2 and published in 1902. This treatise on the psychology of religion is probably the best written of all James's works and the one best known to the general public. In his own way he was as gifted a writer as his younger brother, the novelist Henry James, though their styles were very different. Paradoxically, it is Henry who writes with the careful qualifications and minute attention to detail that one might expect of a psychologist or a philosopher, and William who carries the reader away with his humour and zest and the vividness of his imagery. This very virtue of his writing is in one way a detriment to his philosophy. He did not always take the time and trouble to make his meaning entirely clear or to safeguard his theories from minute criticism.

James's great period of philosophical activity came in the last decade of his life. All but one of the twelve papers which make up his posthumously published *Essays in Radical Empiricism* were first printed in the years 1903–4. His book *Pragmatism*, which was first published in June 1907, was approximately a transcript of lectures which he had delivered during the preceding year, first in Boston and then at Columbia University in New York. The book enjoyed great popular success in the United States, and to a lesser extent in England, but also met with much professional criticism. James enjoyed philosophical controversy, and the essays which made up his book *The Meaning of Truth*, which was published in 1909, are mainly devoted to the defence and restatement of the pragmatic theory of truth, as he envisaged it. 1909 was also the year in which he delivered in Oxford a course of lectures, published under the title of *A Pluralistic Universe*, and began work on the book *Some Problems of Philosophy*, which was published only after his death.

By this time James was internationally regarded as the foremost exponent of the American philosophy of Pragmatism, but he had not in fact been its originator. His friend and contemporary Charles Sanders Peirce, who lived from 1839 to 1914, was the first to give currency to the terms, and it was Peirce who, in a series of papers which he published in the 1870s, set out the basic principles of the pragmatic theory of meaning and truth. Much of Peirce's work, however, remained unpublished in his lifetime, and the papers which he did publish attracted relatively little attention. He was unable to command a regular position at any American university and his main employment was as an official in the United States Coast and Geodetic Survey. It was only in the early 1930s, after Harvard brought out the first six of the eight large volumes of his Collected Papers, that he began to be at all widely recognized as one of the great philosophers of the nineteenth century. It can fairly be argued that he was a more profound, as well as a more inventive philosopher, than William James, but in the actual development of twentieth-century philosophy James is historically the more important figure.

The Character of James's Pragmatism

The main attraction of Pragmatism for James was that he saw it as illuminating and in a large measure resolving the principal issues of philosophical dispute. It allowed him to take one side in the debate, while leaving his opponents enough to save their honour. This was particularly true of his stand on the question of Monism and Pluralism. From a logical point of view his allegiance was wholly given to Pluralism, but he acknowledged the spiritual needs of those who wished to see the universe as One, and he thought that Pragmatism allowed for their indulgence.

The monism to which James was hostile was that of the contemporary followers of Hegel, in particular F. H. Bradley and James's Harvard colleague Josiah Royce (1855–1916). Neither of these philosophers was an entirely orthodox Hegelian, nor did they wholly agree with one another, but they were alike in identifying Reality with a Spiritual Whole, which they called The Absolute. In Bradley's case, this was largely the result of his adopting the view, later to be discredited by G. E. Moore, that all relations are internal to their terms,[1] with the result that he came to see everything as inextricably mixed with everything else. In Royce's case, it depended rather on his inability to see how our thoughts could refer to reality, whether truly or falsely, unless both the thinker and the object of his thought were themselves ideas in an all-knowing Mind, a doctrine which James characteristically parodied as the belief that a cat cannot look at a king unless some higher entity is looking at them both. Bradley and Royce were alike also in taking the Absolute to be perfect, with the difference that Bradley thought of it as necessarily transcending good and evil, whereas Royce believed that it held them in harmony, the existence of evil being, as he saw it, a necessary condition for that of the greatest good.

Theories of this type were offensive to James's feelings as well as to his reason. He was pleased by the show of variety in the world and resented its dismissal as mere appearance. He was morally shocked also by the blandness and callousness displayed in such remarks as Bradley's 'The Absolute is the richer for every discord, and for all the disunity which it embraces', with its implication that pain can be assumed to 'disappear into a higher unity'. Against this, he quotes with approval the protest of the anarchist writer M. I. Swift that when men commit suicide because they cannot find work to keep their

---

[1] See above, pp. 57–8.

families from starving, 'that slain man makes the universe richer, and that is philosophy. But while Professors Royce and Bradley and a whole host of guileless thoroughfed thinkers are unveiling Reality and the Absolute and explaining away evil and pain, this is the condition of the only beings known to us anywhere in the universe with a developed consciousness of what the universe is. What these people experience *is* Reality.'[1] Neither was this only a moral question for James. He was intellectually opposed to a conception of reality which in any way divorced it from actual experience.

Nevertheless, as I said earlier, James did not lack sympathy for the spiritual yearnings which Absolute Idealism was partly designed to satisfy. In Royce's case at least, the underlying motive was overtly religious, and there are passages in *Pragmatism*, and still more in some of James's earlier writing, where James not only shows respect for this motive but appears even to concede that belief in the Absolute is justified by it. How seriously this is to be taken will depend on the way in which one interprets James's pragmatic theory of truth. We shall see later on that there is some ground for thinking that he treated moral and religious questions as a special case. But whatever sympathy he may have felt for the outlook of those to whom the idea of the absolute brought emotional satisfaction, it was not an outlook that he shared. This comes out in a characteristic passage from the earliest of his essays in *Essays in Radical Empiricism:*

Since we are in the main not sceptics, we might go on and frankly confess to each other the motives for our several faiths. I frankly confess mine – I cannot but think that at bottom they are of an aesthetic and not a logical sort. The 'through-and-through' universe seems to suffocate me with its infallible impeccable all-pervasiveness. Its necessity, with no possibilities; its relations, with no subjects, make me feel as if I had entered into a contract with no reserved rights, or rather as if I had to live in a large seaside boarding-house with no private bedroom in which I might take refuge from the society of the place. I am distinctly aware, moreover, that the old quarrel of sinner and pharisee has something to do with the matter. Certainly, to my personal knowledge, all Hegelians are not prigs, but I somehow feel as if all prigs ought to end, if developed, by becoming Hegelians. There is a story of two clergymen asked by mistake to conduct the same funeral. One came first and had got no further than 'I am the Resurrection and the Life' when the other entered. '*I* am the Resurrection and the Life,' cried the latter. The 'through-and-through' phil-

[1] M. I. Swift, *Human Submission*, quoted in *Pragmatism*, p. 21.

osophy, as it actually exists, reminds many of us of that clergyman. It seems too buttoned-up and white-chokered and clean-shaven a thing to speak for the vast slow-breathing unconscious Kosmos with its dread abysses and its unknown tides.[1]

One of the most interesting features of this passage is James's avowal of his suspicion that the motives of his philosophical 'faith' are fundamentally 'of an aesthetic and not a logical sort', and indeed it would seem that he always had a tendency to look upon philosophy as expressing some general attitude towards the world rather than as seeking, and if possible advancing, the correct solutions to a special set of problems. Thus, in the first of his lectures on Pragmatism he characterizes the history of philosophy as being 'to a great extent that of a certain clash of human temperaments'. He does not ignore the fact that philosophers most commonly advance arguments to support their theses, but he thinks that such arguments play a secondary role. The philosopher's temperament 'really gives him a stronger bias than any of his more strictly objective premisses. It loads the evidence for him one way or the other, making for a more sentimental and a more hard-hearted view of the universe, just as this fact or that principle would.'[2] Since these biases are not acknowledged, philosophical discussions have 'a certain insincerity'.

James thinks that this contrast between the more sentimental and the more hard-hearted view of the universe is to be found at work not only in philosophy but in 'literature, art, government and manners'.[3] He presently expands it into his celebrated dichotomy of the tender and the tough-minded, the tender-minded being Rationalistic (going by 'principles'), Intellectualistic, Idealistic, Optimistic, Religious, Free-willist, Monistic, and Dogmatical: the tough-minded correspondingly being Empiricist (going by 'facts'), Sensationalistic, Materialistic, Pessimistic, Irreligious, Fatalistic, Pluralistic and Sceptical.[4] James does not name any philosopher as fitting into either category, though it can fairly be assumed that he counted Hegel and his followers as tender-minded, while Hume and perhaps John Stuart Mill might serve as models for the tough. In most instances the strains are mixed, though one or other of them may predominate. Indeed,

---

[1] *Essays in Radical Empiricism*, pp. 276–8.
[2] *Pragmatism*, p. 7.
[3] ibid., p. 12.
[4] ibid.

James himself is conspicuously such a mixture. In some ways he was very tough-minded: a radical empiricist, a sensationalist in his theory of being as well as in his theory of knowledge, a good deal of a materialist in his psychology and, if not a sceptic, not at all dogmatical. On the other hand, he was optimistic, temperamentally religious, anxious to find some opening for free will, and not a philosophical materialist. In sum, he was tough-minded in his approach to questions of natural facts but tender-minded when it came to morals and theology. It was not so much a question of his having a divided temperament as of there being a conflict between his sentiments and his reason. He wanted to retain his tender-minded beliefs, but not at the price of relaxing his intellectual standards. What chiefly attracted him to pragmatism was that it seemed to him the only philosophy that made this possible.

In the course of explaining 'what pragmatism means', James defined its scope as covering first a method and secondly a theory of truth. The method is based on a principle which Peirce had put forward in a paper, published in the 1870s, called 'How to make our ideas clear'. In James's reformulation it runs: 'To attain perfect clearness in our thoughts of an object . . . we need only consider what conceivable effects of a practical kind the object may involve – what sensations we are to expect from it, and what reactions we must prepare. Our conception of these effects, whether immediate or remote, is then for us the whole of our conception of the object, so far as that conception has positive significance at all.'[1] In a similar vein he speaks of the pragmatic method as forbidding us to rest content with a 'solving name' like 'God', 'Matter', 'Reason', 'the Absolute' or 'Energy'. Rather, 'You must bring out of each word its practical cash-value, set it at work within the stream of your experience. It appears less as a solution, then, than as a program for more work, and more particularly as an indication of the ways in which existing realities may be *changed*.'[2]

These descriptions of the pragmatic method are more vivid than precise. It is not clear what we are to count as the effects of an object, or what the cash value of a word comprises, or how words like 'Matter' and 'the Absolute' can be set at work, or how the process of setting them at work can lead to change in existing realities. Similar

[1] ibid., p. 29.
[2] ibid., pp. 31–2.

statements are to be found in Peirce's writings, and in his case the prevailing idea appears to be that the meaning of a concept is to be sought in the observational tests by which the presence of what falls under it is scientifically detected. As scientific theories change, and new evidence becomes available, the meaning of a concept may evolve, and indeed Peirce regards the laws of nature themselves as subject to evolution. The observations, by which the meaning is fixed at any given stage, are at the physical level and are publicly repeatable. That James's approach is different, especially on this last point, is shown by his illustrating the effects of an object as 'the sensations we are to expect from it' and by his associating the cash-value of a word with the stream of one's experience. From this and from similar clues which occur in other passages of his works, we may infer that he meant to analyse one's conception of an object not, like Peirce, in scientific terms but rather in terms of the difference to one's sense-experiences which the object's existence or non-existence would be expected to make. If we apply the idea of cash-value to statements rather than to individual words, the cash-value of a statement may be taken to consist in the experiences that one would have if the statement were discovered to be true. A word is set at work by one's belief in the various statements in which it figures, and it is by setting out to verify or falsify these statements that we make a change in existing realities.

Radical Empiricism

By interpreting James's pragmatic theory of meaning in this way, I am fulfilling what I believe to have been his intention of bringing it into harmony with his Radical Empiricism. The cardinal feature of this empiricism, which we have seen that Russell also adopted at one point in his career, is that what Russell called the ultimate furniture of the world is taken to be experience. As such, experience is neither mental nor physical. The theory is that both mind and matter can be constructed out of it. The distinction between 'thoughts' and 'things', like the distinction between 'the knower' and 'the known', is to be analysed wholly in terms of the different relations in which the elements of experience stand to one another. Just as the same geometrical point can lie at the junction of two intersecting lines, so the same item of experience can be a member of two different groups of experience, one of which constitutes a physical object and the other a mind.

To illustrate this, James invites us to consider a typical case of sense-perception; for instance, that of his reader's present perception of the room in which he is sitting. Philosophers may tell him that the physical objects, which he takes himself to be perceiving, are not directly presented to him; the immediate data of perception are subjective impressions to which it is inferred that external objects correspond. But the trouble with such theories is that 'they violate the reader's sense of life, which knows no intervening mental image but seems to see the room and the book immediately just as they physically exist'.[1]

On this issue James sides with his reader. He suggests that the reason why philosophers have had recourse to representative theories of perception is that they have thought it impossible that 'what is evidently one reality should be in two places at once, both in outer space and in a person's mind'.[2] But he argues that this difficulty vanishes once it is realized that the object's being in two different places is simply a matter of its belonging at the same time to two different groups, or, as James prefers to say, its entering simultaneously into two different processes. His account of these processes is worth quoting for its own sake:

One of them is the reader's personal biography, the other is the history of the house of which the room is part. The presentation, the experience, the *that* in short (for until we have decided *what* it is it must be a mere *that*) is the last term of a train of sensations, emotions, decisions, movements, classifications, expectations, etc., ending in the present, and the first term of a series of similar 'inner' operations extending into the future, on the reader's part. On the other hand, the very same *that* is the *terminus ad quem* of a lot of previous physical operations, carpentering, papering, furnishing, warming, etc., and the *terminus a quo* of a lot of future ones, in which it will be concerned when undergoing the destiny of a physical room. The physical and the mental operations form curiously incompatible groups. As a room, the experience has occupied that spot and had that environment for thirty years. As your field of consciousness it may never have existed until now. As a room, attention will go on to discover endless new details in it. As your mental state merely, few new ones will emerge under attention's eye. As a room, it will take an earthquake, or a

----

[1] *Essays in Radical Empiricism*, p. 12.
[2] ibid., p. 11.

gang of men, and in any case a certain amount of time to destroy it. As your subjective state, the closing of your eyes, or any instantaneous play of your fancy will suffice. In the real world, fire will consume it. In your mind, you can let fire play over it without effect. As an outer object, you must pay so much a month to inhabit it. As an inner content, you may occupy it for any length of time rent-free. If, in short, you follow it in the mental direction, taking it along with events of personal biography solely, all sorts of things are true of it which are false, and false of it which are true if you treat it as a real thing experienced, follow it in the physical direction, and relate it to associates in the outer world.[1]

This passage is both characteristically vivid and characteristically careless. On the face of it, it is full of contradictions. How, for example, can it be true of one and the same entity both that it has just come into existence and that it has existed for many years past? But the contradictions lie only on the surface. They are due to James's failing to take the trouble to distinguish between a given experience and the different groups of which it may be a member. The experience itself is ephemeral: the persistent object, with which James identifies it in one of its aspects, is not any single experience but a group of actual and possible experiences of which the given experience is one. In fact, everything that James here says about the experience in its physical aspects should be construed as applying to the group. On the mental side also, he goes beyond the experience when he says such things as that fire can play over it without effect, since they refer to the play of imagination on it. In this way it is 'collected' by another member of the mental group.

But while these emendations may show that James's story can be freed from contradiction, they do not show that it illustrates a tenable theory. For this, much more would be needed. We should have to be told what are the relations between different experiences that make them, respectively, elements of the same physical object or elements of the same mind, and in James's exposition these requirements are not met. Indeed, on the physical side he makes no serious attempt to meet them. He lets it be understood that what distinguishes a 'physical experience' from a merely mental one is the regularity of the association of experiences of its sort with other experiences of the appropriate type; but he does not

[1] ibid., pp. 13–15.

say what these associations are or what are the salient characteristics of the experiences which they are supposed to relate. He also sees that our actual percepts are too fragmentary to constitute a physical world on their own. They form a nucleus which has to be supplemented by 'a lot of conceptual experiences'. But again we are not told in any detail how this is to be achieved.

James does make a more serious effort to deal with the problem of personal identity. His theory that minds are constructed out of items of experience echoes Hume's view of the self as 'a bundle of perceptions'. Like Hume, he sees no reason to assume the existence of what is variously called a pure ego, or soul, or mental substance. Not only is the existence of such a substance not verifiable, but 'the substantial view' is not required 'for expressing the actual subjective phenomena of consciousness as they appear'.[1] It explains nothing that cannot be equally well or better explained without it. Where James parts company with Hume is in refusing to be discouraged by the fact that our perceptions are distinct existences between which the mind perceives no 'real connection'. Our perceptions are indeed distinct existences, in the sense that they are logically independent of one another, but this does not mean that there cannot be any factual connections between them. What unites them, in James's view, is primarily the fact that 'within each personal consciousness, thought is sensibly continuous'. That is to say, 'the changes from one moment to another in the quality of consciousness are never absolutely abrupt' and 'when there is a time-gap the consciousness after it feels as if it belonged together with the consciousness before it, as another part of the same self'.[2] In other words, the work of unification is carried out within the series through the appropriation by later thoughts of earlier experiences with which they feel the right affinity. The trouble is that, when there are gaps in consciousness so that the relation of sensible continuity fails, this feeling of affinity may be deceptive. An appeal to the continuity of the body, to which they are all similarly related, still seems to be requisite to bring all the experiences of one and the same person into a single fold.

James also follows Hume in accepting the distinction between what Hume called 'relations of ideas' and 'matters of fact', and like Hume he attributes the necessity of *a priori* propositions to their

---

[1] *The Principles of Psychology*, I, p. 344.
[2] ibid., p. 237.

being concerned only with relations of ideas. 'Our ready-made ideal framework,' he says in *Pragmatism*, 'for all sorts of possible objects follows from the very structure of our thinking. We can no more play fast and loose with these abstract relations than we can do so with our sense-experiences. They coerce us, we must treat them consistently, whether or not we like the results'.[1] This is at variance with an earlier statement in *The Principles of Psychology* according to which 'The eternal verities which the structure of our mind lays hold of do not necessarily themselves lay hold on extra-mental being, nor have they, as Kant pretended . . . a legislating character even for all possible experiences. They are primarily interesting only as subjective facts. They stand waiting in the mind, forming a beautiful ideal network; and the most we can say is that we hope to discover outer realities over which the network may be flung so that the real and the ideal may coincide'.[2] Perhaps the two groups can be reconciled, if we attribute to James the view that the structure of the mind is not fixed once for all but is capable of being modified in the course of experience. *A priori* propositions would indeed be 'eternally' true of the current set of 'mental objects', but the 'mental objects' which make up our 'ideal framework' at any given moment might be liable to change in the light of further experience.

James's Theory of Truth

For James, the central feature of Pragmatism was what he took to be its theory of truth. Unfortunately, his exposition of this theory, as he understood it, again sacrificed accuracy to vigour. He did himself a particular disservice by making remarks which seemed to imply that he was equating truth with expediency, that he was willing to count any belief as true if it satisfied the interest of the person who held it. This made things easy for his critics, of whom there were many. With greater good will they could have detected that his actual theory, although vulnerable to criticism, was not nearly so simple.

James introduces it in the sixth lecture of *Pragmatism* by the application of the pragmatic method. 'Grant,' he says, 'an idea or belief to be true . . . what concrete difference will its being true make in anyone's actual life? How will the truth be realized? What

[1] *Pragmatism*, pp. 210–11.
[2] *The Principles of Psychology*, II, pp. 664–5.

experiences will be different from those which would obtain if the belief were false? What, in short, is the truth's cash-value in experiential terms?' The answer which he immediately gives is that '*True ideas are those that we can assimilate, validate, corroborate and verify. False ideas are those that we cannot.*' It follows, he thinks, that 'The truth of an idea is not a stagnant property inherent in it. Truth *happens* to an idea. It *becomes* true, is *made* true by events. Its verity *is* in fact an event, a process: the process namely of its verifying itself, its veri-*fication*. Its validity is the process of its vali-*dation*.'[1]

This does not mean, as one might think, that James limits true ideas to those that are actually verified. He speaks also of our having 'a general stock of *extra* truths, of ideas that should be true of merely possible situations'. It is of any instance of these extra truths that he remarks, misleadingly, that one can say that 'it is useful because it is true' or that 'it is true because it is useful', and that these phrases mean the same thing. But what they both mean, he explains, is simply 'here is an idea that gets fulfilled and gets verified'. In short, the utility of the idea consists in its being found to be true.

There has, then, to be verifiability, if not actual verification. When replying to the objection, ascribed by him to a 'rationalist' opponent, that truth is something that 'absolutely obtains', James admits that the quality of truth obtains beforehand, but allows this to mean no more pragmatically than that in the world as we find it 'innumerable ideas work better by their indirect or possible than by their direct and actual verification'.[2] We do not have to keep verifying them 'any more than a wealthy man need be always handling money, or a strong man always lifting weights'.[3] It is, however, only because of their similarity to ideas which actually are verified that they are counted as verifiable.

James is not seriously troubled, as perhaps he should be, by the problem of one's right to attribute experiences to persons other than oneself. He takes it to be a fact that 'all things exist in kinds and not singly' and infers from this that what holds good in one person's experience will normally hold good in the experience of

[1] *Pragmatism*, p. 97.
[2] ibid., p. 105.
[3] ibid., p. 106.

others. This enables him to take advantage of testimony. As he characteristically puts it: 'Truth lives, in fact, for the most part on a credit system. Our thoughts and beliefs "pass" so long as nothing challenges them, just as bank-notes pass so long as nobody refuses them. But this all points to direct face-to-face verification, without which the fabric of truth collapses like a financial system with no cash-basis whatever. You accept my verification of one thing, I yours of another. We trade on each other's truth. But beliefs verified concretely by *somebody* are the posts of the whole superstructure'.[1]

Ideas that are verified work, both as fulfilling our expectations and as contributing to the success of the actions which are taken in accordance with them. No doubt this is what James had in mind when he spoke of 'the true' as being 'only the expedient in the way of our thinking'.[2] The expediency consisted not in conformity with whatever it suited us to believe, but in finding that our ideas accorded in the long run with the actual course of our future experiences. The fact, however, that 'what meets expediently all the experiences in sight won't necessarily meet all farther experiences equally satisfactorily'[3] puts truth indefinitely on probation. 'The "absolutely" true, meaning what no farther experience will ever alter, is that ideal vanishing-point towards which we imagine that all our temporary truths will some day converge.'[4]

This characterization of absolute truth, which is substantially the same as that originally given by Charles Sanders Peirce, effectively implies that 'truth', as we ordinarily use the term, is not to be understood in an 'absolute sense'; from which it follows that James was not a realist in his conception of truth. He himself was reluctant to admit this; so much so that at the start of his essay 'The Meaning of Truth' he actually says, 'My account of truth is realistic, and follows the epistemological dualism of common sense'[5] and in reply to one of his critics concedes that 'Truth is essentially a relation between two things, an idea, on the one hand, and a reality outside of the idea on the other'.[6] It turns out,

[1] ibid., p. 100.
[2] ibid., p. 106.
[3] ibid.
[4] ibid., pp. 106–7.
[5] 'The Meaning of Truth', p. 117.
[6] ibid., p. 91.

however, that this is not an 'external' reality, as realists conceive it: it is composed of possible experiences. For instance, in the case of what James calls 'phenomenal knowledge', his considered view is that 'Truth here is a relation, not of our ideas to non-human realities, but of conceptual parts of our experience to sensational parts'.[1]

Since James takes phenomenal knowledge to cover all matters of fact, we can conclude that reality there consists for him in the experiences by which our beliefs are verified or falsified. Does this apply also to our moral and religious beliefs? I believe that it does, in spite of James's accepting 'the notion of an *absolute* reality' and his admission, in replying to a critic, that just 'as our private concepts represent the sense-objects to which they lead us, these being public realities independent of the individual, so these sense-realities may, in turn, represent realities of a hypersensible order, electrons, mind-stuff, God, or what not, existing independently of all human thinkers'.[2] For even if we are led to entertain such notions, James never suggests that we are required, or even entitled, to regard them as being cognitively true, independently of our power to verify them.

But what in their case constitutes their being verified? Their working satisfactorily: but in what does this consist? To what do they lead us, in the way that our 'private concepts' lead to sense-realities? Obviously not to supra-sensible realities, of which we can have no experience. Rather, I suggest, to the satisfaction of our spiritual and moral needs. Thus, to take the most conspicuous example, there being or not being a God is not, for James, a straightforward matter of fact. He can allow the belief that God exists to be true because in this special case he takes the statement that God exists to mean no more than that men have spiritual requirements which religious belief may be found to satisfy.

It is, indeed, only in the domains of morals and theology that James can fairly be accused of making this simple equation of truth with expediency. His overall equation is rather that of truth with verifiability, and the more subjective interpretation which he puts upon some tender-minded beliefs results from his desire to make it possible that they too can be verified. He is right in claiming to be a

[1] ibid., p. 51.
[2] ibid., p. 130.

realist, to the extent that he can admit of there being real objects which exist independently of the actual experience of any particular subject, though not independently of all possible experience. Nevertheless, in modern terms, his theory of truth, with which his theory of reality is intimately connected, is anti-realistic. For all its consequent difficulties, this is not to say that it is untenable.

C. I. Lewis

The most interesting attempt to fill in the outlines of James's version of pragmatism is to be found in the work of another Harvard professor, Clarence Irving Lewis, who lived from 1883 to 1964. Unlike James, Lewis took a serious interest in formal logic, and in collaboration with C. H. Langford published in 1932 a book entitled *Symbolic Logic* in which a system, or rather a set of systems, was developed on the basis of a relation to which the authors gave the name of strict implication. This differed from the relation of material implication, which had sufficed for Russell and Whitehead in their *Principia Mathematica*, in that it was not satisfied, as was the relation of material implication, by any pair of true propositions, or by any pair in which the first was false, or any in which the second was true, but required it to be impossible that the first proposition be true and its implicate false. Their intention was that the main connective in this system should be one at least more closely corresponding to the relation of logical entailment. Thus they avoided what were sometimes called the 'paradoxes' of material implication, according to which a false proposition implies any other, and a true proposition is implied by any other. They had, indeed, 'paradoxes' of their own, in that a contradiction strictly implies any other proposition and a necessarily true proposition is strictly implied by any other, but these were considered to be less offensive to common sense. In fact, there are no paradoxes in either case, but at worst a misleading use of the word 'implication'. The weakness of material implication in no way impairs the system of *Principia Mathematica*, since it starts with logically true axioms, and the relation covers the conveyance of truth from one proposition to another, which is what the system demonstrates. The relation of strict implication is devised for systems of modal logic which come into play not just when we are handling necessary propositions but rather when we are reasoning about their necessity. It is not an internal objection to such forms of logic that there may be some doubt concerning their utility.

His Theories of Knowledge and Meaning

Lewis's most ambitious work was *An Analysis of Knowledge and Valuation*, published in 1946, in which he set out a detailed theory of meaning, and extended his theory of knowledge to include ethics. It was, however, less influential than his *Mind and the World Order*, published in 1929, which also shows greater continuity with the ideas of William James. The main thesis of this book is that all knowledge of the world results from the conformity of what is sensorily given with concepts which are fashioned *a priori*. At first sound, this is reminiscent of Kant, but such resemblance as there is between the two systems is very slight. It hardly goes further than their common agreement that sense-data, intuitions in Kant's terminology, without concepts are blind, and that nothing can be known which goes beyond our possible experience. For Lewis there are no synthetic *a priori* propositions. The propositions of pure mathematics are analytic, and it is a contingent question whether they are applicable to matters of empirical fact. Thus we cannot take it for granted that space is Euclidean. We can know for certain that if there are areas of space which form Euclidean triangles, the sum of their internal angles will be 180°, because this is part of what is meant by anything's being a Euclidean triangle, but whether there are such areas is something that only experience can discover. Or rather, to state the case more accurately, since the figures of pure geometry are anyhow idealizations of measurable areas, it needs to be discovered whether our experience is more conveniently ordered if it is fitted into the framework of Euclidean or some other, say Riemannian, geometry.

Again, unlike Kant, Lewis admits no distinction between things as they appear to us and things as they are in themselves. This is not to say that he does not distinguish at all between appearance and reality, but he conceives of the distinction as falling wholly within experience. One is presented with a sense-quale and one makes the prediction that such and such other qualia will be presented in their turn, or it may be that one simply makes the judgement that one would be presented with them if one were to take certain actions, such as moving in a particular direction, or bringing it about that some other sense modality came relevantly into play. What these further sense-qualia are depends upon the type of thing of which the original presentation is taken to be a sign. It will be a reality of that type if the predictions are fulfilled or the conditional judgements are true. Otherwise the original sense-quale will have proved deceptive and may be set down as an illusion. This is not to say that the sense-quale itself was illusory: that would be meaningless. A sense-quale has no status, other than that of being something 'given' to us in sense experience. It becomes 'illusory' only if it fails to bear the relations to other actual and possible sense-qualia which are conceptually required for there to be even a probability of its presenting something real.

I write 'even a probability' as though the ascription of reality could be certain. But the fact is that in Lewis's view no empirical proposition can ever be certain. The reason for this is that the meaning of these propositions, being equated with the possibility of their verification, extends indefinitely into the future. However strongly our experience confirms them, there is always a chance that future experience will reverse the verdict. Since Lewis takes judgements of probability to be *a priori*, what can be certain, in his opinion, is that relatively to such and such sensory evidence there is a probability of some calculable degree that a particular proposition, implying the existence of some physical object and ascribing such and such properties to it, is true. But the degree of probability never reaches unity, so that the proposition in question never attains a superior status to that of being a well-confirmed hypothesis. Neither is there any difference here, except a difference of degree, between abstract scientific hypotheses, concerning the behaviour of electrons or whatever, and the most commonplace judgements of perception, such as my taking what is currently given to my sense of sight as revealing that there is a book on the table in front of me. My interpretation of the visual datum is fallible since it covers the indefinite totality of the possible experiences in which it could be verified. Correspondingly, while the process of verifying the scientific hypothesis is more cumbrous, it could not acquire any probability unless it made contact with direct experience. Indeed, Lewis goes further, saying: 'If the existence or non-existence of "scientific reality" makes certain verifiable differences in experience, then these empirical differences are the marks of the kind of reality that can be predicated of it. They are the "cash-value" of the category; they constitute what it means to be real in just the way that electrons can be real. "Scientific reality" is either an interpretation of certain parts and aspects of experience or it is a noise, signifying nothing.'[1]

The image of cash-value, as we have seen, is borrowed from William James. As James understood it, the cash-value of a proposition exhausted its factual content. Should we attribute the same view to Lewis? The passage which I have just quoted might allow us to suppose that he was doing no more than making it a necessary condition for something like an electron to be physically real that its existence be 'verifiable in a laboratory'.[2] If this were taken to mean not that an entity could not be introduced into a physical theory until there was experimental evidence for its existence, but only that something should count as such experimental evidence, if certain conditions were fulfilled, it would be open only to the objection that not every element of a scientific theory needs to be independently verifiable, so long as the theory is verifiable as a whole. Unfortunately, however, Lewis goes on to say that 'the totality of the possible experiences in which any interpretation would be verified – the completest possible empirical verification which is conceivable – constitutes the entire meaning which that interpretation has'.[3] This does not, indeed, exclude the idea that what is submitted to verification is a whole body of theory, rather than its constituent items independently of one another, but it does imply that the theory, to the extent that it has any factual content, could be rewritten in purely observational terms. At this point it has to be remarked that such a reduction of a high-level scientific theory has never yet been achieved, but the reason for this could be that the range of observations which would amount to its completest conceivable verification is not finite. If it were finite, the theory could be established once for all, which we have seen that Lewis holds to be impossible. The most that one could do would be to give a full description of the sort of tests to which the theory was perpetually subject, and this might very well be feasible. We should be left with a host of unfulfilled conditionals to the effect that if one set up such and

---

[1] *Mind and the World Order*, p. 32.
[2] ibid.
[3] ibid.

such an apparatus, such and such observations would be made, and it might be objected that we are still in want of a satisfactory theory for establishing the truth-conditions for propositions of this type. But this is not a special objection to Lewis's treatment of scientific entities. It is one that he encounters in any case, since he holds that all empirical statements are hypotheses. Nor does he appear to think that it poses any serious difficulty. According to him 'What is *normally* meant by saying "If an observer were there he would observe so and so" is verifiable by the fact that, other conditions being altered at will, whenever an observer *is* there he *does* see this' or, more generally, 'The hypothetical "If x were there y would be" means "However conditions be varied, and condition x being similarly supplied at will, whenever x is, y is" '.[1] But the trouble with this is that it yields no criterion of truth for the numerous cases in which no observer actually is present, or the requisite conditions are not in fact supplied.

From what I have so far said it might be inferred that Lewis was a thoroughgoing phenomenalist, but this would not be correct. He describes his method of philosophy as reflective, and explains that 'The reflective method is empirical and analytic in that it recognizes experience in general as the datum of philosophy', but then he at once goes on to say that 'it is not empirical in the sense of taking this experience to coincide with data of sense which are merely given to the mind'.[2] For there to be experience, the mind has to make its contribution. The primitive data have to be interpreted, and it is only when they have received some interpretation that they play a cognitive role. The experience which verifies a hypothesis is in part the product of an interpretation, which is not free from the requirement that it should itself be verifiable. On this count alone it can be seen that the process of verification is prolonged indefinitely. For practical purposes, we need to treat a great number of empirical propositions as though they had been conclusively established, but there can be no guarantee that this verdict will not be revised.

There are several problems here. For instance, where do we draw the line between propositions which are reports of experience and more purely theoretical hypotheses? How, if at all, do we distinguish the 'given' element in an experience from the interpretation which we

[1] ibid., p. 65, fn.
[2] ibid., p. 33.

put upon it? How is the transition made from private experiences to a public world? If the meaning of every empirical proposition extends indefinitely into the future, how do we deal with propositions which are ostensibly about the past?

Lewis pays no attention to the first of these questions, and we are left to assume that he draws the line where common sense would draw it. Objects like desks and fountain pens, which it would ordinarily be said that we perceived, fall within the boundaries of experience; objects like alpha-particles do not, though of course there must still be some empirical evidence for their existence. No doubt Lewis saw no point in trying to sharpen the distinction, since he accords no special privilege to reports of experience with regard to their need for being verified.

But do not sense-qualia occupy a special position? They do indeed, but not as objects of knowledge. Lewis thinks it legitimate to speak of knowledge only in cases where there is a possibility of error, and in the case of sense-qualia there is no possibility of error. They just are what they are felt to be. This does not imply that one can give an infallible or even a true description of them, catching them as it were in their native state. For any description will involve interpretation. The resulting proposition may be true, but it will still give hostages to the future and so be liable to error.

This does not mean, however, that the given is inextricably entangled with our interpretation of it. It is indeed an abstraction, but still an element in experience which we can identify. It remains qualitatively the same, however we interpret it, and this indeed is its distinguishing mark. As Lewis puts it, in the course of developing an example in which the item of his current experience is something which he would describe as a fountain pen if his purpose was to write, or else as a cylinder if he was explaining a problem in geometry or mechanics, or perhaps as 'a poor buy' if he was concerned with his habits of expenditure, 'the distinction between the element of interpretation and the given is emphasized by the fact that the latter is what remains unaltered, no matter what our interests, no matter how we think or conceive. I can apprehend this thing as pen or rubber or cylinder, but I cannot, by taking thought, discover it as paper or soft or cubical.'[1] In the same situation 'an infant or an ignorant savage'[2]

[1] ibid., p. 52.
[2] ibid., p. 50.

might not have the concepts to interpret the data in any of the ways that Lewis cites as legitimate possibilities, but the given element in his experience would be qualitatively the same. It has a nature of its own which is independent of what the mind contributes to the experience, and therefore sets a limit to it.

But might not one be hypnotized into believing that the pen which one was actually holding was something soft and cubical? One would be mistaken of course, and no doubt the mistake would come to light. But would it simply consist in one's falling foul of future experience? Would it not rather be that one's interpretation did not accord with the given? This is not like the example of the drunkard who sees hallucinatory snakes. In his case, his experience is wayward, but his interpretation of what is given to him is natural. In the other, the interpretation is not authorized by the datum itself. Lewis seems not to envisage this distinction, and perhaps he would have denied its legitimacy. He might have tried to explain away the hypnotic example by saying that the hypnosis would affect what was actually given to the subject, rather than merely distort its interpretation. But then what would have become of his criterion for distinguishing the given? He could hardly have continued to describe it as 'that which remains untouched and unaltered, however it is construed by thought'.[1]

The fact is that Lewis needs the given as a check on the freedom of our thought. It supplies the element of brute reality that is a necessary ingredient of perceptual experience. As such, it must have a character of its own, which limits the interpretation that can legitimately be put upon it. But then why can not this character be named or described? Lewis's answer is that a name which was a pure demonstrative would carry no significance; a description would relate the quale to other items of experience and so involve interpretation. It would also incur the risk of error. The given is immune from error but only at the price of being ineffable. 'All that can be done to designate a quale is, so to speak, to locate it in experience, that is, to designate the conditions of its recurrence or other relations of it. Such location does not touch the quale itself; if one such could be lifted out of the network of its relations, in the total experience of the individual, and replaced by another, no social interest or interest of action would be affected by such substitution. What is essential for

[1] ibid., p. 53.

understanding and for communication is not the quale as such but that pattern of its stable relations in experience which is what is implicitly predicated when it is taken as a sign of an objective property.'[1]

But what are the terms of the network of relations in which the quale participates if not other qualia? Why should the complex be nameable and not its elements? I am seated under the branches of a tree and when I look up I am presented with qualia which I interpret as green leaves. I am forbidden to say of any such quale that it is green, because that would be to confuse it with the physical leaf. But why should I not say that it looks green? Lewis's answer to this is that it would violate common usage, which treats even the show of colours, shapes and the like as 'objective properties'. 'A thing is said to "look round" when it presents the quale which a really round object does when held at right angles to the line of vision; and a thing is said to "look blue" when it looks the way a really blue thing does under usual or standard illumination. In general, the name of the property is also assigned to the appearance of it under certain optimum conditions.'[2] Well, that may be so. But where in these cases does the object get its property from, if not from its privileged appearances? And in that case why should it not be ascribed to the appearance, whether or not this accords with common usage? For that matter, common usage does allow colour and shape to be ascribed to after-images. It does not assign them to qualia because qualia do not figure in its vocabulary. But now if we return to Lewis's vocabulary, we can substitute for 'the way a thing looks' 'the quale it presents'. And if we then ask what coloured quale a green leaf presents under standard conditions, what better answer can we give than that it is green?

I conclude that Lewis was at fault in making his qualia ineffable. I suppose that the reason he did so was that he thought of all descriptions as being fallible and predictive. But, as I said earlier, qualia have to be assigned a character if they are to do the work of confirming or refuting the predictions, and there seems no reason why such characters should not be described in a sense which did not refer beyond them. It would also follow that they could be misdescribed; but whether such misdescriptions would consist in anything

[1] ibid., pp. 124–5.
[2] ibid., p. 122.

more than a misuse of language is a question that I am not able to decide. It is not in any case a question of major importance, since the qualia which one may claim to describe with factual certainty would be of short duration, and there is no suggestion that one's memory of their character is infallible.

The stress which Lewis lays on relations between qualia, as opposed to the nature of what they relate, is explained by his view that our common knowledge, say of the physical world, is due not to our having similar impressions, which may or may not be the case, but to our apprehending similar relations between them. I say that these relations are apprehended because it is a matter of objective fact that our concepts are satisfied, but I could also have said that the relations were imposed inasmuch as they sustain the order which our common concepts bring to what is severally given. Lewis concedes that we have no means of knowing how disparate our several sense-data may be, even when we refer them to the same object. 'That,' however, he says, 'will in no way impede our common knowledge or the conveying of ideas. Why? Because we shall still agree that there are three feet to the yard; that yellow is lighter than blue; and that middle C means a vibration of 256 per second. In other words, if we *define* any one of the unit-ideas or concepts which enter into the expression of our thought, we shall define it in the same or equivalent fashion, and we shall apply the same substantives and adjectives to the same objects. So far as we fail in *these* two things, our knowledge will be really different and the attempt to convey our thought will break down. These, then, are the only practical and applicable criteria of common knowledge; that we should share common definitions of the terms we use, and that we should apply these terms identically to what is presented.'[1]

But how can we be assured that we do share common definitions and that we do make an identical use of the terms so defined? Only through congruence of behaviour. If I can interpret your utterances in a way that concurs with my sensory contents, and if your responses to my utterances are correspondingly appropriate, then I can justifiably conclude that we share a community of meaning, reflected by a common reality, no matter how disparate our sensory contents themselves may be. There is no question here of any pre-established harmony. We do, indeed, account for our possession of common

[1] ibid., pp. 75–6.

concepts by our being confronted with a common reality. But this common reality is something that we help to create. It is 'in part a social achievement, directed by the community of needs and interests and fostered in the interest of cooperation'.[1] The same line of reasoning leads Lewis to conclude that 'reality itself reflects criteria which are social in their nature'.[2]

I find this answer convincing. There is, however, a lacuna in that it fails to explain how one comes by the idea of there being other persons who have experiences of a pattern comparable to one's own. It might even be argued that Lewis is caught in a circle, since he requires a plurality of minds for the devising of a world of public objects, while it is only through the observation of a class of these objects that one can be led to believe in a plurality of minds. Lewis, indeed, accepts the second of these propositions but avoids the circle by denying the first. 'Genuinely verifiable knowledge,' he says, 'can grasp other minds only as things revealed in the patterns of behaviour of certain physical beings.'[3] On the other hand he claims that 'However much our concepts are shaped by social intercourse and borrowed ready-made by the individual, a human being without fellows (if such can be imagined) would still frame concepts in terms of the relation between his own behaviour and his environment'.[4] This means that on the basis of his experiences and the relations between them, especially those, as Lewis says, 'into which the knower himself may enter as an active factor',[5] he can erect a conceptual structure in which his own body is melded with these experiences in some unique fashion and distinguished from other physical objects to some of which experiences are similarly attributed. I believe that it is possible to show how this could happen, but it is not an easy problem, as Lewis would have discovered if he had ever tried to work it out in detail.

The idea that one's understanding of a concept is to be equated with one's view of the actual and possible experiences that one would count as witnesses to its application raises difficulties not only with regard to one's knowledge of other minds, where it would seem to impose behaviourism, but also with regard to one's interpretation of

[1] ibid., p. 116.
[2] ibid.
[3] ibid., p. 411.
[4] ibid., p. 117.
[5] ibid.

statements about the past. Lewis does not appear to take his remark that other minds are 'revealed' in patterns of behaviour as committing him to behaviourism, and he pays no further attention to this problem. On the other hand he does deal rather briefly with the question of one's knowledge of the past. He envisages a critic objecting that once knowledge is identified with verification 'the past, so far as it can be known, is transformed into something present and future, and we are presented with the alternatives, equally impossible, that the past cannot be known or that it really is not past',[1] and then oscillates between accepting what amounts to a version of the second of the horns of this dilemma and suggesting that there is a way between them. He admits that 'from the point of view of knowledge' the past is to be identified with its present and future effects, but then tries to hedge by calling it a fallacy 'to attach to epistemological analysis a kind of *exclusive* truth'[2] so that his adoption of the point of view of knowledge does not rob the past of various other 'types of significance'.[3] He fails, however, to make clear what these other types of significance could be. He warns us against drawing the conclusion that 'a past event, verifiable as being so and so by certain present and future possible experiences, is thereby transformed into something present and future'[4] but a few lines further on repeats that the totality of the effects of a past event are obviously all of it that is knowable and adds that to separate the effects from the object would turn the object into some 'incognizable' thing in itself. But how then do we distinguish the past from the present and future? Lewis's answer is that 'the conception that an event is spread throughout the time "after its occurrence" will not abolish the difference between different events occurring at different times: these will be identified through a different totality of effects'.[5] He says nothing further about these differences beyond suggesting that one item, which might mark out the past, would be 'a certain kind of unalterability and unresponsiveness to desire and purpose in which respect what is present or future would not be thus unalterable'.[6] This may, indeed, be a feature of the past, but it is not an exclusive feature. There are many

[1] ibid., p. 149.
[2] ibid., p. 150.
[3] ibid.
[4] ibid., p. 151.
[5] ibid., p. 152.
[6] ibid., p. 153.

events in the present and future that are equally unresponsive to our desires. Lewis does not notice this objection and continues to deal in generalities, repeating that 'The past is known through a correct interpretation of something given, including certain given characters which are the marks of pastness'. 'If this,' he concludes, 'be paradox, then so much the worse for common-sense.'[1]

Or should one say 'so much the worse for pragmatism'? There is no paradox in the idea that the past is known only through the traces which it has left, in memory, through written and photographic records, or as the result of our assigning earlier causes to currently observable effects. There are, indeed, those who say that memory, at least in some cases, makes us directly acquainted with the past, but this is merely to record the fact that the deliverances of memory are often accepted without question. There still remains the temporal gap between the event recollected and the subsequent recollection of it. No more than any other form of record does memory do away with intervals of time. Not that Lewis suggests that it does; he wants to keep the distinction between the past, present and future but make it fall wholly within the present and the future. It is not its explicit temporal reference but the way it is deemed to be verifiable, both now and in the future, that makes a statement into a statement about the past.

Now this really is paradoxical. Admittedly the only reason that I now can have for accepting the historical statement that Napoleon was defeated at the Battle of Waterloo in the year 1815 is that it is vouched for by historians and that it coheres with a great number of other statements, ostensibly referring to events occurring between that year and the present, for which historians also vouch. The consensus is strong enough for it to be foolish to look for further proof, which anyhow could be only of the same character. But surely what makes it true that Napoleon was defeated at the Battle of Waterloo in 1815 is not just the truth of the conditional proposition that if we were to consult such and such books we should find the appropriate sentences written in them. We want to say that these sentences report a historical fact, which, though we interpret them as entailing it, is logically independent of their existence. In other words, the sentences would not express truth unless the battle occurred as they reported it; but it is logically possible that what they

[1] ibid.

express is false, and conversely the battle might have taken place with the same result, even if these reports of it had never been written. We accept these sentences as stating truths because we interpret them as concurring with our interpretations of a great many other sentences which we also accept; but what their truth consists in is the actual occurrence of the battle, as reported by them, at the time which they assign to it.

Such is the view not only of common sense but of historians of all types, as well as the specialists in the numerous sciences which deal wholly or partly with the past. This does not make it sacrosanct, but we need a strong reason for rejecting it. The reason which Lewis gives is, as we have seen, that it treats past events as incognizable things in themselves. The same might be said of all the contemporary events which are spatially remote from the interpreter of the sentences which ostensibly refer to them, unless he takes the sentences to mean that if he were to perform such and such actions he would make the appropriate observations: for by the time he performs the actions the events will be past. If Lewis's argument is accepted, the only tensed sentences in which the temporal reference is to be taken at its face value will be those that make predictions which their interpreter could be in a position to verify and those that report matters which fall under his present observation, if they exist at all.

But are we really obliged to allow that all putative matters of fact which fall outside these very narrow limits are incognizable, unless they are subjected to the pragmatic treatment? Can we not draw a distinction between what lies outside all possible experience, like the Kantian thing-in-itself, and what eludes the observation of a given speaker, because of their relative situation in space and time? I cannot witness the Battle of Waterloo because it took place so long ago, and quite probably I should not have been in a position to witness it even if I had been alive at the time, but it is not an event of an unobservable type. There were many thousands who did witness it. What is the objection to saying that its occurrence and its outcome were verified by their experiences?

This raises the crucial problem for those who wish to connect meaning with verification. On the one hand it is plausible to identify the meaning of a proposition with its truth-conditions and then equate these truth-conditions with the observable states of affairs that would make the proposition true, never mind who is or could be in a position to observe them. According to this view, what makes a state of affairs observable is its intrinsic character, not its featuring in the actual or possible experience of any given person. On the other hand it is also plausible to argue that a sentence has meaning only for an interpreter and that when the sentence is treated as purporting to express an empirical matter of fact the only way that the interpreter can understand it is in terms of the difference that its truth or falsehood would make to his own experience. But quite apart from the difficulties to which we have seen that this view leads in the case of statements ostensibly about the past, it encounters the much more serious, indeed fatal, objection that it cannot coherently be general-ized. For if I can make sense of a sentence which apparently refers to the experiences of another person only in terms of the difference which the truth of what it expresses would make to my own experience, I cannot suppose that the same is true of anyone else. I cannot credit another person with the power of interpreting a sentence in accordance with the difference which the truth of what it expresses would make in his experience, since *ex hypothesi* the reference to his experience means nothing to me except in so far as I can interpret it in terms of my own. Consequently, the thesis that every interpreter of a sentence must construe it in terms of his own experience is one that no philosopher can consistently combine with the assumption that there are other users of language besides himself; for he cannot, on his own principle, attach any sense to this assumption beyond some reference to the behaviour of those others which his own experiences might verify.

It might be suggested that symmetry could be maintained by construing every report of an experience, including one's own, as a reaction to some physical stimulus. The report would then be interpreted as a description of the publicly observable state of affairs which provoked the reaction. Since Lewis supposes that qualia are ineffable, the statements of observation which serve as tests in his system for more abstract hypotheses would presumably take this form. But difficulties arise when it comes to the interpretation of sentences which are designed to report not what one perceives but one's thoughts or feelings or sensations. I do not find it credible that the utterance of such sentences is a way of expressing conditional hypotheses about one's behaviour. Even if mental states were factually identical with states of the central nervous system, which has by no means yet been proved, that is not how their subject would describe them, and the problem of interpreting his descriptions of them would still remain.

This difficulty and the difficulty about the past would both be removed if the meaning of a sentence were identified with the truth-conditions of the proposition which it was understood to express, and these truth-conditions could be the same for any interpreter of the sentence, no matter who he might be and no matter what position he occupied in space and time. Thus, in the case of a sentence interpreted as ascribing a thought or feeling to a particular person at a given time the truth-condition would be that the person in question did at the time in question have that thought or feeling; in the case of a sentence taken as expressing a historical proposition, such as a description of a battle occurring at a specified date, the truth-condition would be the occurrence at that date of a battle which answered to the description. So far as the meaning of the sentences went, it would make no difference in the first case whether the person referred to was oneself or another, and no difference in the second case how the utterance of the sentence was temporally related to the event which it reported. If in the second case it is thought paradoxical that the tense of a sentence should make no difference to its meaning, the paradox could be removed by adding the rider that the event referred to stood in the designated temporal relation to the utterance of the sentence. This would, however, have the awkward consequence of making every tensed sentence partially self-referential. An alternative would be to make use of a demonstrative expression like 'earlier than now'. This would capture the information which is conveyed in this example by the use of the past tense, but would have the drawback that the meaning of a sentence would vary with the time of its utterance. Perhaps the most satisfactory course would be to replace the demonstrative by a date, though it might be objected that this would alter the meaning of the original sentence, by giving more information than was conveyed merely by the use of one or other tense. It would, however, still be faithful to the truth-conditions of the proposition which the sentence expressed. The same would apply to the replacement of other demonstratives, including personal pronouns, by names or descriptions. The elimination of proper names themselves in favour of descriptions, though always feasible, would carry us still further from translation into paraphrase.

A more radical objection to the course we are now exploring is that it threatens the connection between meaning and verification. One way to try to maintain the connection would be to introduce the notion of the privileged witness. Thus, in the case of a proposition ascribing thoughts or sensations or feelings to a particular person at a particular time, the privileged witness would be the person himself at the time in question. In the case of a proposition asserting the existence of an ordinary physical object like a tree, the privileged witness would be someone who perceived the tree at the appropriate time and place under optimum conditions. It is presumed that these optimum conditions, which would include some reference to the state of the observer, could be exhaustively specified, though it is by no means clear that this could be achieved without circularity. His perceiving the tree might in these conditions be a test of his normality. But in any case these are simple examples. The Battle of Waterloo is already more difficult. Is our privileged witness to be a participant in the battle? But even if he survived to the end of it he is unlikely to have seen very much of all that was happening. A civilian spectator, then, like Tolstoy's Pierre at Borodino? Again his evidence would be very incomplete. And these are battles that took place in a single day. What of battles like the Battle of Verdun that went on for months? It looks as if we should have to break such battles down into a set of incidents, different in time and space, for each of which we should require a privileged observer. But merely to assert that a battle took place is not to commit oneself to every detail of it. Just how much first-hand evidence is needed to warrant the assertion that a battle is going on?

So far we have been thinking of our privileged witness as an actual person, but this will not always serve. One obvious reason why it will not is that we want to speak of events which occurred before any human beings existed. We might fall back upon the fiction of an ideal observer, who would have been able to verify propositions about the remote past, or, for that matter, the remote future, or present events which are very remote from us in space, if he were to occupy or have occupied the appropriate spatio-temporal position, but what ground should we have for assuming that his presence would have made no difference to the events in question? Since we have anyway to decide what sorts of events are observable in order to delimit the powers of our ideal observer, we might just as well dispense with him altogether, and require only of events which fall outside the ken of any privileged witness that they be of such a nature as to be observable. This leaves us with the problem of marking out the range of such events, and I confess that I see no way of dealing with it except by drawing up a list of predicates which we are going to count as standing for observable properties, and specifying the ways in which they can be combined with one another. Observable things, or events, will then be those to which such properties can significantly be attributed. We should here be guided by ordinary usage rather than follow Lewis in restricting these properties to qualia.

But what of the particles or other entities which figure in scientific theories, not as perceptible features of the world but only as having perceptible effects? For instance, we do not see photons, though it is because of photons that we see; a photon is a quantum of electromagnetic radiation which is invoked to explain the transmission of light. A dictionary provides the further information that it is 'regarded as a particle with zero mass and charge, unit spin, and energy equal to the product of the frequency of the radiation and the Planck constant'. I do not think that Lewis would have wished to claim that the objects which satisfied this definition could be brought down to the phenomenal level, in the sense that the theories in which they figured could be transformed without residue into a set of conditional statements about the probability of obtaining such and such experiences. For one thing he held that no amount of sensory evidence could ever exhaust the meaning of a physical hypothesis, since its truth was always open to re-assessment. There is, however, no reason to think that he attributed any more factual content to these hypotheses than was to be found in the formulations of the endless series of experiments that would be regarded as confirming them.

One is inclined to protest at this point that the main issue is being evaded. Did he or did he not believe that photons, and other such entities, were real? The easy answer is that he did, since his criterion for the reality of an object was the confirmation of the hypotheses in which its reality was explicitly or implicitly affirmed; and this is a criterion which photons satisfy. What is wrong with this answer is that it still seems evasive. It does not tell us whether Lewis thought that photons and the like were real in an absolute sense. But now we come to an impasse. For Lewis would surely have replied that this absolute notion of reality was pragmatically vacuous.

So far as the theory of knowledge goes, *An Analysis of Knowledge and Valuation* does no more than reinforce the position that is taken in *Mind and the World Order*. As I mentioned earlier, it has far more to say on the topic of meaning. Linguistic expressions are all said to be terms, and every term is credited with meaning in each of four modes: that of *denotation*, which is the class of all actual things to which the term applies; that of *comprehension*, which covers all the possible things to which the term would be applicable; that of *signification*, which is the property or set of properties which a thing must possess for the term to apply to it; and that of *intension*, which is the conjunction of other terms which the term carries with it in the sense that it cannot apply to anything without their applying to it also. In the case of the complex term which Lewis calls a proposition, its denotation is the actual world if it is true, and nothing at all if it is false, its comprehension is the set of possible worlds in which it would be true, its signification is the state of affairs which needs to obtain for it to be true, and its intension is the set of other propositions which it entails. An analytic proposition, being true solely on account of its meaning, holds good in all possible worlds. It therefore has universal comprehension and, correlatively, zero intension. This is not to say that nothing can be deduced from it, though any proposition that can be so deduced will itself be analytic, but rather that neither it nor its consequences make any distinction between possible worlds. They do not mark off the actual world from any other which might have existed instead. Conversely, a self-contradictory proposition has zero comprehension and universal intension, since every proposition, true or false, is a consequence of it.

From this it would seem to follow that all analytic propositions, and likewise all self-contradictory propositions, are equivalent. So far as his four modes of meaning go, this is a conclusion that Lewis has to accept, but he tries to make it less paradoxical by dissociating equivalence from synonymity and making synonymity consist in a concurrence of what he calls analytic meaning. Roughly speaking, two expressions have the same analytic meaning if and only if there is one to one correspondence in the intensions of each of their constituents. Thus, to use two of his own examples, the analytic propositions 'All cats are vertebrates' and 'All felines are creatures having a spinal cord' are synonymous because of the intensional equivalence of the terms 'cats' to 'felines' and 'vertebrates' to 'creatures having a spinal cord'. On the other hand there is no such intensional concordance between the constituents of the propositions 'Iron is a heavy metal' and '$2+2=4$'. So while these propositions are equivalent, in the sense that they both have zero intension, they are not synonymous.

While Lewis consistently adheres to what he calls 'the traditional conception of analytic truth as truth which is determined, explicitly or implicitly, by meaning alone'[1] and resolutely maintains that all true *a priori* propositions are analytic, he strongly insists that he does not take this to imply that *a priori* propositions are made true by linguistic conventions. In his words, 'Intensional meaning can be specified in alternative ways; as *linguistic meaning*, constituted by the pattern of definition and other analytic relationships holding between linguistic expressions; or as *sense meaning*, constituted by the criterion in mind by which what is meant is to be recognized. It is sense meaning which is epistemologically the most important signification of "intension". Linguistic *expression* of what is meant and what is apprehended, is the dependent and derivative phenomenon: it is meaning and apprehension themselves which are the fundamental cognitive phenomena, and these are independent of any formulation in language'.[2]

We may concede at once that it is a contingent fact that the words of a given language have the meanings that they do. It might have been the case that the English word 'cow' was commonly used to denote the class of horses, rather than the class of cows, just as it might have been the case that the English word 'bovine' had the intension of belonging to the family Equidae, rather than that of belonging to the family Bovini; but given that these words are used in the way they are, it is not a contingent but an analytic proposition that cows are bovine. Lewis agrees with this conclusion but wishes to make its validity depend on what he calls the sense meaning rather than the linguistic meaning of the terms involved. This distinction is not easy to grasp. Sense meaning is said by him, as we have seen, to be 'constituted by the criterion in mind by which what is meant is to be recognized', but it is not clear how this is supposed to differ from the criterion by which the proper use of the relevant word is regulated. One might suppose that 'the criterion in mind' consisted in the presence of an image, but this would be open to serious

[1] *An Analysis of Knowledge and Valuation*, p. 37.
[2] ibid.

objections. To begin with, the power of entertaining images does not go *pari passu* with the understanding of sentences, even at the level of possible observation. I am probably not alone in being unable to form an image of sweetness, but this does not prevent me from understanding and assenting to the analytic proposition that sugar is sweet. A more general difficulty would be that of attaching images to abstract terms. One could draw a cartoon to illustrate the truism that honesty is a virtue, but it would at best be an adventitious aid to one's understanding of the words. Again, it is not easy to see what images would do duty for terms like 'meson' or 'photon', which are only indirectly linked to observation. But the decisive objection is that if we do not understand how words can operate as signs, a recourse to images will not help us; for it is only by functioning as signs that images themselves can serve our understanding.

I conclude, then, that Lewis's distinction will not bear the weight that he attaches to it. What he needed here was not a contrast between two different sorts of meaning, but rather that between the contingent choice of certain forms of utterance to fulfil diverse linguistic functions and the consequences that necessarily obtain so long as these decisions are adhered to. The propositions in which these consequences are drawn are *a priori* and analytic, because no possible state of affairs is counted as being incompatible with them.

His Moral Philosophy

Finally we come to Lewis's moral philosophy. He takes this branch of the subject very seriously, partly because of his pragmatic view that knowledge is chiefly to be valued as a guide to action. Nearly 200 out of the 550-odd pages of *An Analysis of Knowledge and Valuation* are devoted to it. His main contentions, however, are very easily summarized. They are stated succinctly in the last two sentences of his book. 'Valuation is always a matter of empirical knowledge. But what is right and what is just, can never be determined by empirical facts alone.'

Of these two propositions Lewis pays far more attention to the first than to the second. His thesis that valuation is always a matter of empirical knowledge is based on the assimilation of what he describes as experiences of value to the direct apprehension of sensory qualities. 'It will hardly be denied,' he says, 'that there is what may be called "apparent value" or "felt goodness" as there is seen redness or heard shrillness.'[1] A few pages later he slightly qualifies this by saying that 'immediately or directly findable value is not so much one quality as a dimensionlike mode which is pervasive of all experience. There is,' he continues, 'not one goodness and one badness to be found in living but uncountably many variants of good and bad, each like every other most notably in being a basis for choosing and preferring. Value or disvalue is not like the pitch of middle C or the seen colour of median red or the felt hardness of steel. It is not one specific quale of experience but a gamut of such; more like colour in general or pitch or hardness in general.'[2] It is important to note, at this point, that value, for Lewis, is always an intrinsic property of an *experience*. It is an extrinsic property of what he usually calls the 'object' on which the experience is focused. As predicated of such objects it may either be inherent, if the object directly gives rise to an experience of value, or instrumental, if it does so indirectly by causing objects to exist in which value is inherent. It may, of course, happen that a particular object has value in both these modes.

Though experiences are the only intrinsic bearers of value, it is not normally predicated of them. Lewis holds that apprehensions of value, like the apprehensions of sensory qualia, as ingredients of experience, are in themselves infallible. They therefore do not provide material for judgement or even for knowledge, since Lewis wants to reserve both judgement and knowledge for cases where there is a possibility of error. Judgements of value are made about objects and their fallible content is that the objects in question are inherently or instrumentally valuable. In this way they are akin to judgements of perception, with the difference that judgements of perception are subject to a greater variety of tests. For an object to be red or heavy, it is not sufficient that it should look red or feel heavy; there are also such criteria as those of the wave-length of the light that it emits or the amount that it is found to weigh. In the case of judgements of value the only test is the extent to which it gives rise to value-experiences.

Lewis has relatively little to say about the character of the objects of which value is predicated. He devotes most space to a review of aesthetic objects, regarding 'only those values [as] distinctively

[1] ibid., p. 374.
[2] ibid., p. 401.

aesthetic which are resident in the quality of something as presented or presentable, and are explicitly enjoyable in the discernment of them and by that pause of contemplative regard which suspends the active interests of further purposes'.[1] At the same time, rather in the fashion of Jeremy Bentham, he allows that 'So far as the quality of experience goes, there is no notable distinction between the transient value of a passing odour of honeysuckle and the enduring value of a symphony; between the appetitive value of a beef-steak and the spiritual value of a Gothic façade; between the innocent value found in a little red wagon and the cultivated value one may find in a sonnet or a Grecian urn'.[2] There is nothing in this catalogue that touches noticeably upon morals, but I think it fairly clear that Lewis would have maintained that the contemplation of certain actions, motives and benevolent states of mind could give rise to experiences of similar quality.

Though he claims no descendance from them, Lewis's position is reminiscent of that of the eighteenth-century moralists, like Francis Hutcheson, who tried to connect our moral judgements with our possession of what they called a moral sense. For my own part, I doubt if there need be, or indeed very commonly is, any close similarity between such experiences as those of responding to one of Cranach's pictures, enjoying a feast of oysters, and admiring, say, an act of self-sacrifice, except that they are all prized, but perhaps no more than this is required. At least one might infer this from Lewis's saying at one point 'The immediately good is what you like, and what you want in the way of experience; the immediately bad is what you dislike and do not want'.[3] If that is what it comes down to, the question whether value and disvalue are present in experience after the fashion of sensory qualities becomes of minor importance.

A much more serious charge, which Lewis repeatedly tries to rebut, is that his theory represents judgements of value as subjective. His pragmatism commits him, as we have seen, to regarding all empirical properties as subjective in the sense that '*Any* property of an object is something determinable through experience, and in that sense definable in terms of the experience which would sufficiently assure it',[4] but this does not prevent them from being objective, in the

[1] ibid., p. 454.
[2] ibid., p. 446.
[3] ibid., p. 404.
[4] ibid., p. 458.

sense that the properties correspond to genuine possibilities of experience, whether or not they are believed to do so, and whether or not the possibilities are actually realized. It is sufficient that they would be realized, if the appropriate tests were carried out. In the sense in which being objective and subjective are properly contrasted, a property is subjective only if its actual or possible realization in the experience of some person is due to a peculiarity in that person's make-up or environment; if in short the experience is such as we should ordinarily characterize as an illusion. But that, Lewis maintains, is not generally true of values. So far as objectivity goes, they are exactly on a level with other properties. To use one of his own illustrations, the beauty of a nugget of gold is no less an objective property of it than its specific gravity, and this remains true even if the nugget is never discovered. All that is required in either case is the truth of the conditional that if such and such conditions were realized, such and such experiences would ensue. The difference lies only in the character of the tests.

But might not this difference be important? Why, after all, are we inclined to say that beauty is in the eye of the beholder, whereas we should be surprised to find this said of specific gravity? May not our reason be, to continue with the same example, that its specific gravity is an intrinsic property of the nugget of gold, while its beauty is not? This distinction could be maintained without prejudice to the pragmatic assumption that the attribution of specific gravity comes down in the end to prediction of the results of hypothetical experiments. In the one case it is taken for granted that the measurements would yield approximately the same result, when carried out by any normal observer. In the other it is a matter of a simple aesthetic reaction which is subject to cultural differences or may even vary from person to person within the same culture.

Lewis attempts to meet this point by requiring that the 'test-observation' be made by 'a connoisseur of beauty in metals',[1] though he does not say how such expertise is to be assessed. In the same spirit he maintains that 'objectivity of a value-apprehension is not dependent on the statistics of general appreciation; and "genuinely and objectively valuable" does not mean simply "conducing to satisfaction on the part of people in general" '.[2] This appears to be his

[1] ibid., p. 514.
[2] ibid., pp. 526–7.

dominant view, though there are passages which imply that an object has some objective value if there is anyone who would find satisfaction in it, so long as it would not give greater displeasure to others. In the main, though, as I have said, he denies that 'an arithmetic of counting noses has any relevance to an inherent value like the aesthetic ones'.[1] And more generally he remarks that the 'naturalistic view' which he is advocating 'does not wish to fall into the arms of a Protagorean relativism. It does not intend to put evaluations which the fool makes in his folly on a par with those of the sage in his wisdom.'[2] This weakens the analogy between judgements of value and judgements of perception, where the counting of noses is a dominant factor. It assimilates judgements of value more to scientific judgements, of which the understanding and appraisal require professional expertise. But then we are brought back to the difficulty of the choice of our mentors in deciding questions of value. Perhaps we could find acceptable criteria for the selection of experts in aesthetics, but it is not at all clear what would warrant the bestowal or refusal of the title of a moral sage.

It is not, however, for this reason that Lewis concludes that 'what is right and what is just can never be determined by empirical facts alone'.[3] It is rather that he distinguishes ' "good" meaning "useful for conducing to satisfaction" ', which he does take to be factual, from ' "good" meaning "morally justified" or "praiseworthy" ',[4] which he does not. He even goes so far as to call them two different words. To conflate their senses would be to commit oneself to utilitarianism, or possibly to egotism, which Lewis is not prepared to do, though he does rather strangely say that 'Be concerned about yourself in future and on the whole' is a categorical imperative 'which requires no reason'.[5] I think, however, that this should be regarded as an injunction to take life seriously rather than to study one's own interest. The only other moral maxims which he propounds are 'Be consistent, in valuation and in thought and action'[6] and 'No rule of action is right except one which is right in all instances, and therefore right for everyone',[7] which he characterizes as a tautology. It can

[1] ibid., p. 460.
[2] ibid., p. 398.
[3] ibid., p. 554.
[4] ibid., p. 552.
[5] ibid., p. 481.
[6] ibid.
[7] ibid., p. 482.

indeed be made into a tautology if one juggles sufficiently with the notion of instances, so that all the differences which might make one think it right for different people to act differently in similar circumstances are ironed out, but then it loses any moral force. As for consistency, it is indeed to be prized in logic, but there seems no compelling reason why a good logician should not be consistently villainous.

Lewis several times refers to the emotive theory of ethics in terms almost of pious horror, but it does not seem to me that the differences between it and his own position run very deep. Emotivists are not committed to denying that the questions of what people want and what would actually conduce to their satisfaction are questions of empirical fact. What they do resist is any attempt to blur the distinction between the descriptive and the normative uses of language. On this point Lewis would appear to have agreed with them, though he may have disliked their particular way of marking the distinction. If he did so agree with them I believe that he was right.

IV   Wittgenstein, Popper and the
Vienna Circle

The Tractatus *and its Sequels*

Ludwig Wittgenstein was born in Vienna in 1889. He came of a family of
rich industrialists who were Jewish by descent but had been converted to
Catholicism. Having studied engineering in Berlin, he enrolled in 1908
in the engineering department of the University of Manchester. He
specialized in aeronautics, and it has been said that he designed a
jet-reaction engine for aircraft. Finding that his interest had shifted from
applied to pure mathematics and thence to the philosophy of mathematics, he went in 1911 to the University of Jena to visit Gottlob Frege, by
whom he was very strongly influenced. Frege advised him to work
under Bertrand Russell, with the result that he spent five terms in
1912–13 at Trinity College, Cambridge. He very soon induced both
Russell and Moore to treat him as at least their intellectual equal. He
left Cambridge abruptly to live alone in Norway in a hut which he built
for himself. He was visited there by Moore, to whom he dictated notes
on the philosophy of logic, and he corresponded with Russell on the
same topic. When war broke out in 1914 he volunteered for the
Austrian army and served as an artilleryman first on the eastern front
and then in the Tyrol, where he was taken prisoner by the Italians in
November 1918. He had lost contact with his friends in Cambridge, and
in a footnote in Russell's *Introduction to Mathematical Philosophy*,
which was published in May 1919, Russell, having acknowledged that
the importance of the concept of tautology for a definition of
mathematics had been pointed out to him 'by my former pupil Ludwig
Wittgenstein', adds that he does not know whether Wittgenstein has
solved the problem of defining 'tautology' 'or even whether he is alive'.[1]

Russell was not left long in doubt about the answer to either of these
questions. Later in 1919 Wittgenstein wrote to him from his prison
camp, sending him a copy of a treatise in which he claimed not only to

[1] op. cit., p. 205, fn.

108

have succeeded in defining 'tautology' but to have solved all the other problems in the philosophy of logic which he and Russell had discussed. Wittgenstein had fashioned this treatise out of a numerous collection of philosophical 'remarks' which he had compiled during the war. A residue of them was picked out by his executors and published after his death. The treatise itself was a series of remarks, but they were systematically ordered and numbered. Wittgenstein, when the Italians released him, wished to meet Russell in order to discuss this work with him. A slight difficulty had arisen because Wittgenstein lacked the money for the journey, having been persuaded by a reading of Tolstoy that he ought not to enjoy wealth, and having accordingly made over his considerable private fortune to other members of his family. The difficulty was overcome by Russell's selling some furniture which Wittgenstein had left in Cambridge and their meeting took place in Amsterdam.

Russell was impressed by what Wittgenstein said and showed to him and agreed to write an introduction to the work, which appeared in 1921 under the title *Logisch-Philosophische Abhandlung* in the final number of the journal *Annalen der Philosophie*. A German translation of Russell's introduction was omitted, because Wittgenstein objected that when shorn of the elegance of Russell's English style the introduction was superficial and full of misunderstanding. He nevertheless allowed it to appear in the version of the work which came out the following year with the German text and an English translation by C. K. Ogden on facing pages. The title, suggested, it is said, by Moore, for this edition was *Tractatus Logico-Philosophicus*. Apart from a short essay entitled 'Some Remarks on Logical Form' which appeared in the *Supplementary Proceedings of the Aristotelian Society* for 1929, it was the only philosophical work that Wittgenstein published during his lifetime.

In the belief, which he expressed in the preface to the *Tractatus*, that he had essentially succeeded in solving the problems with which it dealt, Wittgenstein gave up working at philosophy for a time in order to become an elementary schoolteacher. From 1920 until 1926 he taught in a series of village schools in the mountains a long way south of Vienna. The children seem to have liked him but their parents did not and a legal action was brought against him on the charge that he used excessive physical severity. Though he was acquitted of the charge, he did not resume his teaching but instead spent the next few months in retreat at a monastery near Vienna, working as a gardener. He next turned to architecture and co-operated with his friend Paul Engelmann in designing a house in Vienna for his sister. The house survives in a modified form as the Bulgarian Embassy. I do not know whether he designed or helped to design any other buildings, but it is interesting that in each edition of the Viennese city directory from 1933 to 1938 the occupation attributed to Dr Ludwig Wittgenstein was that of an architect rather than a philosopher.

It was, however, as a philosopher that he obtained his doctorate. His interest in the subject was revived when he gave up schoolmastering and he made contact with several members of the group which came to be known as the Vienna Circle, including its leader, Moritz Schlick. He was also attracted back to Cambridge, mainly by the brilliant young philosopher F. P. Ramsey (1903–30) who, at the age of eighteen, had assisted Ogden in the translation of the *Tractatus* and had reviewed the book for *Mind*. Wittgenstein submitted the work as a doctoral thesis in 1929. His examiners were Russell and Moore, and Moore's report is said to have been 'It is my personal opinion that Mr Wittgenstein's thesis is a work of genius; but, be that as it may, it is certainly well up to the standard required for the Cambridge degree of Doctor of Philosophy'. After obtaining his doctorate, Wittgenstein was elected to a Research Fellowship at Trinity College, Cambridge, and taught classes there during the next six years, returning to Vienna in the summer holidays. During this period he became dissatisfied with the approach of the *Tractatus*. The new direction that his thought was taking is to be seen in two series of notes that he dictated to pupils. Some copies circulated privately at the time but it was not until 1958 that the notes were published under the title of *The Blue and Brown Books*.

After visiting the Soviet Union, where he was tempted to settle, and spending another year in his hut in Norway, Wittgenstein returned to Cambridge in 1937, becoming a British citizen a year later when Germany annexed Austria. In 1939 he was chosen to succeed Moore as Professor of Philosophy, but spent most of the war as a medical orderly in a London hospital and later in a research laboratory in Newcastle. After the war he resumed his duties at Cambridge but found that he disliked being a professor and resigned from the Chair in 1947. He spent the next two years in Ireland working on the second part of his *Philosophische Untersuchungen*. The first and much longer part, on which he had worked for many years, had been completed by 1945. On his return to England in 1949, after a visit to the United States, he discovered that he had an incurable cancer. He continued to work, mostly staying with friends in Oxford and Cambridge, and died in Cambridge in the spring of 1951.

Since his death his literary executors have been assiduous in editing and publishing his philosophical legacy. The *Philosophische Untersuchungen* came out in 1953, with the German text and its English translation by Miss Elizabeth Anscombe on facing pages, as in the *Tractatus*, and the English title of *Philosophical Investigations*. This book, which also takes the form of numbered remarks, more loosely ordered than those of the *Tractatus*, is by far the most important of Wittgenstein's posthumously published writings. In addition to *The Blue and Brown Books* which I have already mentioned, these include *Remarks on the Foundations of Mathematics*, thought to have been written in the years 1937 to 1944 and published, again in both languages, in 1956, a set of fragments dating from 1929 but mostly written in the years 1945–8 and published in both languages under the title *Zettel* in 1967, and some notes, *Über Gewissheit*, translated as *On Certainty*, published in the same format in 1969, and representing work on which Wittgenstein was engaged in the last eighteen months of his life. There have been various other posthumous publications, and a number of commentaries both on the *Tractatus*, of which a fresh translation by David Pears and Brian McGuinness, preserving the German text and Russell's introduction, appeared in 1960, and upon the later tendencies of Wittgenstein's thought.

When I first read the *Tractatus* as an undergraduate at Oxford in 1931, it made an overwhelming impression on me. In the intervening years I have come to find much of it obscure and to disagree on many points with what it appears to be saying, but I then took what I wanted from it and did not mind the rest. Its main theses, taken at their face-value, can be very briefly summarized. They were that the world is a set of facts which themselves consist in the existence of what in the original German are called 'Sachverhalten', translated by Ogden as 'atomic facts' and perhaps more accurately by Pears and McGuinness as 'states of affairs'. These states of affairs are composed of simple objects, and are represented by elementary propositions which are logically independent of one another. To have any literal significance a sentence must express either a true or false elementary proposition or one that assigns a certain distribution of truth or falsehood to elementary propositions. In that case the compound proposition is said to be a truth-function of the elementary propositions in question. There are two limiting cases. A proposition may disagree with all the elementary truth-possibilities, in which case it is a contradiction, or it may agree with them all, in which case it is a tautology. The true propositions of logic are all tautologies, in this sense, and so virtually are the propositions of pure mathematics, though Wittgenstein preferred to call them identities. Tautologies and identities serve a purpose in that they facilitate the drawing of deductive inferences, but in themselves they say nothing about the world. A genuine proposition pictures a possible state of affairs. These pictures themselves are facts and share a pictorial and a logical form with what they represent. Failure of representation occurs when a sentence, laying claim to truth or falsehood, depicts no possible state of affairs, whether simple or complex. Inasmuch as they are themselves neither elementary propositions nor truth-functions of elementary propositions, metaphysical pronouncements fail to represent anything. They are nonsensical. At their best they are attempts to say what cannot be said but only shown. This applies to ethics and aesthetics. It applies also to any attempt to describe the conditions of representation, so that the propositions of the *Tractatus* are themselves nonsensical. Wittgenstein compared them with a ladder which the reader must throw away when he has climbed up it. He will then see the world rightly. Among the things that he will realize is that philosophy is not a body of doctrine but an activity, the activity of clarifying the propositions of natural science and exposing metaphysics as nonsense. The book ends with the much-quoted sentence: '*Wovon man nicht sprechen kann darüber muss man schweigen*' ('What we cannot speak about we must consign to silence').

Even at the time when I was most impressed by the *Tractatus* I did not wholly accept the author's claim that the truth of all the thoughts that were put forward in it was 'unassailable and definitive'.[1] I wholeheartedly endorsed his conclusion that metaphysical utterances were nonsensical but did not count the utterances of the

[1] *Tractatus Logico-Philosophicus* (Pears and McGuinness), p. 4.

Tractatus itself among them. I did not see, and still do not see, how a sentence could at one and the same time express a pseudo-proposition and an unassailable truth. I agreed rather with Ramsey that 'if the chief proposition of philosophy is that philosophy is nonsense . . . we must then take seriously that it is nonsense, and not pretend, as Wittgenstein does, that it is important nonsense'.[1] Avoiding this conclusion, as Ramsey himself did, I looked upon philosophy as an activity of analysis and the propositions of the *Tractatus*, in most cases, as analytic truths. In fact they belong to what would nowadays be reckoned as the domain of general semantics, and I see no reason why this in itself should make them nonsensical. There is no doubt that one can significantly ask about the relation of sentences in a given language to what they are used to signify, and I do not see why this question cannot be generalized, so that we enquire into the general conditions of stating a possible fact.

Wittgenstein gives no example of an elementary proposition, nor consequently of an atomic fact, or state of affairs. He makes the mysterious assertion that 'in a state of affairs objects fit into one another like the links of a chain'[2] and argues that the reason why the objects must be simple is that they make up the substance of the world. 'If the world had no substance,' he continues, 'then whether a proposition had sense would depend on whether another proposition was true'[3] and 'in that case we could not sketch out any picture of the world (true or false)'.[4] The reasoning is cryptic but the assumption behind it seems to be that the most primitive signs, those that combine to express the elementary propositions, must be guaranteed a reference. If this condition is to be fulfilled, none of them can refer to a complex object, because the complex object in question might not exist: the proposition in which it was asserted that its elements were combined in the requisite way might be false. But then the sign which was supposed to name it would lack a reference and consequently could not contribute to the expression of an elementary proposition. The sentence into which it had been inserted would be meaningless.

The trouble with this argument is that there seems to be no good reason to accept its underlying premiss. Wittgenstein himself was later to point out that it is a mistake to identify the meaning of a name

---

[1] F. P. Ramsey, *The Foundations of Mathematics*, p. 263.

[2] *Tractatus Logico-Philosophicus*, 2.03.

[3] ibid., 2.0211.

[4] ibid., 2.0212.

with its bearer, and once this is admitted we are freed from the dilemma of having to say of a sign which fails to name a simple object that it either names a complex object or is meaningless. Not that this leaves us very much the wiser. We are frustrated by our not knowing even what sorts of objects are in question or what is the criterion of their simplicity.

This frustration was not felt by the earliest recruits to Wittgenstein's standard. They took it for granted that the elementary propositions of the *Tractatus* were descriptions of sense-experience; the objects which they signified were what Russell and Moore had made it fashionable to call sense-data; their configurations made up the structure of sense-fields. The result was that Wittgenstein was credited with a philosophical standpoint hardly differing from Hume's. His states of affairs, whether simple or compound, corresponded to Hume's matters of fact; his tautologies and identities expressed Hume's relations of ideas. They agreed that these two categories exhausted everything that could significantly be said. Not only that, but Wittgenstein also seemed to share Hume's attitude to causality, asserting, as he did, that 'the procedure of induction . . . has no logical justification but only a psychological one'[1] and that 'there is no compulsion making one thing happen because another has happened. The only necessity that exists is *logical* necessity.'[2]

The main obstacle to this interpretation is that it is not consistent with the logical independence of elementary propositions. It allows for the logical independence of actual states of affairs, so long as these are viewed as being altogether specific, but it does not prevent the truth of one elementary proposition from falsifying another, if, say, they ascribe incompatible colours to the same sensory area at one and the same time. Nor will the requirement of independence be satisfied if the predicates of the elementary propositions are quantitative: the assignment of some measure to a given item will not be reconcilable with its being accorded a different measure at the same time in the same dimension. In any case, if the elementary propositions referred to the contents of sense-experiences, the predicates which they contained would be qualitative rather than quantitative. The fact that the requirement of logical independence is violated by quantitative predicates also rules out the suggestion that Wittgen-

[1] ibid., 6.3631.
[2] ibid., 6.37.

stein's elementary propositions should be taken as referring to physical events. But what possibility then remains?

The only one I can think of is that the objects which combine to make up the primitive states of affairs are all universals. This would accord with the conception of elementary propositions as pictures representing possible states of affairs. To assent to such a picture would amount to asserting that there existed a state of affairs which matched it; the denial that the depicted state of affairs existed would correspondingly be conveyed by dissent. The fact that the pictures differed in whatever respect would not make them incompatible, since there would be no internal reference to bring them into conflict. Each would be conveying the information that there was some state of affairs which it matched, but neither would carry the mark of any attempt to pin-point the state of affairs in question otherwise than by describing its qualities.

It would, indeed, be possible to use such a language, provided that there was some convention in force which set limits to the area in which its propositions would be tested. For instance, if the language were phenomenal, it might be tacitly understood that the depicted states of affairs were to be sought in some limited set of sense-fields. It is not, however, clear that this would genuinely preserve the logical independence of elementary propositions. It is true that no two of them would be formally incompatible, but any picture which completely filled the conventionally imposed limits would exclude all the rest.

There is little point, in any case, in pursuing this idea, since it not only runs counter to the symbolism of the *Tractatus*, where variables appear to be distinguished according as they take particulars, qualities or relations for their values, but falls directly foul of Wittgenstein's objecting to Russell's definition of identity, that it prevents us from saying of two objects that they have all their properties in common, adding that 'Even if the proposition is never correct, it still has *sense*'.[1] This is a point on which Wittgenstein may well have been mistaken, but it does disprove the suggestion that he regarded objects as collections of properties.

In these circumstances, I think that we are driven to saying that Wittgenstein's requirement that elementary propositions be logically independent of one another just cannot be satisfied. Indeed, he

[1] op. cit, 5.5302.

himself fairly soon came to the same conclusion. In his short paper on Logical Form, he dismissed the possibility that different colour predicates could be true of the same particular at the same time. He did not recant to the point of saying that elementary propositions could for this reason be mutually incompatible, but, what appears to come to the same thing, he did speak of the 'grammar' of colour-predicates as being such that one colour could 'exclude' another: and of course the same would apply to sizes and shapes. This does not entail a sacrifice of atomicity, since it can remain true that all actual states of affairs are logically independent.

Another difficulty, which is mentioned in Wittgenstein's note-books as standing in the way of his inclination to treat the elementary propositions of the *Tractatus* as descriptions of phenomena, is the vagueness, if not of the phenomena themselves, at least of any concepts in which we might try to capture them. Thus, it is notoriously not a sufficient condition for two patches to be of the same shade of colour that there is no visible difference of colour between them. The reason for this is that discernibility of difference in colour is not a transitive relation. There may be a series of colour patches A, B, and C, such that A is indiscriminable from B and B from C but A is discriminable from C. So if x and y are to be accounted exactly alike in colour, they have to satisfy the strong condition that there is no specimen z which one of them exactly matches but the other does not. It would be of no advantage to us here to substitute roughly matching for exactly matching, for the relation of roughly matching is also not transitive. It would seem to follow, therefore, that in some cases at least our bestowal of a colour predicate upon a sensory datum will have to be provisional. There may, however, be a way of escaping this conclusion. In my example of the ABC series, we might make the ruling that if an instance of B was presented with instances of both A and C, it was to be assigned a different colour predicate from either of the others; if it were presented with an instance of either A or C in the absence of the other, it was to be assimilated to its companion; and if it appeared without either it could be given whichever of the three appellations we pleased. This would have the advantage of avoiding actual contradiction and of our being able to assign a definite truth-value in each case to the elementary proposi-tion. Nevertheless, it would hardly satisfy the demands of the *Tractatus*, since B would not be available to enter into different combinations as the same definite object.

Perhaps this point was hardly worth pressing so far, since the problem of vagueness arises in a more acute form when it comes to the assessment of the compound propositions which are supposed to be truth-functions of the elementary ones. Presumably we want to make full use of mathematics in our theories, but once we do so, then, as Wittgenstein himself admits when he deals explicitly with mathematics, the extension of our concepts becomes indeterminate. For instance, if our physical theory incorporates Euclidean geometry, there may well be lengths to which it assigns irrational numbers, like $\sqrt{2}$, as values: yet no actual operation of measurement can have an irrational number as a result. Again, our theory may well allow for an infinite number of possible differences in weight, but the observable differences that we can distinguish will always be finite. The result is that there is not always a sharp division between the elementary propositions, considered as reports of observation, with which a more abstract proposition concurs and those with which it does not. The states of affairs which are taken as verifying a theory fall within a certain range, but the boundaries of the range are not precisely drawn.

Another obvious objection to Wittgenstein's system is that it makes no provision for unfulfilled conditionals. In a purely truth-functional scheme, admitting only the values 'true' and 'false' and assigning one or other of these values to every proposition, the formula 'if p then q' is equivalent to 'not-p or q', with the result that among the outcomes which are sufficient for its truth are all those in which p is false. But, as we have seen in discussing the work of C. I. Lewis, we do not wish to be put into the position of having to assent to any possible result of an experiment, just so long as the experiment is not actually carried out. It may be feasible to develop a theory of conditionals which avoids allowing them to be true in cases where their antecedents are not satisfied, but the problem is not one that should simply be overlooked, especially if one is taking one's basic propositions to be phenomenal. If things are to be treated, in John Stuart Mill's terms, as permanent possibilities of sensation, we have to set limits to what we are taking to be possible.

It is not clear to me whether the conception of elementary propositions as picturing their senses was meant to ensure that they are definitely either true or false. Perhaps the way in which pictures were held to be composed excluded their being fuzzy; otherwise a degree of fuzziness in the picture might serve to reflect some indeterminacy in the facts. A more serious question is whether we gain any illumination from this idea of propositions as pictures. The model on which it is based is that of a photograph or a map, where there is a temptation to think that what turns these objects into symbols is their similarity of structure or content to some possible state of affairs. A map is an accurate portrayal of a stretch of country if the distances between the points with which it is dotted reflects, according to some uniform scale, the distances between towns, if its various shadings correspond to differences of altitude and so forth. But the choice, say, of a green colour to represent heights of under 600 feet and a purple colour to represent those of over 9,000 feet is obviously a matter of convention. So, less obviously, is the correlation of distances between marks on the map and the distances between features of the countryside. Without the convention according to which the map, or the painting, or whatever it may be, is to be interpreted as a sign of what it resembles, in some fashion or other, we know only the fact that two objects are in some way similar, and this no more makes one of them a sign of the other than the buttons on the right sleeve of my jacket symbolize those on my left. In short, the fact of physical likeness becomes relevant only when it is selected as a method of representation. It comes naturally to us to associate like with like, but it is not the only choice open to us, nor for many purposes the most practical. Most importantly, since it is only one out of many possible methods of representation, it does not serve to explain in what representation consists.

The view that elementary propositions are records of actual or possible experiences is likely to evoke the problem of solipsism. Whose experiences are in question? Must they not be those of the speaker, and in that case how can his utterances convey anything to persons other than himself? For surely one has direct access only to one's own experiences? One may infer from the behaviour of other persons that they have experiences which are analogous to one's own, but this is not something that one can actually verify. Indeed, if the propositions to which I can attach significance are all and only those that are truth-functions of elementary propositions which are descriptive of my experiences, it is not clear how the ascription of experiences to others can have any meaning for me, let alone be justified.

Towards the close of the *Tractatus* Wittgenstein deals with the problem of solipsism in an oracular fashion in which there are echoes of his reading of Schopenhauer. 'What solipsism intends,' he says, 'is quite correct, only it *cannot* be said, but it shows itself. That the world is *my* world shows itself in the fact that the limits of the language (the language, which alone I understand) mean the limits of *my* world.'[1] And later on he says 'The subject does not belong to the world: rather it is a limit of the world',[2] comparing it in this respect with the eye's not being itself a constituent of the visual field. The conclusion is that 'solipsism, when its implications are followed out strictly, coincides with pure realism. The self of solipsism shrinks to a point without extension, and there remains the reality co-ordinated with it.'[3] And finally 'What brings the self into philosophy is the fact that "the world is my world". The philosophical self is not the human being, not the human body, or the human soul, with which psychology deals, but rather the metaphysical subject, the limit of the world not a part of it.'[4]

It is not surprising that commentators on the *Tractatus* have found these passages difficult to explain. To have said that 'the world is my world' is obviously false if it is construed as a claim made by Wittgenstein about himself. The world existed before he was born and has not vanished with his death, and during his life he knew relatively little of it. But it is also obvious that this is not what he intended – it is not just to whoever happens to be speaking but to each one of us that 'the world is my world' applies. But this, as we have seen when we discussed C. I. Lewis's handling of the problem, is surely contradictory. We cannot all of us be so uniquely privileged. Or rather, it would be contradictory if the 'my' in each case referred to a particular human being, but we are told that it does not. It refers to the metaphysical subject. And what is this metaphysical subject? Here we reach the point where nothing further can be said.

This is not at all satisfactory. Even if we allow ourselves to be fobbed off with the remark that the solipsist is trying to say what cannot be said, we need some clear indication of what it is that he

[1] *Tractatus*, 5.62.
[2] ibid., 5.632.
[3] ibid., 5.64.
[4] ibid., 5.641.

intends, and why it is correct. A case can be made for saying that the range of my experience sets limits to my understanding, but if we take this so far as to equate the truth-conditions of any proposition that I understand with the experiences that would lead me to hold it true, we run into inextricable difficulties concerning my attribution of experiences to persons other than myself. A behavioural analysis is no solution since in order to be consistent one has then to deal similarly with one's own experiences, which results in pretending that one does not have them. And here the owner of whoever's experiences are in question is the human being. To suggest that 'my world' is the world of a metaphysical subject makes no sense at all.

Wittgenstein returns to this topic in *The Blue Book*, treating it at greater length and showing far less indulgence to the solipsist. He repeatedly makes the point that the solipsist who proclaims that only he feels pain is not drawing attention to some empirical fact, not even the fact that the pains which he feels are located in his own body. To show that this is no more than an empirical fact, Wittgenstein ingeniously constructs a set of examples which might lead us to say that a man was feeling pain in another man's body, or even that the pain was located in some inanimate object. The point of these fantasies is that they do not disarm the solipsist. Wherever the pain may be located, he still wants to say that it is he who feels it and not anybody else. In this way it becomes clear that he is making it a necessary proposition, a feature of usage, that he alone has experiences. There is no room in his language for the expression of a proposition which assigns a feeling of pain, or indeed any conscious state whatever, to anyone but him. But then, Wittgenstein argues, we can dispose of him simply by indulging him in his foible. We agree to confine our use of terms like 'pain' to the description of his experiences, and invent different terms for characterizing the experiences of others. Alternatively, we might say that his pains are the only real pains, his thoughts the only real thoughts, and so forth. In short, we give him a privileged status in our notation, since this is what he seems to want.

But of course this is not what he wants. He is not claiming any special privilege for himself. He is not conceiving of himself as the only sentient being in the world and of all those others who might appear to be human beings as robots. His image puts him on a level with other people, since it casts us all in the same predicament. Each one of us is confined within the circle of his own experiences. Taken straightforwardly, this image is contradictory, since one would have somehow to stand outside all the circles in order to frame it, but it has a powerful appeal, which is not merely, as Wittgenstein suggests, the result of our being bewitched by our habitual use of language, which makes no provision, or not the right sort of provision, for the sharing of experiences. It is all very well to say that we come up against a point of grammar when we complain that we cannot know about our friend's thoughts and feelings in the way that he knows about them; or, what comes to the same thing, that we have to depend upon physical evidence in a way that he does not and in a way that we do not when it is our thoughts and feelings that are in question. The fact remains that the point of grammar is not the effect of a merely wanton choice. The ground for making it a necessary fact that I cannot have your experiences lies in the different way that propositions about thoughts and feelings and sensations are verified by any given person, according as they are or are not his own.

Moritz Schlick, Otto Neurath and Rudolf Carnap

The thoughts which are distilled into *The Blue Book* were developed by Wittgenstein not only in Cambridge but also in his meetings with the members of the Vienna Circle. They are most clearly traceable in the contemporary work of Moritz Schlick, who had founded the Circle in 1925. Schlick, who was born in 1882, was not an Austrian but a German, and like other leading members of the Circle he was originally trained in physics. His doctoral dissertation, which he completed at the University of Berlin in 1906 under the supervision of Max Planck, was about the reflection of light in a non-homogeneous medium. He first attracted notice with a paper on 'The Philosophical Significance of the Principle of Relativity', written as early as 1915, and two years later published a small book on *Space and Time in Contemporary Physics*, which drew praise from Einstein. He decided, however, to pursue an academic career in philosophy rather than in physics and held philosophical posts at Rostock and at Kiel before accepting an invitation in 1922 to occupy a Chair of the History and Philosophy of the Inductive Sciences at the University of

Vienna. This was the Chair which had been founded in 1895 mainly for the purpose of attracting the celebrated physicist Ernst Mach from Prague to Vienna. Mach had been greatly interested in the philosophy of physics, in regard to which he held a radically positivist position. One of his most important books was entitled, in its English translation, *Contributions to the Analysis of Sensations*. Mach was obliged, as a result of a stroke, to resign from the Chair in 1901, and his successor, the equally famous physicist Ludwig Boltzmann, adopted the different title of Professor of Theoretical Physics and Natural Philosophy. Boltzmann did not sympathize with Mach's philosophy of physics and the change of title enabled him to claim that he had no predecessor, so that he was able to avoid the courtesy of paying any tribute to Mach in his inaugural lecture. It was characteristic of Schlick's attitude to philosophy that he restored Mach's title.

In fact, Schlick's philosophical interests were exceptionally wide, embracing ethics and aesthetics as well as the philosophy of science and the theory of knowledge. The first book that he published, as early as 1908, was entitled *Lebensweisheit: Versuch einer Glückseligkeitslehre*, and was, as the title indicates, concerned with the achievement of happiness. But the book which made him famous was his *Allgemeine Erkenntnislehre* (*General Theory of Knowledge*) which he first published in 1918, bringing out a second and a considerably revised edition in 1925. Rather surprisingly, it was only in 1974 that it was translated into English.

Soon after he assumed the leadership of the Vienna Circle Schlick was converted to a view of science which was substantially the same as Mach's, and he had also come to think, again agreeing with Mach, that the basic statements of observation were statements about sense-data. In his *General Theory of Knowledge*, however, he had adopted a more realistic standpoint. He insisted that every scientific statement or theory must be capable of being verified, in the sense that it had to have consequences which were capable of corresponding to observable facts, but the observable facts could have physical objects for their constituents. He agreed with Mach in rejecting psycho-physical dualism, arguing that to speak in mental or in physical terms was just to adopt one or other way of describing the same phenomena, but he tended to treat the phenomena as physical, in some degree anticipating the current fashion of identifying mental occurrences with processes in the central nervous system. This was another view which he was later to revise in favour of neutral monism. Perhaps the most remarkable feature of Schlick's book was that he anticipated Wittgenstein, with whom he had not yet made contact, in rejecting Kant's view that there could be such things as synthetic *a priori* truths and holding that all true *a priori* propositions, such as those of logic and pure mathematics, were analytic, or, in other words, tautological. He did not give the word 'tautological' the technical meaning that we have seen that Wittgenstein had in store for it, but characterized true analytic, or tautological, propositions as owing their truth solely to the meaning of the signs which were used to express them. This equally led to the conclusion that they were devoid of any factual content.

While Schlick remained the titular leader of the Circle until his death in 1936, its most militant member, one who aspired to make it not only the mainspring of an international movement in philosophy, but also a left-wing political force, was the Austrian, Otto Neurath. Neurath, who was the same age as Schlick but of a very different temperament, as untidy and rumbustious as Schlick was elegant and urbane, a giant of a man who used to sign his letters with a drawing of an elephant, was not officially attached to the University of Vienna but was the director of a Social and Economic Museum which he himself had founded in 1924. He had been educated at the Universities of Vienna and Berlin, first studying mathematics and then proceeding successively to linguistics, law, economics and sociology. The thesis with which he obtained his doctorate in Berlin in 1906 was on the subject of the economics of the Ancient World. At the end of the First World War, in which he served in the Austrian Army Service Corps, he sacrificed an opportunity to become a lecturer in Max Weber's department of sociology in Heidelberg in order to aid the Social-Democratic government which had been set up in Bavaria. He was put in charge of its central planning and continued in this office when the government was replaced by the so-called Spartacist government, consisting of Communists, left-wing Socialists and Anarchists. Neurath was not a member of any of these groups, though he showed sympathy for Marxism in his writings. When the Spartacists were overthrown in their turn by right-wing forces, Neurath was sentenced to imprisonment but released on the intervention of the Austrian government. He again escaped imprisonment in 1934, when the right-wing clerical government of Dollfuss, soon himself to be murdered by the Nazis, overthrew the Socialist Municipality of Vienna. Neurath was in Moscow at the time on business connected with his museum, which was mainly devoted to the display of pictorial statistics, and succeeded in making his way to The Hague where he had already established an International Foundation for Visual Education. He remained in Holland until the Nazi invasion of 1940, when he and the lady who was to become his third wife found passages in a small boat which took them to England. After a short period of internment as an enemy alien, he re-established his statistical institute in Oxford, where he lived until his death in December 1945.

Though he published only one book of any length, his *Empirische Soziologie*, which appeared in 1931 in a series of *Contributions to the Scientific Conception of the World* (*Schriften zur wissenschaftlichen Weltauffassung*) which were sponsored by the Circle, Neurath was an extremely prolific writer, mostly on applied economics but also on a varied set of topics, ranging from formal logic through history, politics and methods of education to the theory of warfare. A bibliography was attached to the English edition of his collected works, which was published in 1973, and the number of items included in it was 277. Not many of them dealt with what would ordinarily be reckoned as philosophical questions, but those that did went about it in an extremely trenchant fashion. His political platform consisted of an extreme hostility to metaphysics and a proclamation in favour of the unity of science. He did not always make it entirely clear in what he took the unity of science to consist, but it mainly appeared to be a combination of the theses that, so far as their grounds for acceptance are concerned, there is no difference in kind between the natural and the social sciences, and that all scientific statements are inter-subjectively testable. This made him take a realistic view of observation-statements and brought him into conflict with Schlick, who came, as we have seen, to construe them as referring to sense-data. In one way, however, Neurath's view of observation-statements was insufficiently realistic, since his ban on metaphysics was so stringent as to exclude any talk of comparing statements with facts, or indeed with anything external to them. Statements, he asserted, could be significantly compared only with other statements. The unhappy result of this was that he was driven into upholding a coherence theory of truth.

This was true also for a time of Rudolf Carnap who, though not a founder member of the Circle, became its best-known representative. A younger man than either Schlick or Neurath, Carnap was born in north-west Germany in 1891 and educated at the University of Jena, where he was one of the very few students to attend Gottlob Frege's courses on mathematical logic. His main interest, however, was in physics, and he started work on a doctoral thesis concerning the behaviour of electrons. He was prevented from completing the thesis by the outbreak of the First World War, in which he served as an officer in the German army. Returning to Jena after the war, he gave up his experimental work and obtained his doctorate in 1921 with a fresh thesis on the topic of space, the work being subtitled 'a Contribution to the Philosophy of Science'. Like Schlick, he had been struck by the philosophical importance of Einstein's Theory of Relativity, and, in addition to a pamphlet concerning the part played by the concept of simplicity in physics and another on the different levels of the construction of physical concepts, the passage from the qualitative to the quantitative and from the concrete to the abstract, he published articles on the topics of space, time and causality. His position at that time appears to have been closer to that of Mach than to Schlick's earlier realism, and in the intellectual autobiography which he contributed to the Schilpp volume, *The Philosophy of Rudolf Carnap*, he acknowledges the influence of the conventionalism of Henri Poincaré.

Meanwhile, the interest in mathematical logic which Frege had aroused in him developed and branched out. Through Frege, he had learned of Russell's and Whitehead's *Principia Mathematica* and he went on to study and be greatly influenced by Russell's work on the theory of knowledge, written during the period of Russell's neutral monism. Carnap had read the *Principia* when he was at Jena but could not afford to buy a copy and could not find one to borrow in Freiburg, to which he had moved. He wrote to Russell to ask where he could buy a second-hand copy and received in answer a thirty-six-page letter in which Russell wrote out all the most important definitions on which the proofs in the *Principia* were founded. This enabled Carnap to compile his *Abriss der Logistik* (*Outline of Mathematical Logic*), of which he wrote the first draft in

1924, though it was not published until 1929. It may well have been the first German handbook to do justice to the expansion of logic for which Frege had been responsible fifty years before.

Carnap was invited to become an instructor at the University of Vienna in 1926. He remained there, attending meetings of the Circle, until 1931, when he accepted a professorship at the German University in Prague. His main achievement during the years which he spent in Vienna was the publication of *Der Logische Aufbau der Welt* (in English, *The Logical Construction of the World*, though it was more than forty years before it appeared in an English translation). An exceedingly ambitious work, displaying, as all Carnap's work did, enormous industry and very great technical accomplishment, it adopted the standpoint of what Carnap called methodological solipsism. The use of the word 'methodological' was somewhat disingenuous: it was intended to forestall discussion of the epistemological problems which the choice of a solipsistic basis might be thought to raise. The basis was solipsistic inasmuch as Carnap, following Mach, James and Russell, after his own fashion, took as his starting-point the series of elements each constituting the whole of a person's current experiences at a given moment, and attempted to show how the entire set of concepts needed to describe the world could be constructed stage by stage, by the application of Russell's logic, on the basis of the single empirical relation of remembered similarity. This relation was chosen as being epistemologically primitive. Carnap was persuaded by members of the Gestalt school of psychology that experience comes in undifferentiated wholes. Even if this were so, however, it would not justify him in taking the experiences of a lifetime as the field of his primitive relation, for this includes the future as well as the past, and not all of one's past experience is remembered in detail at every subsequent moment. This is not an objection to Carnap's starting-point as such, but only to his grounds for choosing it. There are those, like Nelson Goodman,[1] who doubt whether any clear sense can be given to the claim that any type of statement is epistemologically primitive.[2] In constructing his 'language of appearance' Goodman borrows the term 'qualia' from C. I. Lewis, but does not share Lewis's assumption that the apprehension of qualia is logically prior to the perception of physical

---

[1] See Chapter IX below, p. 257.
[2] See his *The Structure of Appearance*, 2nd edn., pp. 136-40.

objects. On this point I am disposed to side with Lewis, on the ground that no physical object can be perceived unless the presentation of some quale or set of qualia has been at least implicitly noted, whereas the converse does not hold. For the purpose, however, of any sort of 'constitution' of the physical world on such a basis one would almost certainly need qualia of a wider range of types than the colours, places and times to which Goodman restricts himself.[1]

Carnap's system is purely extensional. Sensory qualities, such as colours, are equated with the classes of elementary experiences in which they occur, the qualities themselves being picked out on the basis of relations of partial similarity between the primitive units, so that there is only a structural difference between one quality and another, that is to say, a difference in the extensions of the classes with which they are respectively identified. Sense classes are defined in similar fashion in terms of the similarity of qualities and distinguished in terms of their dimensions. The middle and higher levels of the construction, such as the development of the physical out of the perceptual world through the replacement of sense-qualities by the purely mathematical operation of the assignment of quantities to spatio-temporal points, the constitution of one's own body, and of other people's minds, and the arrival at cultural 'objects' are sketched only in outline. Carnap's ingenuity is mainly displayed in his construction of sensory objects, but here he comes to grief, as Goodman shows,[2] by failing to see that it is possible for there to be sets in which every pair of things has a quality in common without there being any quality which is common to all the things in the set. In the case of colours, the set composed of the three combinations blue-red, red-green, blue-green would be a simple example.

In 1929 the Circle published a manifesto entitled *Wissenschaftliche Weltauffassung: Der Wiener Kreis* (*The Scientific Conception of the World: The Vienna Circle*). It was mainly drafted by Neurath, though Carnap and the mathematician Hans Hahn also signed the preface as editors. Schlick, to whom the manifesto is dedicated, had been away teaching in California, and the work was presented to him on his return, in gratitude for his decision to remain in Vienna rather than accept the offer of a professorship at Bonn. This may partly account for its making a larger concession to phenomenalism than Neurath

[1] See my *The Central Questions of Philosophy*, Chapters IV and V.
[2] op. cit., pp. 163–4.

might have been expected to yield. For instance, it is said that 'the meaning of every statement of science must be statable by reduction to a statement about the given',[1] and a similar possibility of reduction is required for every concept, in accordance with the hierarchy of Carnap's *Aufbau*, the lowest layers of which are said to contain 'concepts of the experiences and qualities of the individual psyche'.[2] This has, however, to be read in the light of the ensuing statement that 'a scientific description can contain only the *structure* (form of order) of objects, not their essence' and that 'subjectively experienced qualities are as such only appearances, not knowledge'.[3] This accords with Schlick's argument, developed in a set of three lectures delivered in London in 1932,[4] that only structure but not content can be communicated. Here one can also detect an echo of Wittgenstein, since Schlick feels himself obliged to say that nothing significant can be said about content, so that strictly speaking he is talking nonsense when he distinguishes it from structure or pronounces it ineffable. Even so, again like Wittgenstein, he expects his words to be understood. For my part, I am not sure that I do understand them, but if what is meant is that talk about qualities can be replaced by talk about the purely numerical ordering of classes, after the fashion of Carnap's *Aufbau*, then I believe that the thesis is not indeed meaningless but simply false. A part, however, of what Schlick may have had in mind is that, for the purposes of communication, the character of another person's experiences need not concern me, so long as I can put an interpretation on his utterances and his actions that accord with my own experience: and this, as I have already indicated in discussing the views of C. I. Lewis, seems to me not only meaningful but true.

Three theses which are stressed in the manifesto are the rejection of metaphysics as nonsensical, there being 'no such thing as philosophy as a basic or universal science alongside or above the various fields of the one empirical science',[5] and the tautological character of the true propositions of logic and mathematics. The grounds for accepting this last thesis were the belief that it had been proved by Wittgenstein and, in Schlick's case at least, the untenabili-

---

[1] See O. Neurath, *Empiricism and Sociology* (1973), p. 309.
[2] ibid.
[3] ibid, pp. 309–11.
[4] Published in Moritz Schlick, *Philosophical Papers*, (1979) II, pp. 285–369.
[5] op. cit., p. 316.

ty of what were regarded as the only possible alternatives, that these propositions were empirical generalizations, or synthetic *a priori* truths in the sense devised by Kant. There seems to have been no doubt within the Circle of the tenability of the analytic-synthetic distinction. They would not have denied that a sentence, taken to express an analytic proposition as, for example, the law of excluded middle, could be rejected; but they would have regarded this not as an abandonment of the proposition but as a decision to change the meaning of the sentence, in our example by giving a different meaning to the disjunctive sign. Rightly, as I see it, they did not attach any sense to saying that an *a posteriori* proposition was necessarily true.

The close connection between pragmatism and Viennese positivism is shown by the fact that C. I. Lewis's conception of meaning, which I have already criticized, could be fully expressed by the Viennese slogan that the meaning of a proposition is its method of verification. This principle is no more than implicit in the manifesto, but it occurs explicitly in Schlick's lectures and in more than one article in *Erkenntnis*, which became the journal of the movement in 1930 under the joint editorship of Rudolf Carnap and the leader of the small Berlin group of positivists, Hans Reichenbach. I have already shown that the principle operates differently, according as the possibility of verification is or is not affected by the identity and the spatio-temporal position of the speaker. Schlick does not enter into this question, but in general he appears to have actual speakers in view rather than ideal observers. He may have supposed that the difficulty about attributing experiences to others was resolved by his distinction between structure and content; he does not seem to have noticed that his interpretation of the principle raised any problem concerning statements about the past.

In the appendix to the manifesto the members of the Circle are listed as fourteen in number. Besides Schlick, Carnap and Neurath, they consisted of the philosophers Gustav Bergmann, Herbert Feigl, Victor Kraft, Marcel Natkin, Theodor Radakovic and Friedrich Waismann, the mathematicians Kurt Gödel, Hans Hahn, Karl Menger and Olga Hahn-Neurath, who was Neurath's second wife and Hans Hahn's sister, and the physicist Philipp Frank. Ten persons were listed as sympathizers, of whom the most notable were Hans Reichenbach and Kurt Grelling in Berlin, E. Kaila in Finland, and F.

P. Ramsey in England. Three 'leading representatives of the scientific world conception' were also mentioned in the persons of Albert Einstein, Bertrand Russell and Ludwig Wittgenstein.

It is interesting and even surprising to find the name of Kurt Gödel included in the Circle's membership. At the time that the manifesto was written he was only twenty-three, and it was two years later that he published in a German scientific periodical an architéchtonic paper, the modest title of which, translated into English, was 'On Formally Undecidable Propositions of *Principia Mathematica* and Related Systems'. In it, by a highly ingenious method of mapping statements about arithmetic into statements of arithmetic, he demonstrated not, as is sometimes alleged, that the consistency of arithmetic cannot be proved, but at least that no proof of the consistency of any deductive system, which was rich enough for the expression of arithmetic, could be represented within the system. He also showed that any such system will contain true propositions, which the system does not have the means to demonstrate. There is, therefore, a sense in which Gödel proved that arithmetic is essentially incomplete. This conclusion is not incompatible with the credo of the Circle that all the true propositions of mathematics are tautologies, but it does create a difficulty in that it stands in the way of a proof that being tautological is a property which all the true members of a deductive system can inherit from its premises. I can vouch for the fact that Gödel regularly attended meetings of the Circle in the winter of 1932–3 and that he then allowed their received view of logic and mathematics to pass without protest. By 1940, however, when he contributed a paper on 'Russell's Mathematical Logic' to the Schilpp volume *The Philosophy of Bertrand Russell*, he was maintaining that the assumption of classes and concepts, 'conceived as real objects, namely classes as "pluralities of things" and concepts as the properties and relations of things existing independently of our definitions and constructions . . . is quite as legitimate as the assumption of physical bodies and [that] there is quite as much reason to believe in their existence'.[1] There is no evidence that he ever abandoned this form of Platonic realism.

---

[1] *The Philosophy of Bertrand Russell*, p. 137.

Karl Popper on Induction

One who was not admitted to the Circle but maintained close relations with some of its members, notably Feigl and Carnap, was Karl Popper, who was born in 1902 and taught at a high-school in Vienna until 1937, when he accepted a lectureship at a university in New Zealand. After the war he was to become Professor of Logic and Scientific Method at the London School of Economics. His first book, *Logik der Forschung*, translated into English twenty-five years later as *The Logic of Scientific Discovery*, appeared in 1934 as number nine in the series of *Schriften zur wissenschaftlichen Weltauffassung* (*Contributions to the Scientific Conception of the World*), which were jointly edited by Moritz Schlick and Philipp Frank, who by 1931 had moved, like Carnap, to the University of Prague. Both editors contributed to the series, Schlick a book called *Fragen der Ethik* (*Questions of Ethics*), in which he treats ethics as a branch of psychology, attempting to explain how moral principles are selected and why people act in accordance with them, and Philipp Frank one called *Das Kausalgesetz und seine Grenzen* (*The Law of Causality and Its Limitations*), in which he treated causality in Humean fashion and applied the results to contemporary physics. The book advertised as the first volume in the series, *Logik, Sprache, Philosophie* (*Logic, Language, Philosophy*) by Friedrich Waismann, never appeared. The reason was that it was intended to reflect the current views of Wittgenstein and Wittgenstein was never satisfied with any of the drafts that Waismann submitted to him.

The appearance of Popper's book in the series was notable for several reasons. To begin with, he rejected the Principle of Verifiability, and indeed condemned the attempt to put forward any general criterion of meaning. Instead, he suggested a criterion which would serve as a principle of demarcation between statements that were scientific and those that were not. He was willing to say of statements which failed to pass his test for being scientific that they were metaphysical, but did not take this to imply that they were meaningless. On the contrary, he held that in certain cases metaphysical statements might fulfil a valuable heuristic function. The criterion he chose was that of falsifiability. Its superiority to a criterion of verifiability, even if one was looking for nothing more than a principle of demarcation, was supposed to consist in the fact that whereas no finite number of positive instances can fully establish a generalization whose range extends beyond them, one negative instance can definitely refute it.

This distinction is valid and important, but in practice it is not so clear-cut as it might at first appear. The first question that arises is what is to constitute falsification? Popper's answer to this was that a theory or a hypothesis is falsifiable if it is logically incompatible with some set of basic propositions. It is falsified if in conjunction with one or more accepted basic propositions it entails the negation of an accepted basic proposition. What, then, is a basic proposition, and when is such a proposition to be accepted? The answer is that a basic proposition is one that assigns some observable physical property to some region of space-time and that it is accepted by fiat. One's acceptance will indeed be motivated by some sense-experience that one is having, but it cannot so be justified. The reason why it cannot be justified is that the proposition will always contain a law-like element which goes beyond what is sensorily given. An example which Popper gives is the proposition 'Here is a glass of water' where the terms 'glass' and 'water' are not reducible to a single experience or even to a class of experiences. In any case Popper agrees with Carnap and Neurath that one proposition can be justified only by another. This leads to an infinite regress which is brought short only by a common decision, itself not irrevocable, to accept some member of the chain. The state of affairs which this proposition depicts must be repeatable if its occurrence is to be taken as refuting the theory which it serves to test. That is to say, there must be a consensus in favour of accepting a series of basic propositions of the relevant type.

Not all theories are cast in such a form as to be logically inconsistent with some set of basic propositions. In the case where the theories contain terms standing for unobservable objects there will be need of auxiliary hypotheses to bring this about. The same difficulty arises in the case of theories which contain assignments of probability. Since Popper identified probabilities with the frequency limits of open sequences of events, no finite series of events could rule out a predicted frequency; there was always the possibility that the balance would be restored if the series were prolonged. There had, therefore, to be a convention that a statement of probability was to count as being falsified if, at a certain stage, the recorded frequency differed from the predicted frequency by more than an agreed amount.

The upshot of these various factors is that a theory can always be protected from falsification, whether by one's making a different assessment of probability, or by one's rejecting some auxiliary hypothesis, or even by one's refusing to accept some basic proposition, however much favour it may have found with other judges. Popper admits that this is so and has to fall back on saying that someone who so cherishes his theories that he makes them immune from falsification is simply not playing the scientific game. The game consists in framing hypotheses which square with the accepted evidence but make large further claims so that they are highly vulnerable to being falsified, in subjecting them to the severest possible tests, in retaining them so long as they pass these tests, in rejecting them when there is an agreement to accept some set of propositions which refutes them, in framing new hypotheses which accord with these propositions and the previous evidence but also give the maximum number of hostages to fortune, and so continuing the cycle. There never comes a point where a theory can be said to be true. The most that one can claim for any theory is that it has shared the successes of all its rivals and that it has passed at least one test which they have failed.

A startling claim which Popper and his adherents have made for his account of scientific procedure is that it solves the problem of induction. Hitherto it had been believed that favourable evidence lent some credibility to the theory which it supported, but no satisfactory answer had been found to Hume's argument that reasoning from the particular to the general, or in any other way from past to future experience, cannot be justified by any means that do not beg the question. On this point Popper does not dissent from Hume, but he tries to cut the knot of the problem by denying that induction features in scientific method. There may be cases in which we are led to entertain a hypothesis by generalizing from experience, but how we come by our hypotheses is of no importance, except perhaps to psychologists. What matters is whether they are testable and how they meet the tests.

This last remark is one with which an inductivist might well agree. He might see it as his business to show how a theory was confirmed by positive instances, in the sense that they rendered it more credible. For instance, Carnap devoted the last years of his life to developing a system of inductive logic. In Popper's view this could serve no useful purpose, since he denies that hypotheses are in any way strengthened by the accumulation of positive instances. He therefore has no truck with any talk of confirmation. All the same, he is willing to say that a hypothesis is corroborated if it passes a severe test. We are not, however, supposed to infer that its being corroborated makes it any the more credible.

But this is very strange. For what would be the point of our testing our hypotheses at all if they earned no greater credibility by passing the tests? It is not just a matter of our abiding by the rules of a game. We seek justification for our beliefs, and the whole process of testing would be futile if it were not thought capable of providing it.

Not only that, but the whole pretence that we do not reason inductively becomes ridiculous when we consider how much inductive theory is built into our ordinary ways of speaking. My beliefs in the existence of the house in which I live, the clothes I am wearing, the pen with which I am writing, the cat sitting on my table, and indeed almost anything else that it might occur to me to mention, alike involve the assumption that a set of properties habitually go together; these assumptions are founded in my past experience, and however difficult it may be to devise a satisfactory account of confirmation, there is surely no doubt that they are justified. It might be said for Popper that these cases are covered by his account of basic statements; they add nothing to his example of the glass of water. But the most that such examples prove is that our judgements of perception are fallible. They do not prove that we are never justified in making them. This is not to deny that Popper gives a luminous account of at least one form of scientific procedure, but the basis of his system is insecure.

The Concentration on Syntax

The eighth volume of the *Schriften zur wissenschaftlichen Weltauffassung*, appearing in the same year as Popper's *Logik der Forschung*, was Carnap's *Logische Syntax der Sprache*, translated into English in 1937 as *The Logical Syntax of Language*. One purpose of this book, in opposition to the view attributed to Wittgenstein, was to show that a language could significantly be used to express its own syntax.

Another was to make good Carnap's claim that philosophy, to the extent that it could be a cognitive discipline, had to consist in the logic of science, which was itself identified with the logical syntax of a scientific language. I put it in this way because Carnap, while sharing Neurath's conception of the unity of science, allowed for the possibility of alternative language systems. The choice between them would be a matter of convenience. He thought that a language was completely characterized by its formation-rules, which would specify what sequences of signs were to count as proper sentences of the language, together with its transformation-rules, which would lay down the conditions under which sentences were validly derivable from one another. Unless the language were intended to be purely formal, one would expect there also to be meaning-rules, which would correlate some of its expressions with observable states of affairs, but at this stage Carnap saw no need for them. He believed that statements of verbal equivalence could do the work not only of semantic statements but even of ostensive definitions.

This makes it clear why Carnap was bound to uphold a coherence theory of truth. To the obvious objection that many incompatible systems of sentences could each be internally coherent, he replied that the true one was that which was accepted by the scientists of our culture circle. But this, as I pointed out at the time,[1] was a fudge. Each one of the competing systems might consistently contain the sentence that it alone was accepted by contemporary scientists. What Carnap meant was that only one of them was so accepted in fact. But this was to surrender his position. For why should this be the only instance in which an appeal to fact is authorized?

It was in *The Logical Syntax of Language* that Carnap made his famous distinction between the material and formal modes of speech. He distinguished three kinds of sentences: 'object sentences', such as '5 is a prime number' or 'Babylon was a big town'; 'pseudo-object sentences', such as 'Five is not a thing but a number', 'Babylon was treated of in yesterday's lecture'; and 'syntactical sentences', such as ' "Five" is not a thing-word, but a number-word', 'The word "Babylon" occurred in yesterday's lecture'. I am using his own examples, though it is clear that a sentence like 'Five is a number-word' is not a syntactical sentence at all, on a par with sentences like

[1] See my 'Verification and Experience' in *Proceedings of the Aristotelian Society* (1936–7), 37.

' "Big" is an adjective' or 'The word "Five" contains four letters'. The pseudo-object sentences were so called because they were held to be syntactical sentences masquerading as object-sentences. As such, they were also said to be syntactical sentences expressed in the 'material mode'. Translating them into the 'formal mode' revealed their syntactical character. Actually, if one looks at Carnap's examples, the sentences said to be in the formal mode are either not translations of their supposed counterparts or are not syntactical. Thus, if the sentence 'The word "Babylon" occurred in yesterday's lecture' is construed syntactically, the word 'Babylon' might be a name for anything. The sentence clearly does not entail what would ordinarily be understood by the sentence 'Babylon was treated of in yesterday's lecture' and equally clearly it is not entailed by it. Again, the sentence referring to 'experience-expressions' which is offered as a translation of the sentence 'The only primitive data are relations between experiences' is only masquerading as syntactical. What makes an expression an experience-expression is not its having any particular form but its being used to stand for an experience. It was Carnap's ambition to show that the respectable propositions of philosophy, as commonly formulated, were syntactical propositions misleadingly expressed in the material mode. The most he succeeded in showing, though he would not then have admitted it, was that some of them at least belonged to semantics.

Tarski's Theory of Truth

Carnap's negative attitude to semantics was dramatically changed at a congress organized by the Circle in Paris in 1935, at which the Polish logician Alfred Tarski presented an abstract of his paper 'The Concept of Truth in Formalized Languages'. Tarski belonged to a group of Polish philosophers and mathematical logicians with whom the Circle had long been associated. Its other leading members were Lukasiewicz, Leśniewski, Chwistek, Kotarbinski, and Ajdukiewicz. Tarski's article, which had already appeared in Polish, was made generally known by the appearance of a German translation in 1936. An English translation was included in a collection of Tarski's papers, translated by the biologist Professor J. H. Woodger, which was published in 1955.

Tarski begins by showing that any attempt to give a general definition of truth, which would apply to all natural languages, falls foul of the paradox of the liar; such definitions always allow the possibility of constructing sentences which say of themselves that they are not true, with the consequence that they are not true if they are and true if they are not. He maintains that in order to avoid this paradox it is necessary to distinguish clearly between a language, L, and a meta-language in which statements are made about L and to treat the terms 'true' and 'false' only as predicates of the meta-language. By a formalized language he means a language, like those of Carnap's *Logical Syntax*, which is fully characterized by its formation- and transformation-rules. He then defines truth for one such language, the language of the class-calculus. His method is first to define the concept of 'satisfaction' in such a way that any two classes *a* and *b* satisfy the function 'x is included in y' if and only if *a* is included in *b*, and eventually to arrive at the definition that x is a true sentence if and only if x is a sentence and every infinite sequence of classes satisfies x. He then goes on to show that 'a formally correct and materially adequate' definition of a true sentence can be constructed in the meta-language for every formalized language of finite order.

From a philosophical point of view, the greatest interest has attached to Tarski's two conditions of 'material adequacy'. One, which is relatively unimportant, is that truth is predicated of sentences. There are, indeed, those who insist on predicating truth of statements or propositions, but it is open to them to say that a statement or a proposition is true if it is expressed by a sentence which satisfies Tarski's definition. The substantial part of what Tarski calls 'Convention T' is that for a definition of truth in the meta-language of a language L to be adequate it must have for its consequences all the sentences of L which are obtained from the expression 'x is true if and only if p' by substituting for 'x' a name or structural description of any sentence of L and for 'p' the expression which is the translation of that sentence into the meta-language. If an attempt is being made to apply this convention to a natural language, the terms of the meta-language may, but need not, be drawn from the same natural language. Thus, an example current in the literature is 'The English sentence "Snow is white" is true if and only if snow is white'. But 'La phrase anglaise "Snow is white" est vraie si et seulement si la neige est blanche'

137

satisfies the convention equally well. If greater interest has been taken in examples of the former type, where the translation is homophonous, it is because of the currently fashionable belief, originally fostered by the American philosopher Donald Davidson,[1] that one can propound a theory of meaning for a given language by advancing a set of axioms from which all of the sentences satisfying Convention T in its meta-language would follow. It cannot, however, be said that this enterprise is very far advanced.

The Fate of the Circle

The Circle had held previous congresses, two in Prague and one in Königsberg, but the Paris congress marked the summit of its influence. It had already been weakened by Neurath's exile to Holland, and it suffered its most serious blow as an organized movement in 1936, when Schlick was murdered in Vienna. He was shot on the steps of the university. It was not a political act, but the work of a demented pupil. The right-wing press duly deplored it, but there was a faint suggestion that this was the sort of fate that radically anti-clerical professors might expect to suffer.

I myself, after obtaining my first degree at Oxford, attended meetings of the Circle in the winter of 1932-3, and my book *Language, Truth and Logic*, which was first published in January 1936, did something to spread its ideas. The influence of the book was felt most strongly after the war when it was re-issued with a new introduction. It then enjoyed a large sale in the English-speaking world and was translated into many foreign languages. In the original preface I said that my views were derived 'from the doctrines of Bertrand Russell and Wittgenstein, which are themselves the logical outcome of the empiricism of Berkeley and David Hume', acknowledged my kinship with G. E. Moore and his disciples, and claimed the closest affinity with the members of the Vienna Circle of whom I said that I owed most to Rudolf Carnap. In fact, my position was closer to that of Schlick, since I maintained that all empirical statements were reducible to statements about sense-data, but I presumably had in mind the Carnap of the *Logische Aufbau* rather than the Carnap who

[1] See Chapter VI below, p. 187.

had by then been converted to physicalism. Re-reading the book now, I think that it stands closest of all to C. I. Lewis's pragmatism, except on the question of values, where I took the view that ethical and aesthetic judgements were not cognitive but emotive, expressions of and incitements to feeling. This view is much more adequately developed by the American philosopher Charles Stevenson in his book *Ethics and Language*.

The Circle did not admit many visitors to its meetings but one who attended them at the same time as I did was W. V. Quine,[1] who, having taken his doctoral degree at Harvard, was successively visiting Vienna, Prague and Warsaw in furtherance of his researches into mathematical logic. He was more critical than I of the doctrines of the Circle, and indeed raised some incisive objections to their account of *a priori* truths in an article entitled 'Truth by Convention', which he contributed to a volume of Philosophical Essays for A. N. Whitehead in 1936.

At this time Neurath had largely taken over the movement. His main ambition was to produce an International Encyclopaedia of Unified Science, and he visited Chicago in 1938 to arrange for its publication by the University Press. An organizing committee was set up consisting of himself, Carnap, Frank, Charles Morris, who was teaching at Chicago, the Danish professor Jørgen Jørgensen, whom the war was to turn into an ardent Marxist, and Louis Rougier, almost the only French neo-positivist of the time, who was to become an emissary of the Vichy government. The encyclopaedia dwindled into a number of brochures, of which the most interesting were Carnap's 'Logical Foundations of the Unity of Science' and the American philosopher Ernest Nagel's 'Principles of the Theory of Probability'.

By 1938, when the Germans invaded Austria, the Circle was almost wholly dispersed. Feigl had been established in the United States for nearly a decade, and Carnap, Frank, Menger and Gödel had also found positions there in the preceding two years. Waismann fled to England, and after spending a brief period at Cambridge in the shadow of Wittgenstein obtained a Readership at Oxford, where he remained until his death in 1959. The Berlin group also escaped, Reichenbach and Von Mises to California, after a stay in Istanbul, and Carl Hempel early on to Brussels and then to the United States.

[1] See Chapter IX below, p. 242.

Of the Poles, Kotarbiński and Ajdukiewicz remained in Poland and survived the war, Lukasiewicz was sheltered by his pupil Scholz at Münster and subsequently became a professor in Dublin, and Tarski settled in the United States.

Even after 1938 Neurath still tried to keep the movement in being. He took over *Erkenntnis*, renamed it 'The Journal of Unified Science' and arranged for it to be published at The Hague but only a few numbers appeared. A final congress 'For the unity of science' was held at Girton College, Cambridge, in the summer of 1938. It was attended mainly by affiliates of the Circle, such as the Norwegian Arne Naess and members of the Dutch group, led by G. Mannoury, who engaged in the pursuit of what they called 'Significs'. The British delegates included the veteran pragmatist F. C. S. Schiller. G. E. Moore gave a short address of welcome and was seconded by my old Oxford tutor, Gilbert Ryle, who characteristically queried the point of trying to unify the language of science. What purpose was this supposed to serve? I do not remember what answer he received. Of the original members of the Circle, only Neurath, Waismann, Frank, and Feigl were present, Neurath coming over from Holland and Frank and Feigl from the United States. This was the last occasion on which it made an attempt to function as a group, though individual members, notably Carnap and Gödel, continued to produce important work.

Philosophy progresses, in its fashion, and few of the principal theses of the Vienna Circle survive intact. Metaphysics is no longer a term of opprobrium and it has been recognized that some metaphysicians at least have been led to their outlandish conclusions by their appreciation of difficult conceptual problems. The pragmatic treatment of scientific theories is less in favour than scientific realism. Both the analytic-synthetic distinction and the very concept of sense-data have been put in question, and, among those who believe that the concept of sense-data or something like them serves a useful purpose, there are few, if any, who believe that every empirical statement can be reformulated in their terms. On the other hand there remains considerable support for the connection of meaning with the possibility of verification and still stronger support for the connection of meaning with truth-conditions. Finally, I think it can be said that the spirit of Viennese positivism survives. In its re-accommodation of philosophy with science, its logical techniques, its insistence on clarity, its banishment of what I can best describe as a strain of woolly uplift from philosophy, it gave a new direction to the subject which is not now likely to be reversed.

V Wittgenstein, Carnap and Ryle

The later Wittgenstein

It was in the lectures, circulated in *The Brown Book*, that Wittgenstein first made extensive use of the concept of a 'language-game'. He first describes a 'language' used by a builder and his mate. The builder calls out the name of some item of equipment, such as 'brick' or 'slab', and his mate brings him the item in question. A more sophisticated form of this game is for the players to have learned the series of numerals from one to ten. When the builder's mate is given the order 'five slabs' he recites the numerals in order from one to five, takes up a slab for each numeral and carries it to the builder. Both the words for the items of equipment and the numerals are taught to the builder's mate ostensively. In the case of the numerals, he learns, say, the word 'three' by having trios of bricks or slabs or whatever pointed out to him; or he may be taught the difference between 'three' and 'four' by having them correlated respectively with a triad or a quartet of bricks. It would be wrong, however, to say that he was being shown numbers in the way he was being shown specimens of building materials. The difference lies not in the different character of the 'objects', but in the different roles that the two sorts of signs play in the language game.

This point is taken up again in Wittgenstein's *Philosophical Investigations*, the first and major part of which was considered by him nearly enough fit for publication for him to write a foreword to it in January 1945. He begins with a quotation from St Augustine which presents a picture of language in which, says Wittgenstein, 'we find the roots of the following idea: Every word has a meaning. This meaning is correlated with the word. It is the object for which the word stands.'[1] It will be remembered that this is very much the picture

[1] *Philosophical Investigations*, I, I.

142

of language with which Wittgenstein operated in the *Tractatus*. Its fault is that it exalts one use of language at the expense of a whole host of other uses. To the question how many kinds of sentence are there Wittgenstein now wants to say that there are countless kinds. He gives a list of examples which is not meant to be exhaustive: 'Giving orders, and obeying them – Describing the appearance of an object, or giving its measurements – Constructing an object from a description (a drawing) – Reporting an event – Speculating about an event – Forming and testing a hypothesis – Presenting the results of an experiment in tables and diagrams – Making up a story; and reading it – Play-acting – Singing catches – Guessing riddles – Making a joke; telling it – Solving a problem in practical arithmetic – Translating from one language into another – Asking, thanking, cursing, greeting, praying.'[1] When one goes through this list, one sees that what counts as a particular use of language, or a separate language-game, is fairly arbitrary. The sense of a sentence is not distinguished from the circumstances which attend its utterance, the question whether what it expresses is susceptible of truth or falsehood and the interest that this might have, the motive from which it is constructed, the effects that it is intended to produce. I think that we are meant to infer that if we try to impose even such large-scale distinctions we shall be giving an excessively simple account of the facts. Even the activities that figure in the list can be performed in a multitude of different ways.

Consideration of his primitive language games leads Wittgenstein to review the variety of processes which might come under the heading 'Comparing an object with a pattern'.[2] Let us suppose that it is a question of matching some material. It may be that the person who carries out the task has a sample with him, puts it alongside various bolts of cloth and chooses a length from the bolt which it seems to him most closely to resemble in colour, or texture, or whatever it may be. A similar procedure might take place if he had undertaken to choose some material that was darker, or sturdier than the sample. Alternatively, he might make the comparison from memory. This might involve his retaining a mental image, say, of the colour which he was required to match and choosing the piece of cloth which resembled the image. Alternatively, without having any

---

[1] ibid., I, 23.
[2] *The Brown Book*, p. 85, ff.

mental image, he might examine a number of pieces of cloth of different shades of colour, hesitate over them, reject one as being too light, another as being too dark, and eventually decide that one of them was the right shade. Or else, again without having any mental image, he may immediately pick out the one he wants.

It sounds a little odd to talk of comparison in the last case, since the piece of cloth that he selects as matching the sample he had been shown may be the only one that he ever looks at. He recognizes it as matching without going through any process of comparing. There is, however, nothing odd about the situation as described. One may use a mental image to facilitate recognition, but it is not necessary that one should, and most commonly we don't. I did not have to set any mental machinery in motion in order to identify the familiar objects in this room. I did not have to call to mind the previous occasions on which I had perceived them. I just sat down at my writing-table in my customary chair, took my fountain pen from my pocket, re-filled it from the inkpot in front of me, picked out my manuscript from a scattered set of papers, prepared to start writing at the place where I had left off, and that was that.

'But surely you were not functioning as an automaton?' No. I knew all the time what I was doing, inasmuch as I should have had no difficulty in describing my actions if I had been asked to do so. This is not, however, to say that I was monitoring what was going on. Moreover, I did not compare my current actions with previous actions of the same sort or the objects in question with any mental images.

Still, someone may say, even if you were not conscious of delving into your past experience, you must have been doing something of the sort, else how could you have recognized the objects that you did? It is very important to distinguish what is true from what is false about this remark. What is true is that there is a causal connection in cases of this sort. I should not be able to recognize the objects in question unless I had seen them before, or had seen objects closely resembling them, or at the very least had had them described to me. I should not have been able to deliver my report in English, unless I had been taught the language. One may conjecture that my previous perceptions and my training in the use of English have left traces in my brain which my present perceptions activate. What is false is that the actual process of recognition is bound to involve even an unconscious process of comparison with a sample. Let us suppose that the sample is an image. Then the proof is that the image would not serve its purpose unless it were identified. If we say that this requires a comparison with yet another image, we run into an infinite regress; we must at some point light upon an image which is directly identified. But this makes the whole adventure nugatory. If we can identify an image directly, we can recognize an object directly without having recourse to an image, or indeed any other kind of sample. Wittgenstein makes the point very neatly by bringing up the case where one is asked to imagine such and such an object or occurrence. It is obvious that we can straightforwardly do what is asked of us. We do not need to conjure up a whole series of images, each of which is supposed to check the accuracy of its predecessors.

Just as Wittgenstein came to reject the 'Augustinian' conception of language which he had so wholeheartedly embraced in the *Tractatus*, so he ceased to maintain that reality consists of simple objects. These two discarded doctrines go together since, as we have seen, the simple objects were supposed to be the elements named by the signs which conjoined in expressing the atomic propositions. Now Wittgenstein argues, surely with good reason, that the distinction between what is simple and what is composite depends upon the way in which the question is raised. In Wittgenstein's terminology, it has no meaning except within the rules of some language-game. 'Isn't a chessboard,' he asks, 'obviously and absolutely composite – You are probably thinking of the composition out of thirty-two white and thirty-two black squares. But could we not also say, for instance, that it was composed of the colours black and white and the schema of squares? And if there are quite different ways of looking at it, do you still want to say that the chessboard is absolutely composite? – Asking "Is this object composite" *outside* a particular language-game is like what a boy once did, who had to say whether the verbs in certain sentences were in the active or passive voice, and who racked his brain over the question whether the verb "to sleep" meant something active or passive.'[1]

This is not to say that one cannot devise language-games to which the conception of names corresponding to simple elements would be suited. Wittgenstein suggests an example where the sentence 'RRBGG-GRWW' describes an arrangement of three rows of squares, coloured

[1] *Philosophical Investigations*, I, 47.

red, black, green, or white in the order which the sentence indicates. Here it would be natural, though even so not obligatory, to count the coloured squares as primary elements. As for the question whether the sentence consists of four or nine letters, and whether its elements are tokens or types, it clearly does not matter what we say so long as we make ourselves understood.

Whereas Wittgenstein previously searched for the general form of propositions, something that might be called the essence of language, he now wants to say that there is no such thing. His language-games have no one thing in common. If they are brought under the same heading it is because they are related to one another in various ways. To make clear what he has in mind he invokes the analogy of games. There is no one feature or set of features that is common to all games. Not all of them are played for fun. There is not always competition between different players. When we look closely at the details of the different proceedings that we lump together as games 'we see a complicated network of similarities overlapping and criss-crossing: sometimes overall similarities, sometimes similarities of detail'.[1] Wittgenstein refers to these similarities as 'family resemblances' and concludes that games form a family.

I think that this is a happy analogy. One might, however, object that we have not been told what we are to count as the possession of a common feature. Why should we not be content to say that what all games have in common is that they are games? This would not be incorrect but it would also not be illuminating. The same applies to numbers, which are also said by Wittgenstein to form a family.

When it comes to numbers, Wittgenstein is chiefly exercised by the questions what it is to understand a formula or to follow a mathematical rule. An example on which he dwells in the *Investigations* is that of a man seeing another write down the numbers 1, 5, 11, 19, 29, and exclaiming 'Now I can go on'. Various things may have happened in such a case. The man might have tried out various formulae as the sequence was being written out until he hit upon the formula $a_n = n^2 + n - 1$. That 19 was followed by 29 would confirm this hypothesis. Or he might not have thought of formulae but noted the progression of differences 4, 6, 8, 10 and then felt able to continue. Or it may be that he just continues the series without more ado. It may be already familiar to him or simply present no difficulty. One of

[1] ibid., 1, 66.

the points that Wittgenstein is trying to make is that this man's understanding the principle of the series doesn't simply mean that the formula occurs to him, since one can imagine that the formula occurred to him without his being able to make use of it, but equally that his understanding need not consist in his having a flash of intuition or any other special sort of experience. And this would apply to understanding of all sorts, not only to the case of mathematical formulae.

Another case that Wittgenstein imagines is that of a man whom we train, as we think, to write down the series of even numbers. He adds 2 to each preceding number up to 1000, but at 1000 he continues 1004, 1008, 1012 and so on. When we protest, he says he is doing what he thought we meant him to do. 'It would now be no use,' says Wittgenstein, 'to say: "But can't you see . . . ?" – and repeat the old examples and explanations. – In such a case we might say, perhaps: It comes natural to this person to understand our order with our explanations as *we* should understand the order: "Add 2 up to 1000, 4 up to 2000, 6 up to 3000, and so on".

'Such a case would present similarities with one in which a person naturally reacted to the gesture of pointing with the hand by looking in the direction of the line from finger-tip to wrist, not from wrist to finger-tip.'[1]

But if these cases are analogous, then the man who goes from 1000 to 1004 rather than 1002 can be considered eccentric but not exactly mistaken. When it comes to the point, we say that he has misunderstood us, but when we gave him his instructions we may not have had that particular application of them in mind. Or if we did have that application in mind, there were countless others that we didn't. The moral which we are invited to draw is that the acceptance of a rule does not put us into a strait-jacket. We are left free to decide at any given point what the rule enjoins or forbids.

In a more generalized way this appears to be the outlook of Wittgenstein's *Bemerkungen über die Grundlagen der Mathematik* (*Remarks on the Foundations of Mathematics*), which came out in 1956, and his *Lectures on the Foundations of Mathematics*, which were delivered at Cambridge in 1939 and also posthumously published. Here again Wittgenstein appears to take the position that the result of a process of calculation is never determined in advance.

[1] ibid., I, 185.

Even though we may be following what seems to us a clear procedure we cannot predict where it will lead us. We cannot prejudge the question what verdict we shall characterize as correct. This is not to deny that our employment of mathematical and other concepts is subject to rules, but our obedience to those rules is like the unrolling of a carpet. The floor is covered only to the extent that the carpet has actually been unrolled.

It was in much the same spirit that Wittgenstein conceived of mathematical proof as changing the meaning of the concepts at issue. He drew an analogy here between the propositions of logic and mathematics, in their capacity as rules of deduction and conventions of measurement. He was quoted by Moore as saying in a lecture, ' "3+3=6" is a rule as to the way in which we are going to talk. It is a preparation for a description, just as finding a unit of length is a preparation for measuring.' So, a mathematical proof is a new paradigm. Mathematical propositions do not themselves describe anything, but they help to fix the criteria for the application of concepts which do have a descriptive use. Since they are antecedent to description, there is also a sense in which they are antecedent to truth.

This is not to say that the choice of mathematical rules, any more than that of standards of measurement, is altogether arbitrary. They have to be such that their application accords with empirical observation. The empirical observations come first, as it were, and the rules give their sanction of 'necessity' to what would otherwise be inductive generalizations. The ascendancy then passes to the rules, since they supply criteria for deciding whether our empirical investigations have been correctly carried out. It seems, however, to be implied that if there were a constant discrepancy between our empirical results and those that the rules prescribed, it is the rules that would be changed.

That we have at least the option of changing the rules was a conclusion later to be reached by W. V. Quine.[1] It was one of his arguments against the preservation of the analytic-synthetic distinction. Wittgenstein, however, cleaves to this distinction by continuing to hold, as he had in the *Tractatus*, that the propositions of logic and mathematics 'say nothing'. He has slightly shifted his ground, in that

[1] In his 'Two Dogmas of Empiricism', reprinted in his *From a Logical Point of View*. See Chapter ix below.

he has abandoned the scheme according to which tautologies agree with all the truth-possibilities of elementary propositions, but he achieves the same end by making them true by convention. He shares what we have seen to be C. I. Lewis's view that *a priori* propositions owe their necessity to the fact that their truth is ensured simply by the meaning of the signs which are used to express them.

Wittgenstein, however, carries his conventionalism further than Lewis. It seems to have been Lewis's assumption that once a meaning had been conventionally assigned to the requisite operators, the deductive work of logic and mathematics could proceed without further ado. And indeed this was also the view of the members of the Vienna Circle who dismissed *a priori* propositions as tautologies. It does not, however, square with Wittgenstein's view that we are free not only to choose our rules but also to decide what counts as following them. What other philosophers represent as the logical consequences of conventions, thereby seeming to grant some independent power of constraint to logic, he treats as the applications of further conventions. Such radicalism is heroic, but it is hard not to feel that it grants us more liberty than we actually possess.

The view of philosophy which Wittgenstein takes, or believes that he takes, in his later writings is clearly set out in one of the paragraphs of the *Philosophical Investigations*. 'We may not,' he there says, 'advance any kind of theory. There must not be anything hypothetical in our considerations. We must do away with all *explanation*, and description alone must take its place. And this description gets its power of illumination – i.e. its purpose – from the philosophical problems. These are, of course, not empirical problems; they are solved, rather, by looking into the workings of our language, and that in such a way as to make us recognize those workings: *in despite* of an urge to misunderstand them. The problems are solved, not by giving new information, but by arranging what we have always known. Philosophy is a battle against the bewitchment of our intelligence by means of language.'[1]

One of the principal errors into which we are led, according to Wittgenstein, by our failure to understand the workings of our language, is that of supposing that someone could use words to refer to his private thoughts and sensations, so that only he could understand what he was saying. There has been a great deal of

[1] *Philosophical Investigations*, I, 109.

discussion of this thesis of Wittgenstein's, but no universal agreement as to its import. An important point, which tends to be overlooked, is that he does not deny that we have sense-experiences, including sensations of pain and feelings of movement, or that these experiences are private in at least one reputable sense of the term. There is plenty of evidence for this in the latter part of his *Zettel*, published in 1967, and containing fragments which mainly date from the years 1945–8. For example, note 472 runs: 'Plans for the treatment of psychological concepts. Psychological verbs characterized by the fact that the third person of the present is to be verified by observation, the first person not. Sentences in the third person of the present: information. . . . The first person of the present akin to an expression. Sensations: their inner connexions and analogies. All have genuine duration. . . . Place of feeling in the body: differentiates seeing and hearing from sense of pressure, temperature, taste and pain.' And later note 479: 'We feel our movements. Yes, we really *feel* them; the sensation is similar, not to a sensation of taste or heat, but to one of touch: to the sensation when skin and muscles are squeezed, pulled, displaced.'

Neither does Wittgenstein suggest that a man's sensations or feelings, let alone his thoughts and images, are identical with physical events. He does not follow the line, taken by Carnap[1] and intermittently by Ryle,[2] that it is only if they are interpreted in physical terms, whether as referring to physiological states, or as dispositions to overt behaviour, that statements about one person's experiences can be made intelligible to another. He shows no signs of holding even the milder thesis, which has more recently come into fashion, that what are ordinarily classified as mental states are factually identical with states of the central nervous system.

What then are the pitfalls from which Wittgenstein thinks that we need to be guarded when we philosophize about experience? I find them to be two in number. The first is that of forgetting that one's references to one's private experiences are made within the framework of a public language; they are made in accordance with linguistic rules and there must be public criteria for deciding whether these rules are being complied with. The second is that of supposing that one can know what one's own experiences are but can do no

---

[1] See his *The Unity of Science*.
[2] See his *The Concept of Mind*.

more than surmise, not really know, what are the experiences of others.

Let us consider each of these points in turn. The argument on which the first of them rests is substantially contained in a well-known paragraph of the *Investigations*: 'Let us imagine the following case. I want to keep a diary about the recurrence of a certain sensation. To this end I associate it with the sign "E" and write this sign in a calendar for every day on which I have the sensation. – I will remark first of all that a definition of the sign cannot be formulated. – But still I can give myself a kind of ostensive definition. – How? Can I point to the sensation? Not in the ordinary sense. But I speak, or write the sign down, and at the same time I concentrate my attention on the sensation – and so, as it were, point to it inwardly – But what is this ceremony for? for that is all that it seems to be! A definition surely serves to establish the meaning of a sign. – Well, that is done precisely by the concentration of my attention; for in this way I impress on myself the connexion between the sign and the sensation. – But "I impress it on myself" can only mean: this process brings it about that I remember the connexion *right* in the future. But in the present case I have no criterion of correctness. One would like to say: whatever is going to seem right to me is right. And that only means that here we can't talk about "right".'[1]

At this point someone might object that one could rely on one's own memory for a criterion of correctness. One could also check one memory by another. But Wittgenstein will not allow this. He imagines his interlocutor's suggesting that he could check his memory of the time of a train departure by calling to mind an image of the time-table, and rebuts this suggestion on the ground that 'this process has got to produce a memory which is actually *correct*. – If the mental image of the time-table could not itself be *tested* for correctness, how could it confirm the correctness of the first memory? (As if someone were to buy several copies of the morning paper to assure himself that what it said was true.)'[2]

This is a striking simile, but I do not think that the argument which it serves is sound. The point which Wittgenstein seems to have overlooked is that any check upon the use of language must depend sooner or later on what I call an act of primary recognition. To revert

[1] *Philosophical Investigations*, I, 258.
[2] ibid., I, 265.

to his own example, it is supposed not to be sufficient for me to check my memory of the time at which the train is due to leave by visualizing a page of the time-table. I have to check the memory in its turn by actually looking up the page. But unless I can trust my eyesight at this point, unless I can recognize the figures that I see written down, I am still no better off. I can, indeed, appeal to the testimony of other persons, but then I have to understand their responses. I have to identify correctly the signs that they make. The point here is not the trivial one that the series of checks cannot continue indefinitely in practice, even if there is no limit to them in theory, but rather that the whole series counts for nothing unless it is brought to a close at some stage. Everything hangs in the air unless there is one item that is straightforwardly identified. Wittgenstein is mistaken also in suggesting that the corroboration of one memory by another is an inferior substitute for some other method of verification. There is no other method. Whatever I have to identify, whether it be an object, an event, an image or a sign, I have only my memory to rely on. The difference lies only in the degree to which the memories are cross-checked.

It is worth remarking that, so far as the present argument goes, there is no essential difference between one's use of signs to refer to 'public' objects and one's use of signs to refer to one's 'private' experiences. If my reference to some public object seems to my fellow speakers to be deviant, various courses are open to them. They may judge that my perception is at fault, or that I am trying to deceive them, or that I am making a linguistic error. Which explanation they adopt will depend upon the circumstances of the case. They have equally to decide whether it is my words or my feelings that are deviant if I issue reports of my sensations which do not consort with their observation of my behaviour. This does, indeed, concede the point, on which Wittgenstein insists, that we should not, in practice, be able to learn and teach the words for our sensations unless they had characteristic 'outward' manifestations. It does not follow that when we refer to our sensations we are referring to these manifestations, or indeed that there is any logical connection between them. It is a contingent fact that the congruence between the experiences of our 'outer' senses, which permits the objects of perception to be conceived as public, is not matched by a congruence between our respective feelings. It is a contingent fact even that few, if any, of us are endowed with telepathic powers.

The second of the theses which I chose to examine can also be illustrated by a paragraph from the *Investigations*. 'In what sense,' Wittgenstein asks, 'are my sensations *private*? – Well, only I can know whether I am really in pain; another person can only surmise it. – In one way this is false, and in another nonsense. If we are using the word "to know" as it is normally used (and how else are we to use it?), then other people very often know when I am in pain. – Yes, but all the same not with the certainty with which I know it myself! – It can't be said of me at all (except perhaps as a joke) that I *know* I am in pain. What is it supposed to mean – except perhaps that I *am* in pain?

'Other people cannot be said to learn of my sensations *only* from my behaviour – for *I* cannot be said to learn of them. I *have* them.

'The truth is: it makes sense to say about other people that they doubt whether I am in pain; but not to say it about myself.'[1]

In the light of the attention which we have seen that Wittgenstein paid in *The Blue Book* to the philosophical problem of one's knowledge of other minds, the summary fashion in which this problem is dealt with here is rather surprising. Neither is its abrupt dismissal at all convincing. Even if it were true that I cannot be said to learn about my sensations, nothing would follow about the way in which other people get to know about them, as Wittgenstein says that they very often do, and in particular it would not follow that they had other means of acquiring this knowledge than through observation of my behaviour. This is not to say that they do not have other means – they may have physiological or even telepathic evidence – but only that the question is left entirely open by Wittgenstein's argument.

Wittgenstein may be right in saying that it makes no sense for me to say about myself that I doubt whether I am in pain, though this is a view that has not gone undisputed. For instance, we have seen that C. I. Lewis held that all judgements, including judgements about one's present sensations, were fallible. One can certainly be in doubt as to the correct description of an experience, say a sensation of colour, that one is undergoing, but such examples may perhaps be set aside on the ground that the doubt relates only to one's choice of words, not to any matter of fact. For our present purpose this question may be left open, since however it be decided the consequence cannot be that it is only as a joke that I can be said to know that I am in pain. What Wittgenstein presumably had in mind is that it is very difficult

[1] ibid., I, 246.

to think of contexts in which there would be any point in saying 'I know that I am in pain'. One can imagine its being said to a sceptical doctor, though some such phrase as 'I assure you, it really does hurt' would be more natural. But the reason why there is little or no occasion for saying that one knows that one is in pain is not that one would be talking nonsense but that if one were speaking seriously one would be almost bound to be telling the truth. I do not want to say that being in pain and knowing that one is in pain are simply equivalent, since I believe that sentient creatures without the command of language can truly be said to be in pain without knowing it, but I do not deny that the information which we gain from someone's saying 'I know that I am in pain' is no more than we should already have inferred from his making what we took to be the honest avowal 'I am in pain'. But what follows from this is that he really can know that he is in pain, so that the sentence in which he expresses his knowledge, so far from being senseless, is true.

In his book *On Certainty*, first published in 1969, eighteen years after his death, and consisting of notes which he composed in the last eighteen months of his life, Wittgenstein carries the same line of thought a good deal further. The peg on which he hangs the argument which runs through these notes is that of G. E. Moore's defence of common sense. Wittgenstein does not deny the truth, or even the certainty, of propositions of the sorts that Moore took for his examples. On the contrary, he maintains that to express any doubt of their truth, in normal circumstances, would be nonsensical. At the same time he argues that if it were significant to doubt them, it would not be sufficient to allay the doubt for anyone just to say that he knew them to be true. Not only that, but he takes Moore to be at fault in saying this. His ground for reproaching Moore is not that the propositions themselves are any less certain than Moore took them to be but that to say, in the circumstances in which Moore did say them, such things as 'I know that this is a hand' or 'I know that the earth has existed for many years past' is a misuse of the expression 'I know'.

Wittgenstein's thought here is the same as that which prompted him to say that sentences like 'I know that I am in pain' are nonsensical. He believes that in both sets of instances one is expressing not an ordinary empirical proposition but what he chooses to call 'a proposition of grammar'. What one is really saying is 'There is no such thing as doubt in this case' or 'The expression "I do not know" makes no sense in this case'. From which, Wittgenstein infers, it follows 'that "I know" makes no sense either'.[1]

We have already seen that this conclusion is fallacious. Even when the use of the expression 'I know that' serves no purpose, indeed even when its use is misleading, as suggesting that the circumstances are exceptional when in fact they are not, it still does not follow that its use is senseless, or even that it is not used to state what is true. It may perhaps be worth illustrating this by another example. Although people most commonly believe what they assert, the conventional effect of prefacing an assertion with the words 'I believe that' is to weaken its force. It suggests that one is not entirely sure of what follows. If I say, for instance, 'I believe that Smith has been elected', I commit myself less than if I had said outright: 'Smith has been elected.' Nevertheless, it certainly does not follow that when I do assert something outright, I do not believe it. In exactly the same way, the fact that it may be pointless or even misleading for me to say such things as 'I know that this looks red to me' or 'I know that these are my hands' in no way entails that what I am saying is not true.

There is more at stake here, however, than the implications of our use of the verb 'to know'. Wittgenstein's reason for refusing to say that he knows the truth of such propositions as 'This is a human hand' is exactly the same as Moore's reason for saying that he does know them to be true, namely that under the appropriate conditions there can be no doubt of their truth. They both also accept the consequence that there can be no doubt of the existence of the physical world of common sense. We have already touched on this question in connection with Moore's approach. The present point of interest is the degree to which Wittgenstein shared it. What is there about our belief in the physical world that made him take it to be sacrosanct?

The answer is that he regarded it, not as an ordinary factual belief, but rather as part of the framework within which the truth or falsehood of our factual beliefs is assessed. In his own words, 'All testing, all confirmation and disconfirmation of a hypothesis takes place already within a system. And this system is not a more or less arbitrary and doubtful point of departure for all our arguments: no, it belongs to the essence of what we call an argument. The system is not so much the point of departure, as the element in which arguments have their life.'[2] This does not prevent the system from being

[1] *On Certainty*, para. 58.
[2] ibid., 105.

susceptible to change, but its propositions are protected from doubt inasmuch as it does not occur to us to doubt them so long as they hold their place in the system. 'What prevents me,' asks Wittgenstein, 'from supposing that this table either vanishes or alters its shape and colour when no one is observing it, and then when someone looks at it again changes back to its old condition? – "But who is going to suppose such a thing!" – one would feel like saying.'[1] And then he continues: 'Here we see that the idea of "agreement with reality" does not have any clear application.'[2] I assume that what he means by this is that it is only in the light of certain assumptions that the notion of agreement with reality comes into play. The assumptions themselves neither agree nor disagree with reality. They determine the nature of the reality with which agreement is sought.

What is not clear is how far these assumptions are taken to extend. Wittgenstein speaks of the system which they define as an inherited world-picture and of its propositions as being 'part of a kind of mythology'.[3] 'It might be imagined,' he says, 'that some propositions, of the form of empirical propositions, were hardened and functioned as channels for such empirical propositions as were not hardened but fluid; and that this relation altered with time, in that fluid propositions hardened, and hard ones became fluid. The mythology may change back into a state of flux, the river-bed of thoughts may shift. But I distinguish between the movement of the waters on the river-bed and the shift of the bed itself; though there is not a sharp division of the one from the other. But if someone were to say "So logic too is an empirical science" he would be wrong. Yet this is right: the same proposition may get treated at one time as something to test by experience, at another as a rule of testing.'[4]

This is a very interesting passage in more ways than one. In spite of the injunction not to regard logic as an empirical science, it seems to soften the analytic-synthetic distinction. At least security, even if it is only provisional, is no longer purchased at the price of saying nothing about the world. For it does not appear that the 'hardening' of empirical propositions is thought to deprive them of their empirical content. But what are we to make of his speaking of the elements of our world picture as being part of a kind of mythology? The

[1] ibid., 214.
[2] ibid., 215.
[3] ibid., 95.
[4] ibid., 96–8.

suggestion is not, I think, that the picture is false, but rather that what we count as the nature of things is not independent of the fashion in which we describe them. As Quine was to point out in his *Ontological Relativity* and elsewhere, our judgements about what there is are always embedded in some theory.[1] We can substitute one theory for another, but we cannot detach ourselves from theory altogether and see the world unclouded by any preconception of it. Whether or not Wittgenstein would have approved of this way of formulating it, the impossibility of there being any cognitive process which would require the prising of the world off language appears central to his position. Here he returns to Kant's famous dictum that 'intuitions without concepts are blind' and foreshadows not only Quine but also Nelson Goodman's *Ways of Worldmaking*.[2]

Carnap and Semantics

A similar concession to relativism is to be found in the later work of Rudolf Carnap. I have already described how he was persuaded by Alfred Tarski that the movement from syntax to semantics was not a descent into metaphysics. One result of this was that he himself published three books on semantics: *Introduction to Semantics* in 1942, *Formalization of Logic* in 1943, and *Meaning and Necessity* in 1946. The most important of these is *Meaning and Necessity*, in which Carnap claims to develop a new method for analysing the meanings of linguistic expressions as well as to lay a semantic foundation for modal logic. The new method allegedly consists in doing away with the 'traditional' assumption that linguistic expressions name concrete or abstract entities and in replacing it with the ascription to them of intensions and extensions. Since, however, they are said to 'designate' their intensions and extensions, it is not clear that the change is more than nominal. Carnap claims that every designation, as he calls it, refers both to an intension and an extension. In fact there is some doubt whether his system is not developed in a way that provides only for the designation of intensional entities,[3] but this is not a question

---

[1] See below, Chapter IX.

[2] See Chapter IX below, pp. 259–62.

[3] See Donald Davidson, 'The Method of Extensions and Intension' in *The Philosophy of Rudolph Carnap*.

that we need to argue here. The intensional entities to which individual constants or descriptions, predicates, and declarative sentences are respectively said to refer are individual concepts, properties and propositions, the corresponding extensions being individuals, classes and truth-values. Carnap insists that his intensions, including the individual concepts, are not mental constructs. They are objectively real. At the same time he rebuts the charge of hypostatization. 'As I understand it,' he says, 'a hypostatization or substantialization or reification consists in mistaking as things entities which are not things.'[1] So, individual concepts and properties and propositions must not be considered as things. In Carnap's view, however, this is not a bar to their being genuine objective entities.

This whole approach to the analysis of meaning was severely attacked by Gilbert Ryle, by then Professor of Metaphysics at Oxford, in a discussion of Carnap's *Meaning and Necessity* which appeared in *Philosophy*, volume XXIV (1949). The article is reprinted in volume I of Ryle's *Collected Papers*. Ryle summarizes Carnap's book as 'an astonishing blend of technical sophistication with philosophical naïveté'.[2] He finds the source of the naïveté in Carnap's tacit acceptance of Frege's doctrine that 'to ask What does the expression "E" mean? is to ask To what does "E" stand in the relation in which "Fido" stands to Fido?' or in other words that 'The significance of any expression is the thing, process, person or entity of which the expression is the proper name'.[3] Ryle calls this 'a grotesque theory' and shows that it does not work even in the case of all nominative expressions. Witness the difficulty by which Frege was driven to identify the meanings ('Bedeutungen') of the expressions 'the evening star' and 'the morning star' while distinguishing their senses ('Sinne') and to treat the senses as objects which the expressions named in oblique or modal discourse. Carnap makes what is in effect the same distinction by giving the two expressions a common extension, the planet Venus, and having them designate two 'individual concepts'. In fact, as Russell had already shown, it makes no difference to the meaning of such expressions what extension they may or may not have. To use Ryle's own example, we perfectly well understand what is meant by the expression 'the first

[1] *Meaning and Necessity*, p. 22.
[2] G. Ryle, *Collected Papers*, I, p. 235.
[3] ibid., p. 226.

American pope', even though there is nobody whom it yet names. To talk of its naming a sense or designating an individual concept is just a perverse way of saying that even though it does not name anything the expression is still meaningful. It is still more perverse to try to apply the model of proper names to expressions which are not even candidates for the function of mentioning anything at all. The answer to the spurious dispute whether predicate-expressions stand for properties or classes is that, not being names, they do not stand for either. Carnap has them standing for both; classes, extensionally, and properties, intensionally. Carnap also follows Frege into the trap of having to find nominees for indicative sentences and, like Frege, settles for 'a queer contraption'[1] known as a truth-value, which is either the object The True or the object The False. He again follows Frege in crediting the sentences with senses, though, as we have seen, he calls these senses intensions, and speaks of their designating propositions, whereas Frege has them naming thoughts. This is not to say that sentences lack senses, or that the use of the word 'proposition' is always objectionable. The fault lies in equating 'having a sense' with 'being a name' and in treating either 'thoughts' or propositions as subsistent entities. Carnap's disclaimer of hypostatization was disingenuous. His denial that individual concepts, properties and propositions are 'things' leaves it wholly mysterious what they are supposed to be.

Carnap responded to this attack in an article entitled 'Empiricism, Semantics and Ontology', which originally appeared in the *Revue Internationale de Philosophie* in 1950, and his defence of his procedure took a very interesting form. It basically depended on his drawing a distinction between what he called internal and external questions of existence. Internal questions, as the name suggests, are questions that arise within the framework of a conceptual system and are settled by the application of the criteria which the system supplies. Thus, if we are speaking at the level of common sense, there are accredited procedures for deciding whether there exist such things as shoes and ships and sealing-wax, silver mines or golden mountains, monkeys or unicorns. If we are speaking at the level of physics, such questions as whether there are protons or whether there is phlogiston are decided ultimately by observation, but also in terms of the acceptability of certain theories. If we are operating within

[1] ibid., p. 228.

mathematics or logic there are formal methods for deciding whether there are prime numbers within such and such a range, or sets with such and such properties. If we are talking about mythology or literature, questions about the existence of characters answering to this or that description are settled by consulting the appropriate texts. This is not to say that there can never be disagreements within science or within other disciplines. There are undecided questions in mathematics as well as in history. There may even be dispute within logic concerning the legitimacy of certain types of proof. The point remains that once the criteria of what is acceptable have been settled, the question whether they are satisfied is internal to the relevant discipline.

Now it is typical of philosophers that the questions which they raise about existence are nearly all at a high level of generality. They are questions like: Are there material things? Are there sense-data? Are there numbers? Are there propositions? The problem is how to interpret them. If they are construed as internal questions, then, as Carnap points out, the answers to them are obvious, according as the conceptual framework within which we are operating does or does not make provision for them. Yes, there are physical objects; this table is a physical object. Yes, there are numbers; 3 is a number. Yes, there are fictional characters; Mr Micawber is a fictional character. On the other hand, if one is speaking within a universe of discourse where the criterion for existence is actual location in space and time, then there are no fictional characters and, for that matter, no numbers either.

How does it happen, then, that these questions about existence have given rise to philosophical dispute? The explanation put forward by Carnap is that they become controversial when they are treated as external questions. They are said by him to be external when they are interpreted, not as questions which arise within a given conceptual or linguistic framework, but as questions which bear on the framework itself. Carnap's own suggestion was that when such questions are posited externally they are to be treated as questions of policy. A philosopher who says that there are propositions is claiming that he finds it useful, say in constructing a system for semantics, to employ a terminology in which propositions figure as objects of reference. A philosopher who denies that there are propositions is claiming that he can manage without any reference to them in his treatment of semantics or, perhaps still more strongly, that the introduction of propositions would diminish the utility of his system. There are indeed supposed to be constraints. Statements which are not analytically true have to be testable by observation. Since, however, the frameworks that we choose to adopt are likely to be provided with their own criteria of testability, the constraints are practically without effect. Carnap's principle of tolerance, as he calls it, leaves us free to employ any language that we find useful, no matter what sort of entities it refers to.

Is Carnap's distinction tenable? I think that it is, to the extent that it is treated as a guide to the different ways in which existential questions can be answered. An internal question is one that can be settled by giving examples of the sort of entity whose existence is under discussion. An external question is one where either no example is admitted at all, or else examples are admitted but are not regarded as probative. Thus, someone who does not believe in angels may simply deny that there are such things, or he may admit Gabriel and Michael as examples of angels, while denying that either of them really exists. Whichever course he takes he is unlikely to be satisfied with Carnap's theory that he is merely rejecting a particular mode of speech. His position is not that talk of angels is inconvenient but that nothing answers to it, possibly even that nothing could answer to it, if he holds that the concept of an angel is incoherent. Nor will he be placated by being told that talk of angels belongs to religious discourse and that religious discourse has its own standards. He will want to put these standards themselves in question. He will need to be shown that the religious discourse in question is not incoherent, and if he can be convinced that it has some meaning he will query the grounds for its acceptance. And here there is no reason why the qualifications for acceptance should be different from those that reign in other fields of enquiry, in science, maybe, or in history.

But is there no case at all for Carnap's principle of tolerance? I am inclined to think that there is when it comes to the admission of abstract entities. One may wish to explore certain logical avenues, without stopping to entangle oneself in the question what it is that gives different sentences or different predicates the same meaning, and then the use of words like 'proposition' or 'property' keeps the question, as it were, in suspense. On the other hand, if, as in Carnap's own case, the introduction of such terms is intended to furnish a theory of meaning, then, as Ryle has shown, the best that can be said for such a theory is that it is empty, the worst that it is spurious.

A different class of cases consists of those in which examples are admitted but the category to which they ostensibly belong is rejected not on the ground that it has no genuine application but that it is capable of reduction. Thus, someone may admit that France is a nation and yet deny that there are nations. He need not be contradicting himself, since what he intends to say in denying that there are nations is that nations are nothing over and above the individuals who compose them. In the same spirit someone who believes that physical objects are logical constructions out of sense-data may admit that this table is a physical object yet deny that there are physical objects; someone who believes that mathematics can be reduced to set-theory may admit that 3 is a number while contending that there are no numbers, only sets. Reverting to Carnap, one may say that when such persons admit the examples they are approaching the question internally; they approach it externally when they deny the category.

In a way, however, this would be misleading, since their handling of external questions is very unlike Carnap's. Their denial of the categories which they are repudiating is not based on considerations of convenience. On the contrary, they would respectively allow that it is nearly always more convenient to speak of physical objects than of sense-data, and, in many contexts at least, more convenient to speak of nations than of individuals and more convenient to speak of numbers than of sets. What is at issue, so far as they are concerned, is not a matter of convenience but a matter of primacy. If physical objects, nations and numbers are to be set aside it is because they are held to be less close to the facts than the categories that supplant them.

But in virtue of what can it be held that the members of one category D are closer to the facts than those of another c? There are various answers to this. One is the belief that statements about the members of c are translatable into statements about the members of D, whereas the converse does not hold. As we saw when we were concerned with the work of Bertrand Russell, there were those who thought this to be true of physical objects and sense-data. They never succeeded, however, in effecting the translation, and it would now seem that the most that can be achieved is to show how the common-sense conception of the physical world functions as a theory with respect to a basis of sense-qualia.[1] This is a relatively weak claim, as the objects which figure in the theory are not defined in terms of the primitive elements but posited.

A stronger claim, which appears to be satisfied in the case of nations and individuals, is that category c is reducible to D in the sense that no statement about the members of c can be true unless some statement, or set of statements, about the members of D is true, though once again the converse does not hold. Thus, while we do not have any set rules for translating statements about France as a nation into statements about Frenchmen, it is obvious that any true statement about France, in this sense, is made true by the behaviour of Frenchmen and other persons, whereas in the case of many truths about individual Frenchmen their nationality is not a factor.

Not only does this condition hold in the case of numbers and sets but, if we revert once more to Russell, it would seem that if sets are interpreted as classes the stronger condition of reducibility by translation is also fulfilled. The trouble here is that at least some of those who hesitate to admit numbers as entities in their own right are equally opposed to the admission of classes. This is true, as we have already remarked, of contemporary nominalists who allow considerable latitude in the choice of the individuals which figure as the basic elements or atoms in the systems which they construct, but disallow the admission of classes, as opposed to individual sums or wholes at the higher levels. Their argument, as we have noted,[2] is that the admission of classes leads to the multiplication of entities without end, thus constantly increasing the population of what Nelson Goodman has called 'a prodigiously teeming Platonic Heaven'.[3]

The nominalist appears to have a strong case. The main objection to it is that if classes are banished a great deal of mathematics is banished with them. To put it more mildly, what has so far been achieved by the nominalistic approach to mathematical logic comes a long way short of what most mathematical logicians would regard as the mass of acceptable results. At this point a follower of Carnap would say that if the results are acceptable, there is no further problem. If true propositions are obtained by construing certain

---

[1] cf. my *The Central Questions of Philosophy*, Chapter v.
[2] See p. 6.
[3] Nelson Goodman, *Problems and Projects*, p. 159. See below, Chapter ix.

entities as classes, that is sufficient proof that classes exist; indeed, the fact that they do enter into these truths may be taken as a criterion for their existence. He is surely right to this extent, that it cannot be a contingent question whether there are classes or not. It must be the very concept of a class that the nominalist disowns; and this means either that he finds some accredited results of mathematical logic unintelligible or that he believes that they can be interpreted in something other than the usual fashion. We are therefore brought to an impasse, which gives us a motive for proceeding along the lines of Wittgenstein. If, in spite of the obvious difficulties, we can manage to conceive of logic and mathematics purely formally as being concerned only with the transformation of symbols, then, so long as we do not contravene our rules, we need not care what substitutions are made in our formulae. We shall be committed only to accept the existence of the entities which figure in the empirical propositions to which the formulae are applied.

Gilbert Ryle and the Concept of Mind

The question of reduction has been especially prominent in discussion of the relations between matter and mind. We have already seen what a wide range of views on this topic has emerged in the history of philosophy. In recent years the tendency has been to give primacy to what is physical. We have found this to be true of Carnap, and it was also true of his critic Gilbert Ryle. Ryle, who lived from 1900–1976, spent the whole of his philosophical career at Oxford. After taking a triple first as an undergraduate at Queen's College, he was appointed a lecturer in philosophy at Christ Church in 1924, and Student and Tutor the following year. He remained at Christ Church until the war, when he obtained a commission in the Welsh Guards and worked in Military Intelligence. He returned to Oxford after the war as Professor of Metaphysics with a Fellowship at Magdalen College, retiring from the Chair in 1967. Apart from the influence of his teaching and writing, he played a dominant part in the development of graduate studies in philosophy at Oxford after the war. He was editor of the journal *Mind* from 1948–71. His essays and reviews, ranging in date from 1928 to 1970, and published in two large volumes in 1971, contain important contributions to the history of philosophy and the philosophy of logic, but his principal work was *The Concept of Mind*, which appeared in 1949. The other two books which he published in his lifetime were *Dilemmas*, in 1954, and *Plato's Progress*, which is partly a venture into Ancient History, in 1966. A small volume of his essays, *On Thinking*, was published posthumously in 1979. I shall here be concerned only with the views expressed in *The Concept of Mind*.

To this day *The Concept of Mind* is probably best remembered for Ryle's coinage of the phrase 'the ghost in the machine'. The phrase was designed to characterize a mythical view, which Ryle attributed to Descartes, of the relation between mind and body, and his avowed purpose was to destroy the myth. In his introduction to the book Ryle says that 'A myth is, of course, not a fairy story. It is the presentation of facts belonging to one category in the idioms appropriate to another. To explode a myth is accordingly not to deny the facts but to re-allocate them.'[1] The first question that arises is what general form this re-allocation takes. Does Ryle effect or try to effect a wholesale transference of the mental to the physical?

There is a good deal of evidence that this is his intention. For instance, he says: 'It is being maintained throughout this book that when we characterize people by mental predicates, we are not making untestable inferences to any ghostly processes occurring in streams of consciousness which we are debarred from visiting; we are describing the ways in which those people conduct parts of their predominantly public behaviour.'[2] Elsewhere he denies that there are mental happenings, if these are equated with 'occurrences taking place in a second-status world'[3] and denies also that a person's life is 'a double series of events taking place in two different kinds of stuff'.[4] He argues that 'the imputation of a motive for a particular action is not a causal inference to an unwitnessed event but the subsumption of an episode proposition under a law-like proposition',[5] that neither perceiving nor imagining entails the awareness of private objects, and in sum that 'to talk of a person's mind is not to talk of a repository which is permitted to house objects that something called "the

[1] *The Concept of Mind*, p. 8.
[2] ibid., p. 51.
[3] ibid., p. 161.
[4] ibid., p. 167.
[5] ibid., p. 90.

physical world" is forbidden to house; it is to talk of the person's abilities, liabilities and inclinations to do and undergo certain sorts of things, and of the doing and undergoing of these things in the ordinary world'.[1]

These and many similar passages suggest that Ryle is committed to the view that all our talk about our mental states and processes can be reformulated in such a way as to eliminate any reference to an inner life. What he would put in its place would be a set of dispositional statements about people's overt behaviour. If this view could be sustained, it would be a boon to philosophers. It would rescue them from the difficulty, which besets all dualistic theories, of explaining how mental and physical processes are related or how one person can ever come to know what goes on in the mind of another. But this simplification has to be justified. It has to be shown that all the ostensible references that we make to inner occurrences really can be eliminated.

As we shall see, Ryle does go some way towards meeting this requirement, but he neither contrives nor even pretends to meet it fully. Thus, he allows that 'much of our ordinary thinking is conducted in internal monologue or silent soliloquy, usually accompanied by an internal cinematograph-show of visual imagery';[2] after claiming that 'Boswell described Johnson's mind when he described how he wrote, talked, ate, fidgeted and fumed', he admits that the description was incomplete 'since there were notoriously some thoughts which Johnson kept carefully to himself';[3] he speaks somewhat disparagingly of 'the sorts of things which people often describe as thrills, twinges, pangs, throbs, wrenches, itches, prickings, chills, glows, loads, qualms, hankerings, curdlings, sinkings, tensions, gnawings and shocks',[4] but makes no attempt to show that references to these feelings or sensations can be rephrased in terms of actual or possible behaviour; while he denies that the various forms of sense-perception are mental states or processes, on the ground that words like 'see' and 'hear' are what he calls achievement words and consequently do not stand for states or processes at all, he does not argue that the activities which culminate in these achievements are not conscious; he denies the existence of mental images, but the

[1] ibid., p. 199.
[2] ibid., p. 27.
[3] ibid., p. 58.
[4] ibid., pp. 83-4.

'fancying' to which he tries to reduce imagination remains a conscious state.

In the face of all these counter-examples it must appear doubtful whether Ryle even aimed at establishing the strong thesis that all our talk about the mind is translatable into talk about behaviour. There is, however, a weaker thesis, which he does consistently maintain, and that is that a correct account can be given, in behaviouristic terms, of a great deal of what is ordinarily classified as talk about the mind. In a great many instances in which a person is said to satisfy a 'mental' predicate, what is being said of him is not only, and perhaps not at all, that he is undergoing some inner process, but rather that he is exhibiting or is disposed to exhibit a certain pattern of behaviour. This can apply to the ascription of intelligence, of motives and purposes, of voluntary actions, of emotions and moods, and of thoughts when they are overtly expressed.

This thesis allows the existence of inner processes but minimizes their importance. When someone acts intelligently, his movements may be preceded or accompanied by some inner planning, but they need not be; the silent thought is not required for the performance to be intelligent. Similarly, when I utter a meaningful sentence, it is possible but not necessary that I have already run through the sentence 'in my head'; even if no such inner process has taken place, the utterance will still express my thought. In the case of the will Ryle goes further: he denies that there are any such acts as the word 'willing' is commonly taken to denote; here too, however, his main point is that even if such acts of volition did take place, their occurrence could not be necessary to make an action voluntary; he uses the argument that if we took it to be necessary we should be drawn into an infinite regress, since it would make sense to ask whether these acts of volition were voluntary in their turn. He is not so successful in his analysis of motives, since his theory that imputing a motive is subsuming an episode proposition under a law-like proposition applies only to the standing motives like vanity and ambition which he takes as his examples; it does not apply to the occurrent motives that one may have for doing a particular action, like taking up one's pen in order to write. He could, however, have argued that to act from an occurrent motive need not involve any covert planning or even any covert avowal of the motive to oneself. When it comes to emotions, the occurrence of some inner feeling, or at least a bodily sensation, does seem to be essential: even so, it could be held that it carries less weight than the behaviour, or at least the behavioural dispositions, with which the emotion is typically associated.

Since there has been a tendency among philosophers to assume that everything that commonly passes for the work of mind consists in, or at least essentially involves, some inner process, Ryle's work, which is here reinforced by Wittgenstein's, is a valuable achievement. It needed to be shown that such things as intending, willing, understanding, desiring, exercising intelligence, even thinking, may, in concrete instances, consist in nothing more than the fact that the person of whom they are predicated is behaving or is disposed to behave in such and such a fashion. All the same we must not overestimate what has been accomplished. There is a great deal of mental activity that remains to be accounted for. It includes a considerable part of the exercise of the memory and the imagination and it includes every form of sentience. Most importantly, it has not been shown that perceiving can be analysed in behavioural terms.

Ryle's failure to make good his stronger claim does not mean that we are brought back to Descartes. We do not have to conceive of minds as substances, or indeed as entities of any kind. We do not have to admit thoughts, or feelings, or sensations, or mental images, or sense-data as objects. The only subjects to which mental predicates need to be ascribed are persons, or other sentient creatures, and anything that one might be tempted to count as a mental object, like an image or a sense-datum, can be transformed into ways in which such subjects are affected, that is, into states or processes which are adjectival to them.

But will not these states or processes have to have their own objects? Indeed, the possession of such objects has often been taken to be the distinctive feature of mental states or processes ever since this view was put forward by Franz Brentano (1838–1916),[1] from whom the school of Phenomenology took its inspiration. Brentano called this feature of the mind 'intentionality', borrowing the term from scholastic philosophy. How, then, do we dispose of 'intentional' objects?

Except in the case of perception and feeling, a simple course would be to make them propositions. As Ryle himself has shown,[2] not all thinking is straightforwardly 'thinking that', but with a little adjust-

---

[1] His *Psychology from the Empirical Standpoint* was published in 1874 (2nd ed. 1918).
[2] 'Knowing How and Knowing That' in *Collected Papers*, II, pp. 212–26.

ment such activities as wondering, musing, speculating, doubting, pondering, even dreaming, can be represented as being directed on to propositions. Without too much strain, the same can be made true of optative activities like wishing, hoping, fearing, desiring, seeking and regretting: their object will be the proposition that such and such a state of affairs does or does not obtain. Imagining, if only in view of the occurrence of after-images, is better assimilated to perceiving, in cases where the perception is delusive. Here, for those who are bent on diminishing their stock of objects, I see no alternative to treating images and sense-data as cognate to their respective types of act. In the same way, expressions which refer to feelings will have to be treated as cognate accusatives of the verbs which govern them. What this amounts to is that one refuses to license the existential inference from 'A has the feeling f' to a proposition of the form 'There is a feeling f which A has'.

Can the same technique be used to eliminate propositions? I am afraid, not entirely. One can of course refuse to license the existential inference, but doubts will remain. For instance, it is hardly plausible to reduce what is believed to a fashion of belief. It is possible that a way can be found of replacing propositions by sentences; and that an account of the use and understanding of sentences could be given in behavioural terms. This would help to free us from intentionality, but not from an acceptance of the mental. Thinking, feeling, imagining, sensing, perceiving and the rest would still be conceived as mental acts.

VI   Physicalism

Broad on Mind and Matter

More than twenty years before Ryle published *The Concept of Mind*, the relations between mind and body had been most thoroughly explored by the Cambridge philosopher C. D. Broad in a book of over 650 pages entitled *The Mind and Its Place in Nature*. Charlie Dunbar Broad, who was born in 1887 and died in 1971, was educated at Cambridge, became a Fellow of Trinity and after holding a Professorship at Bristol returned to Cambridge to occupy the Chair of Moral Philosophy from 1931 to 1953. Originally trained in the physical sciences, Broad approached philosophy in a scientific spirit and treated philosophical theories as capable of being rendered more or less probable by empirical facts. He was influenced by his seniors at Cambridge, Russell, Whitehead and Moore, though he never shared Moore's respect for the judgements of common sense. With Wittgenstein, who was his colleague in the 1930s, he had neither personal nor philosophical sympathy. Apart from *The Mind and Its Place in Nature*, which appeared in 1925, his two most important books were *Scientific Thought*, which was published in 1922, and *Examination of McTaggart's Philosophy*, of which the first volume, running to over 450 pages, was published in 1933 and the second, in two parts, amounting in all to nearly 800 pages, in 1938. His demolition of McTaggart's system, according to which the things which we misperceive as physical objects extended in space and time are really timeless spiritual particulars, is perhaps excessively thorough, but he does show McTaggart to have been a highly ingenious metaphysician, and in the course of restating and for the most part combating his arguments he does bring out many points of philosophical interest. Broad was, in his own terminology, more of a critical than a speculative philosopher, but the range of hypotheses on which he brought his critical powers to bear was unusually wide. Not only was he unfashionably tolerant of metaphysical speculation but, in common with H. H. Price, who held the Professorship of Logic at Oxford from 1935–59, he took an active interest in psychical research. His peculiarity in this respect was increased by the fact that he did not combine the interest with any religious belief or even with a positive desire for personal survival. The sentences with which he concludes his *Lectures on Psychical Research*, which came out in 1962, not only summarize his attitude but are also characteristic of his style. 'I think that I may say that for my part I should be slightly more annoyed than surprised if I should find myself in some sense persisting immediately after the death of my present body. One can only wait and see, or alternately (which is no less likely) wait and not see.'

Broad shares with Moore and Russell the belief that the immediate objects of perception are sense-data, though he prefers to use the term 'sensa'. The assumption on which he operates is that 'Whenever I truly judge that [a physical object] x appears to me to have the sensible quality q, what happens is that I am directly aware of a certain object y [a sensum] which (a) really does have the quality q and (b) stands in some peculiarly intimate relation, yet to be determined, to x'.[1] This peculiarly intimate relation consists partly in the fact that physical objects 'manifest themselves' in sensa and contribute towards causing them. It is because we are presented with these sensa that we unhesitatingly believe in the existence of a world of physical objects, but we do not infer the existence of this world from the nature of our sensa, nor should we be entitled to do so. As Broad puts it: 'If there were no sensible appearances to me, I suppose that I should not judge there to be any physical reality. But, on the other hand, there is nothing in my sensa to force me logically to the conclusion that there must be something beyond them, having the constitutive properties of physical objects. The belief that our sensa are appearances of something more permanent and complex than themselves seems to be primitive and to arise inevitably in us with the sensing of the sensa. It is not reached by inference, and could not logically be justified by inference. On the other hand, there is no possibility of either refuting it logically, or of getting rid of it, or – so far as I can see – of co-ordinating the facts without it'.[2]

[1] C. D. Broad, *Scientific Thought*, p. 239.
[2] ibid., p. 268.

Broad's position, then, is that there is no way of proving that the existence of physical objects has any initial probability. Apart from our awareness of our mental states and acts, we are presented only with sensa which are not such that the notion of a physical object can have been abstracted from them. This notion is defined by a set of postulates and thereby qualifies, in Broad's terminology, for the title of a category. These postulates are that anything worthy to be called a physical object must endure for a certain length of time and must throughout its duration possess 'a certain characteristic unity and continuity', that it is literally extended in space, that it persists and interacts with other physical objects at times when no one perceives it, that it is perceptible, at least in theory, by different observers at the same time and by the same observers at different times, and that it has at least one other intrinsic property besides those that are purely spatio-temporal.[1] Its being perceived, in Broad's view, is its being a special causal factor in the production of sensa. Now if we wish to justify the instinctive belief that these postulates are satisfied, we have to take the unwarranted step of assigning some initial degree of probability to the content of this belief. Once this initial step has been taken, we can draw upon the observed properties of sensa to reach highly probable conclusions concerning the character of physical objects. We are not entitled to assume that physical objects in general 'have the same determinate spatial characteristics as the sensa by which they manifest themselves', but we are able to infer with high probability what determinate spatial properties they do have on particular occasions of perception, by consideration of the nature and correlations of the corresponding sensa, and we can even make less certain inferences about some physical object's 'microscopic structure and the movements of its microscopic parts'. What we have no right to infer is that physical objects are literally characterized, even in determinable form, by the sensible qualities of sensa, like colours, sounds, tastes and smells. The most that we can conclude is that they stand to them in some causal relation.[2]

There is a plain echo here of Locke's distinction between primary and secondary qualities, though Broad makes the point more clearly that the resemblance of what Locke called ideas of primary qualities to their counterparts consists only in the common possession of

[1] See *The Mind and Its Place in Nature*, pp. 146–7.
[2] ibid., pp. 218–19.

spatio-temporal properties and not in any exact matching of the forms the properties assume. They are agreed in holding that external objects cause their appearances, whether they be called sensa or ideas, but Broad makes more of the point that this causation is not direct. 'We may *not* believe,' he says, 'that the shape, size, spatial position, date, or sensible qualities of a sensum by which a certain physical object manifests itself are *directly* determined by this physical object or by processes in it. On the contrary, the *independently* necessary and sufficient condition of all these characteristics of the sensum are within the region occupied by the percipient's body. At best the external object and the processes in it are remote and *dependently* necessary conditions of the sensum and its characteristics.'[1]

These are not the only causal factors which Broad holds to be responsible for the character of our sensa. He thinks that in certain cases at least their properties are also partly determined either directly or indirectly by events in the mind which animates the relevant body. He does not infer from this that sensa are states of mind, partly because he differentiates sensa from the sensing of them. In his own words, he believes that a 'perceptual situation' contains both a subjective and an objective constituent. The objective constituent is a sense-field, visual or other, in which one or more sensa are predominant. The subjective constituent is more complex. It is described as 'a mass of bodily feeling, together with certain specific emotions, muscular sensations, feelings of familiarity, images, etc'.[2] The mental element resides not in the sensing of the sensa, which consists rather in their being brought into a suitable relation with the mass of bodily feeling, but in the effects of past experience which leads us to convert our sensings into particular perceptions, or, as Broad puts it, to give the apprehended sensum 'a certain specific external reference'.[3]

It is not a defining property of sensa that they are private, but they can hardly fail to be so in fact because of their causal dependence on the current bodily and mental states of the observers who sense them. If this is not thought to be a bar to mutual understanding, it is because the existence of a sufficient similarity in the sensa presented to

---

[1] ibid., p. 219.
[2] ibid., pp. 219–20.
[3] ibid.

different persons is supposed to be revealed in the concordance of their behaviour. In any case we have seen this to be a difficulty that arises on any theory of perception. What is particularly obnoxious in a causal theory like Broad's is the multiplication of spaces and times. Each sensum is said to be 'a differentiated part of a bigger and more enduring whole, viz. of a sense-*field* which is itself a mere cross-section of a sense-*history*. Suppose, e.g., that I am aware of a red flash. This is a differentiation of my total visual field at the moment; and my total visual field at the moment joins up with and continues my earlier visual-fields, forming together with them my visual sense-history. The sense-history is a continuant; a kind of substance, though not a *physical* substance.'[1]

One difficulty here is that no account is taken of the gaps that occur in one's visual experience. It is not made clear whether, and, if so, by what criteria, the sense-fields preceding such a gap are to be assigned to the same sense-history as those succeeding it. Neither is it merely a question of visual sensa. Tactual sensa have their own spatio-temporal extensions, and the sensa of the other senses, even if they are not considered to be spatial, at least have temporal duration. In what way are these different sense-histories combined to form the experience of a single person and, if they can be so combined, how is the resulting continuant, or set of continuants, related, other than causally, either to the sense-histories of other observers or to the occupants of physical space-time? I say 'other than causally' because merely to make a sense-field causally dependent upon some set of physical objects is not to provide it with a spatio-temporal location. Somehow the multitude of physical and non-physical continuants have to be fitted into a single spatio-temporal pattern, and I do not see how this is feasible. This is not an objection to starting with sensa or to postulating physical objects, but it is an objection to letting them remain side by side. As I have argued elsewhere,[2] there is no warrant for maintaining a distinction between physical and perceptual space. The physical world in its spatio-temporal setting evolves out of the recurrence of sensa in relatively constant spatial patterns, and when the picture of the physical world has been developed, the sensa on which it was founded are absorbed into it and deprived of any independent existence. They are made cognate to the activities of a

---

[1] ibid., p. 195.
[2] See *The Central Questions of Philosophy*, Chapter v.

sub-class of physical objects, namely those that are credited with minds, or at least with some power of sentience.

Broad does not pursue this line of thought. His alternatives to leaving sensa in a kind of limbo between minds and matter are to make them constituents of a neutral stuff out of which mind and matter are obtainable or identifying the sensing of sensa with certain physical events. The first of these alternatives would be a version of neutral monism, which we have already discussed in connection with the views of Bertrand Russell and William James. The second is a feature of the Emergent Materialism for which Broad expresses a slight preference over either Emergent or Mentalistic Neutralism, these being the three survivors of his critical examination of a total entry of seventeen theories regarding the place of mind in nature. It should at once be made clear that the theory to which Broad gives the name of Emergent Materialism makes no concessions to Behaviourism. Mentality, in his view, is a complex characteristic of which the constituents, in ascending order, in the sense that the later members of the series incorporate the earlier but not conversely, are Sentience, Acquaintance, Intuitive Referential Cognition, as exemplified in Perception, and Discursive Referential Cognition, as exemplified in Thought. Any of these factors may or may not be accompanied by affective attitudes. Now there is no doubt that some living organisms appear to exhibit mentality, and this appearance cannot be universally delusive. The proof is that to say that something is delusive is to say that it is falsely believed to exist, and belief, whether true or false, entails mentality. This still leaves open the possibility that the characteristics which constitute mentality are reducible to physical characteristics, but Broad has no difficulty in showing that they are not. Even in the most favourable case of perception there is no form of overt behaviour that is uniquely associated with the perception of this or that physical object. Moreover, there is the sensational element in perception to be accounted for. In this case, if there were to be a reduction, the behaviour would have to be molecular. 'Let us suppose,' says Broad, 'for the sake of argument, that whenever it is true to say that I have a sensation of a red patch it is also true to say that a molecular movement of a certain specific kind is going on in a certain part of my brain. There is one sense in which it is plainly nonsensical to attempt to reduce the one to the other. There is a something which has the characteristic of being my awareness of a red patch. There is a something which has the characteristic of being a molecular movement. It should surely be obvious . . . that, whether these "somethings" be the same or different, there are two different *characteristics*.'[1] The proof, if any proof be needed, is that what can significantly be said about the one cannot significantly be said about the other. 'About the awareness of a red patch it is nonsensical to ask whether it is a swift or a slow awareness, a straight or a circular awareness, and so on. Conversely, it is reasonable to ask about an awareness of a red patch whether it is a clear or a confused awareness, but it is nonsense to ask of a molecular movement whether it is a clear or a confused movement.'[2]

The fact, however, that these characteristics are demonstrably different does not prevent them, in Broad's view, from belonging to the same subject. On the contrary, the emergent materialism, which Broad himself favours, requires that the characteristic of mentality belongs only to events which also possess an elaborate conjunction of material characteristics. The point of saying that the factor of mentality is emergent is that its presence is not deducible from the constitution and conduct of the material factors, considered independently of one another, or in combination with different characteristics. This is not incompatible with holding that the mental characteristics of the events which possess them are causally dependent upon the material characteristics which these events also possess, when these material characteristics are combined as they are. For this is only to concede that a particular organization of matter is sufficient to produce mentality. If we also hold that nothing has only mental characteristics, we shall not be committed to holding that this particular organization is also necessary for mentality to emerge, at whatever level is in question, for some other form of material organization might be sufficient as well.

We have already alluded to Broad's interest in psychical research, and this had already affected his opinions by the time that he wrote *The Mind and Its Place in Nature*. He believed that the evidence in favour of paranormal phenomena was strong enough to favour the adoption of what he called the 'Compound Theory'. This is the theory that mentality is an emergent characteristic composed of a living brain and nervous system and something which he calls a

---

[1] *The Mind and Its Place in Nature*, p. 622.
[2] ibid., p. 623.

psychic factor.[1] This psychic factor, which is assigned an indeterminate status as between mind and matter, is credited with the power to enter into various compounds and to carry the traces of previous experience. The possession of it would not guarantee personal survival, though it might contribute towards it. If anyone thinks this theory worth exploring I can do no more than refer him to Broad's *Lectures on Psychical Research*.

An objection which has been brought against the theory of emergent materialism in its simpler form is that it cannot account for the logical possibility of disembodied existence. It may well be the case that we have no very good reason for believing that there are purely mental entities, whether or not they are at some stage embodied, but at least the hypothesis is intelligible. I am inclined to agree that the hypothesis is intelligible, though not inclined to think it true, but there is no need to argue the point in the present context, since the theory of emergent materialism does not encroach upon it. The theory no more excludes the possibility of there being events which have purely mental characteristics than it excludes the possibility of there being events which have purely material characteristics. It merely declares that as a contingent matter of fact every event which has a mental characteristic has a material characteristic as well.

A much more serious difficulty is that it is not at all clear on what principles the members of a set of characteristics, whether mental or material, are ascribed to the same event. Broad says in *Scientific Thought*[2] that 'By an *event* I am going to mean anything that endures at all, no matter how long it lasts or whether it be qualitatively alike or qualitatively different at adjacent stages in its history'. This is contrary to common usage since, to employ Broad's own example, it allows the cliffs of Dover to count as an event, but that need not worry us. The trouble is that it supplies us with no criteria for individuating events. How is it to be decided whether the property of being a molecule of the requisite type and the property of being the awareness of a red patch characterize one and the same event or two concurrent events? It would seem that any such judgement must be the outcome of a theory. It might, for example, be established that the awareness of the red patch was causally dependent, in some

[1] ibid., p. 651.
[2] op. cit., p. 54.

unique fashion, upon the behaviour of just those molecules, and then it would simply be a matter of scientific convenience to speak of there being one event rather than two. But there is a difficulty in this suggestion which it is easy to overlook. Even if it could be established that an experience of a particular kind was always the outcome of some molecular disturbance, and it could also be discovered that the right molecular motions were occurring at a given time in some nervous system, they might be temporally accompanied by many different instances of that sort of experience. We need to select the instance which the theory picks out. Evidently it is one which 'belongs' to the same body as the nervous system in question. But how is this to be determined? What are the criteria for assigning experiences to one body rather than another?

Strawson's Concept of a Person

This last question sounds strange. It is not as if experiences were like playing-cards which have to be sorted into different packs. Experiences, it may be said, are individuated by reference to the persons whose experiences they are and persons are individuated by their bodies. At least for the sake of argument, let both these claims be granted. Our problem does not vanish, but merely reappears in an inverse form. On the basis of what criteria does a particular body 'appropriate' one series of experiences rather than another?

It is not immediately obvious that even this is a significant question. It would not be thought to be so by those who ascribe experiences to spiritual substances, though we might reasonably look to them, if not for some account of the relation of subject to attribute in this instance, at least from some account of the relation of these spirits to the bodies in which they are housed; and it would not be thought to be so by those who ascribe both material and mental properties to persons and take the concept of a person to be logically primitive.

The view that the concept is logically primitive has been notably developed by Sir Peter Strawson in the third chapter of his book *Individuals*, which was published in 1959. Strawson, who was born in 1919, is currently Professor of Metaphysics at Oxford, in succession to Ryle. His argument presupposes, what he has attempted to prove in the earlier chapters of his book, that material bodies 'in our actual conceptual scheme' are what he calls 'basic particulars'. What he meant by this was, in his own words, 'that material bodies could be identified and re-identified without reference to particulars of other types or categories than their own, whereas the identification and re-identification of particulars of other categories rested ultimately on the identification of material bodies'.[1] Thus, persons are identified through the identification of their bodies. This would be consistent with viewing them as compounds of material bodies and spiritual substances, but Strawson maintains that if this were our concept of a person one would never have any ground for ascribing experiences to others or even to oneself, for he holds it to be 'a necessary condition of ascribing states of consciousness, experiences, to oneself, in the way that one does, that one should also ascribe them, or be prepared to ascribe them to others who are not oneself'.[2] This means that we must be able to pick out individuals of the requisite type, and the distinguishing mark of such individuals is that both states of consciousness and corporeal characteristics must be ascribable to them. Strawson refers to the ascription of corporeal characteristics as the ascription of M-predicates and in this he sees no problem. In the case of the ascription of states of consciousness, which he calls the ascription of P-predicates, he simply asserts that 'it is essential to the character of these predicates that they have both first- and third-person ascriptive uses, that they are both self-ascribable otherwise than on the basis of observation of the behaviour of the subject of them, and other-ascribable on the basis of behaviour criteria'.[3] And later he maintains that the behavioural criteria on the strength of which we ascribe P-predicates to others are 'logically adequate' for the purpose.

I have discussed Strawson's theory at some length elsewhere[4] and attempted to show that he does not succeed either in showing that the concept of a person is logically primitive or in removing the possible grounds for scepticism concerning one's knowledge of other minds. I do not, however, wish to revive these criticisms here. The point which I now wish to make is that it is hardly an explanation of the relation between material and mental properties to say that there is

[1] *Individuals*, p. 87.
[2] ibid., p. 99.
[3] ibid., p. 108.
[4] See *The Concept of a Person*, Chapter IV.

just one type of entity to which they are both attributable. Strawson does indeed raise the question 'How are P-predicates possible?' but interprets it only as a way of asking how one is led to ascribe P-predicates to oneself and to others on the basis of observation in the second case and not in the first. His answer, that it is primarily through viewing both oneself and others as agents, may very well be correct. It is, however, of little or no assistance to us in answering the different question which I have raised.

Armstrong's Materialism

A variant of the answer that mental and material properties can characterize the same event, a theory which we did not reject but found to be obscure, is that mental events, or states, or processes are contingently identical with events, or states, or processes of the central nervous system. This form of physicalism has been defended by a number of philosophers, especially in Australia and the United States. If I pick out for special discussion a book entitled *A Materialist Theory of the Mind*, which appeared in 1968, by Professor D. M. Armstrong (*b.* 1926) of the University of Sydney, it is because it makes the most serious effort to deal with the difficulties which any view of this type entails.

Armstrong begins by defining a mental state as a state of the person apt for bringing about a certain sort of behaviour or, in some cases, as a state of the person apt for being brought about by a certain sort of stimulus.[1] These definitions are intended to leave it an open question what these causes and effects are, and allow it to be a scientific discovery that they are physical states of the central nervous system. The puzzle, on this approach, is to see what else they could be if they exist at all. The natural answer that they might be mental processes has been ruled out of court by the definition of mentality. All that we are allowed to understand by it is that the 'inner' causes of our propensity to behave in certain ways or the 'inner' effects of certain stimuli are what they are. Armstrong does indeed use the word 'spiritual' as if it could conceivably fit his definition of mentality. He does not say what he means by it, but I suspect that it is a substitute

[1] *A Materialist Theory of the Mind*, p. 82.

for the ordinary use of the word 'mental' which his definition denies him.

I think that Armstrong believes that he allows for the possible existence of mentality, in some such sense as Broad defines it, but I also think that he deceives himself. He writes freely enough of consciousness, introspection, bodily sensations, perception, sensory appearances, dreams and mental images: one even comes across passages where the sentence 'I seem to be seeing something green' is described as 'a phenomenological report on my visual experience'[1] or where it is allowed that 'In the case of all perceptions, we can distinguish between sensory appearances and physical reality'.[2] Nevertheless, the main thesis of the book is that mental items, in their ordinary guise, and in particular such things as images, or sensations, or feelings, or perceptions, taken as involving sensory experiences, simply do not occur. What they really are is something quite different from what they appear to be, and it is the business of materialist philosophers like Armstrong to explain these appearances away.

If I am right in thinking that this is what Armstrong is attempting to achieve, I am equally convinced that he comes nowhere near succeeding. Let us consider the crucial case of perception. Armstrong's thesis is that 'perception is nothing but the acquiring of true or false beliefs concerning the current states of the organism's body and environment'.[3] This still leaves us with the psychological concept of belief, but the burden is removed by our being told that while the beliefs in the acquisition of which perception consists may not themselves impel us to do anything, 'perception supplies a *necessary precondition* for appropriate behaviour'.[4] The only example we are given is that of a baby displaying its ability to distinguish between blue and green blocks by sorting them into different piles. This example is generalized to the point where we are told that 'Exhibition of a capacity for such selective behaviour is all the evidence needed for saying that the perceiver has acquired the particular belief'.[5] No notice is taken of the fact that the perception may occur without any exhibition of the capacity, or that in the absence of the perception there may be other evidence that the capacity is possessed. When it

[1] ibid., p. 109.
[2] ibid., p. 311.
[3] ibid., p. 209.
[4] ibid., p. 249.
[5] ibid., p. 340.

comes to beliefs 'of a more abstract sort, or about situations that are remote from us in time and place', Armstrong is reduced to saying that 'the only behaviour that seems to have any very intimate relationship to such beliefs is *verbal* behaviour'.[1] But verbal behaviour is just the production of noises and inscriptions. We need, what we are not given, some behavioural account of the way in which the utterances acquire their meaning. Next to no notice is taken either of the notorious difficulty in the way of a behavioural analysis of belief that our behaviour depends upon a combination of beliefs and a connection between beliefs and desires, neither of which is constant as between different persons or even as affecting the same person at different times. It is no wonder that Armstrong has to confess that he has been 'unable to work out an account of the nature of belief in the concrete detail that would be desirable'.[2]

But let us return to his definition of perception. It can readily be conceded that perception, at least in the cases where attention is paid to it, is capable of resulting in the acquisition of true or false beliefs concerning the current state of parts of the percipient's own body and parts of its environment. This is not an invariable result, since the belief may be one that is already held, but Armstrong gets round this obstacle by saying that in such cases the belief in question would have been acquired if the percipient did not already know it to be true. Let us allow this manoeuvre to pass. The important question is why Armstrong says that perception is nothing but the acquisition of a belief. What is the force of the 'nothing but'? The astonishing answer is that it serves to deny that the belief is acquired through sensory experience. Armstrong does indeed partially disguise this intention by speaking of beliefs as acquired by the use of the sense-organs, such as the eyes or the ears, but the use of the sense-organs is represented as a purely physical transaction between parts of one's body and material objects which display no manifest properties. 'I saw a mouse' is transmuted into 'I acquired a belief that a mouse was there by using my eyes' without its being granted that I used my eyes to *see* anything and without the implication that the belief arose as a result of my being presented with the visual appearance of a mouse. This absurd attempt to do away with phenomena extends even to bodily sensations. 'We recognize by bodily perception that the class of felt

[1] ibid.
[2] ibid., p. 339.

disturbances called "bodily pains" all have something in common. But bodily perception does not inform us what this feature is',[1] except for its tending to evoke the desire that the perception should cease. Why not simply admit that we experience sensations of pain?

Armstrong is too sensible a philosopher to be able to maintain this point of view consistently. For instance, he treats the case of seeing an object in a looking-glass as one in which the potential acquisition of the belief that the object is behind the glass is inhibited by one's previous knowledge of the effects of reflection. But why should we have any inclination at all to believe that the object is behind the glass unless that is where it appears to be? Again, he suggests at one point, quite rightly in my opinion, that there is 'a concealed element of inference'[2] in such perceptions as yield the belief that 'there is a cat's head over there'. His reason is that cats' heads have more than merely visual properties, which is a way of allowing that the belief claims more than is vouchsafed by the visual data on which it is based. To give only one more example, his account of mental images is that they are 'doubly eccentric'[3] perceptions, neither the effects of the stimulation of our sensory-organs, nor such as to involve even 'potential' beliefs. But if we adhere to Armstrong's definition, this implies that they are not perceptions at all. His recourse is to say that they resemble the central cases of perception, but he does not say how. If he did he would have to admit that they resembled them phenomenologically.

Armstrong gets into these straits because he cannot find room in his system for secondary qualities. This comes out most clearly in his treatment of colour, where he is driven to call it an illusion that perception gives us an acquaintance with such qualities as redness.[4] He allows that 'red objects all have a property in common which all normal observers can detect', but goes on to say that 'we normal observers are not aware of the nature of this property. We can only identify the property by reference to the way it is detected (by the eyes) and by mentioning objects that happen to be red.'[5] This is reminiscent of the thesis propounded by his associate, Professor J. C. C. Smart, that 'This is red' means 'something roughly like "A normal

[1] ibid., p. 314.
[2] ibid., p. 234.
[3] ibid., p. 300.
[4] ibid., p. 276.
[5] ibid.

percipient would not easily pick this out of a clump of geranium petals though he would pick it out of a clump of lettuce leaves" ' and I can only repeat, what I have written elsewhere, that 'apart from the fact that there are any number of reasons for which one might pick an object out, this analysis simply puts the cart before the horse. Geranium petals and lettuce leaves are not presented to us as collections of colourless atoms; they are differentiated by their perceptible qualities, including their colour. I do not judge my scarf to be red because I associate it with geranium petals rather than with lettuce leaves. I associate it with geranium petals rather than with lettuce leaves, because the lettuce leaves look green to me and the geranium petals and the scarf look red. To suggest that it is the other way round is merely disingenuous.'[1]

The definition of colour that Armstrong would like to give is that it is contingently identical 'with a certain physical constitution of the surface or object such that, when acted upon by sunlight, surfaces or objects having that constitution emit light-waves having certain frequencies'.[2] In the same way he wishes to identify the sound made by an object with the sound-waves that it emits and its temperature with the mean kinetic energy of the molecules which compose it. In the case of colour, however, there is the difficulty, pointed out by Smart, that 'a huge and idiosyncratic variety of different combinations of wave-lengths may all present exactly the same colour to the observer'.[3] What Smart and Armstrong can suppose themselves to mean by the presenting of colour has become a mystery, but let that pass. The question that worries Armstrong is whether it is possible to find a 'unifying formula' under which different combinations of wave-lengths could be grouped. If it should turn out that no such formula can be found, he is prepared to conclude that colour is a 'pseudo-quality'. At least, that is what he says, but once again his good sense triumphs over his physicalistic theorizing. For the ground which he adduces for this startling conclusion is nothing more than that the 'causes in the physical surfaces bringing about identical colour appearances for human observers' may be 'irreducibly diverse'.[4]

Though, in practice, he cannot avoid admitting that we have experiences of colour and other secondary qualities, Armstrong does have an argument to show that what he calls 'sensory items' do not exist.

---

[1] *The Central Questions of Philosophy*, p. 129.

[2] *A Materialistic Theory of Mind*, p. 283.

[3] ibid., p. 288.

[4] ibid., p. 289.

The argument applies to the data of all the senses, but we can safely continue with the example of colour. There the argument is based on the empirical circumstance that the relation of appearing to be the same colour, or even the relation of appearing to be exactly the same shade of colour, is not transitive. That is to say, there may be three colour patches A, B and C such that the keenest observer can detect no difference in colour between A and B or between B and C but can detect a difference between A and C.[1] This may prove no more than that the indiscernibility in colour of A and B is not a sufficient condition of their being exactly the same shade of colour. What is also required is that there be no third item, like C, from which one of the pair is discriminable and the other not. It might, however, be thought to raise a difficulty for those who think that there are objects, like sensa, which really have the sensible quality that things appear to have: for whereas there is no *a priori* reason why the relation of looking exactly alike in some respect should be transitive, to say that the relation of being exactly similar in a given respect was not transitive would be a contradiction.

Broad had already considered this case and found nothing in it. 'We must distinguish,' he says, 'between failing to notice what is present in an object and "noticing" what is not present in an object.'[2] The latter is excluded by his theory, since 'a sensum is at least all that it appears to be', but the former presents no special difficulty. It is obvious that we may sense an object without being aware of all its relations to some other object which we are sensing at a different or even at the same time. 'Consequently, there is no difficulty whatever in supposing that sensa may be much more differentiated than we think them to be, and that two sensa may really differ in quality when we think that they are exactly alike.'[3]

My objection to this dismissal of this problem is that Broad gives us no criteria for deciding what properties his sensa have, beyond what we succeed in noticing. A suggestion, which I have made elsewhere,[4] is that there is no inconsistency in supposing that two instances of colour, which satisfy the strong condition that no further instance exactly resembles one of them but not the other, should not still be assigned different colour predicates when they appear severally in

[1] See above, p. 116.
[2] *Scientific Thought*, p. 244.
[3] ibid.
[4] See p. 116.

different visual contexts. We may not be able to avoid a certain degree of vagueness in our descriptions of sensible appearances, but that in itself is unobjectionable.

It is strange that materialists like Armstrong should make such desperate efforts to do away with secondary qualities, since they could make them cognate to states of mind, and their thesis is that states of mind are only contingently identical with states of the central nervous system. The trouble is, it would seem that they believe that everything that happens in the world is physically determined, so that the admission of mental states, as something non-physical, would be a gratuitous anomaly. I cannot see any merit in this argument, unless it is so reformulated as to include mental states among the items for which there is a physical explanation. If that were the case, one might take the decision to identify mental states with their correlates in the brain, in the same way as we find heat identified with molecular motion or water with H_2O. There would be no compulsion to take this step, but it might be thought convenient. In fact, there is strong evidence that states of mind are causally dependent, in a general way, upon states of the brain, in the sense that the operations of the brain are necessary for their existence, but no strong evidence of this being a one-to-one correspondence, in the sense that every thought or every shade of feeling has its uniquely typical counterpart. There has been dispute over the question whether there is interaction between the mental and the physical to the extent that mental events play the role of causes as well as effects. At first sight it seems obvious that they do, if only in the realm of human actions. One's actions are the result of one's perceptions and decisions. But actions are also physical movements, and it might be held that all physical movements were fully covered by physical laws. From this point of view, the mental events and processes that accompany the chain of physical events which lead to the physical movements are causally superfluous. The thesis that they are not causal factors is known as epiphenomenalism. Given the assumptions on which it is based, it could not be refuted experimentally, and one might argue for its acceptance on grounds of economy. I see no reason, however, why there should not be more than one way of explaining a given state of affairs, so that the fact, if it be a fact, that a person's actions are explicable in purely physical terms, would not preclude their also being explicable, at least partly, in terms of such mental items as his desires and beliefs.

Davidson's Argument

The thesis that the events that take place in a person's mind are factually identical with events located in his central nervous system has commonly rested on the acceptance of psycho-physical parallelism. Scientific precedents are offered as a justification for transmuting a constant concomitance into an identity. It is interesting, therefore, to come upon a philosopher, the American professor Donald Davidson (*b.* 1917), who bases his physicalism on just the contrary assumption. The denial of the possibility of there being psycho-physical laws is an essential step in his argument in favour of identifying mental with physical events. His argument, as set out in an essay entitled 'Mental Events', first published in 1970 as a contribution to a volume of essays by various authors entitled *Experience and Theory*, runs as follows: We assume for a start that some mental events at least are causes or effects of physical events. A second assumption is 'that each true singular causal statement is backed by a strict law connecting events of kinds to which the events mentioned as cause and effect belong'.[1] This is not to say that every true singular statement of causality instantiates a law, but rather 'that when events are related as cause and effect, they have descriptions that instantiate a law'.[2] Under other descriptions they may not. Next, it is assumed that physical theory is capable of yielding a closed system in which every event answering to a physical description is subject to law. The mental, on the other hand, does not constitute a closed system. Neither can there be psycho-physical laws. The reason for this is that mental concepts do not mesh suitably with physical concepts. 'It is a feature of the mental that the attribution of mental phenomena must be responsible to the background of reasons, beliefs, and intentions of the individual.'[3] And these cannot be pinned down. 'There is no assigning beliefs to a person one by one on

[1] *Experience and Theory*, p. 99.
[2] ibid., p. 89.
[3] ibid., p. 97–8.

the basis of his verbal behaviour, his choices, or other local signs no matter how plain and evident, for we make sense of particular beliefs only as they cohere with other beliefs, with preferences, with intentions, hopes, fears, expectations, and the rest.'[1] Consequently, we have constantly to revise our assignments of mental traits in the light of new evidence. But this leaves us without a partner to pair with some type of physical event in such a way as to arrive at a psycho-physical law. It has, however, already been assumed that mental events are causes and effects. Since this implies that they are subject to strict laws, and neither purely mental nor psycho-laws are available, these laws must govern them under physical descriptions to which they must answer. It follows that any mental event that is causally related to a physical event is itself a physical event. Davidson does not actually attempt to prove that this is true of all mental events, but he implies that he believes it, since he says that the position which he wishes to occupy is that of 'anomalous monism', and says of anomalous monism that it 'resembles materialism in its claim that all events are physical'.

Many people have been convinced by this argument, but I think that it can easily be shown to be fallacious. To begin with, the ground for concluding that events viewed as answering to mental descriptions cannot be governed by strict laws is that there are not enough clues to be obtained from the behaviour of the person in question for the remainder of us to be sufficiently confident that the description is accurate. It does not in the least follow that there is no accurate mental description of the event or that its accuracy is not known to the person himself. The most that could be argued would be that the occurrence of events answering to mental descriptions was not publicly verifiable to an extent that would warrant the formulation of psycho-physical laws; but then, since the establishment of physical laws relies ultimately on perceptual testimony, itself arising out of mental events, the same would apply to them. Moreover, if mental events cannot be sufficiently pin-pointed to be candidates for subsumption under strict laws, why should it be thought that they can be sufficiently pin-pointed to be identified as causes and effects? In fact, the only reason that Davidson can have for assuming that events do function as causes and effects under mental descriptions in relation to physical events is that they are habitually conjoined with

[1] ibid., p. 96.

them. It is observed that someone who is struck commonly suffers pain, that someone who wishes to buy a newspaper usually visits a newsagent, that someone who feels insulted is apt to show resentment, and so forth. Now it is at least very doubtful whether any of these pairings are supported by strict laws. Yet Davidson has no hesitation in taking them to be causally connected: and it is only on the basis of this assumption that he holds them to be subject to physical laws, for the operation of which he has no independent evidence; indeed, he is nowhere near being able to formulate them. Clearly his argument has gone astray. Its proper conclusion is either that events under mental descriptions do not stand in causal relations at all, or, more plausibly, that in order to stand in such relations they do not need the backing of strict laws. It is enough, as I have argued elsewhere,[1] that they claim the support of general statements of tendency. But this comparatively weak requirement can be satisfied by psycho-physical statements. What goes by the board is the argument for physicalism.

Summary

If we are not prepared to take the notion of a person as primitive, and associate mental and physical properties simply on the basis of their being ascribed to the same person, then we are still faced with the question how a given series of experiences is to be allocated to one body rather than another. The position from which I approach this question[2] is that of an observer who has developed a physical theory on the basis of what Hume called 'the constancy and coherence' of his percepts. He distinguishes what I call the central body, which is in fact his own body, from other physical objects and in particular from the other objects the behaviour of which permits him to regard them as being also the sources of signs. It is because he can so regard them that he can think of them as sharing with the central body the property of being the focus of experience. But in what does this property consist?

I have no very clear-cut answer to this question. It seems to me that there are various factors at work. One undoubtedly is causal. The observer's percepts are associated not only with the objects which they

---

[1] See *Probability and Evidence*, p. 132, ff.
[2] See *The Central Questions of Philosophy*, Chapter VI.

manifest but also with what is for him the central body, because of such things as the double location of percepts which belong to the senses of taste and touch, because of the association of visual percepts with the movements of his eyes, the dependence of auditory data on his state of hearing, and so forth. A fact that is relevant here is that the part played by his body is found to a great extent to be under the control of his will.

Another important factor is the occurrence of observations which he is able to construe as the attribution by others of experiences to him. This enables him to think of his body not only as helping to cause his percepts but also as the medium through which not only his sensations and perceptions but also his experiences in general are made known to others.

Finally, I now tend to think the most important factor of all is the compresence of experiences of all other kinds with bodily sensations. It is seldom that these sensations are explicitly attended to, but it seems that they are usually present as forming a relatively constant background to more prominent items of experience. And even in the cases where our experience lacks this background, it is probable that they have a relation of direct or indirect sensible continuity to experiences which possess it. Nevertheless, I doubt if this is a strong enough factor to make the attachment of a series of experiences to a particular body depend on it alone. It would be very much easier for us if we could simply accept Broad's theory of emergent materialism. But the question what is implied by saying that one and the same event has both mental and physical characteristics still waits for a sufficient answer.

VII   The Philosophy of R. G. Collingwood

Gilbert Ryle's predecessor in the Chair of Metaphysics at Oxford was Robin George Collingwood, who lived from 1889 to 1943. Except during the First World War, when he joined a section of Admiralty Intelligence but still found time to publish a book on *Religion and Philosophy* in 1916, Collingwood spent the whole of his working life at Oxford, being a Fellow of Pembroke College for many years before he was elected in 1935 to his professorship, from which he resigned in 1941. He was an ancient historian and an archaeologist, besides being a philosopher, and specialized in the history of Roman Britain. We shall see that his historical studies exercised a considerable influence upon his view of the purpose and method of philosophy.

Apart from his historical works, the early work on religion and a short *Outline of the Philosophy of Art*, Collingwood published six books in his lifetime, ranging in date from *Speculum Mentis* in 1924 to *The New Leviathan* in 1942, and comprising *An Essay on Philosophical Method*, which was published in 1933, *The Principles of Art* in 1938, *An Autobiography* in 1939, and *An Essay on Metaphysics* in 1940. The Autobiography is mainly an exposition of his historical and philosophical principles. Two other books appeared posthumously, *The Idea of Nature* in 1945 and *The Idea of History* in 1946, both edited by Collingwood's pupil, T. M. Knox. *The Idea of Nature* was published with little alteration to Collingwood's manuscript. *The Idea of History* required more extensive editing, and seven separate essays by Collingwood on the philosophy of history were also included in the volume. The editor apologizes in his preface for 'the rather lecturing style of the later books', but the best of them, *The Idea of Nature*, is not exposed to this charge and Collingwood always wrote well, whether or not he was writing polemically.

R. G. COLLINGWOOD

The Influence of Croce

Speculum Mentis is something of a curiosity. Though Collingwood says of it in a footnote to his autobiography that 'there is not a great deal that needs to be retracted' though 'much of it needs to be supplemented and qualified',[1] its approach is markedly different from that of his later work. At the time at which he wrote it he was reacting against the Oxford 'realism' of the school of Cook Wilson, in which he had been educated, and favouring a form of idealism which stemmed partly from the Italian philosopher Benedetto Croce (1866–1952) and indirectly from Hegel. Art, Religion, Science, History and Philosophy are represented as competitors in a sort of obstacle race towards the winning-post of Truth. Art is the first to fall. A work of art is real in so far as it is imagined, but it also aspires to meaning and is thus led into contradiction, for meaning is conceptual and 'a concept can only be conceived, not intuited';[2] it cannot be 'fused or identified with its sensuous vehicle'. Religion goes next. Its development 'when it proceeds healthily according to the law of its own dialectic, results in the ideal of a single supreme God worshipped by a single universal church',[3] but it never succeeds in saying what it means. The reference, even to God, which it construes literally, 'is in reality a texture of metaphor through and through'.[4] Science comes closer to a grasp of literal truth, but its defect lies in its being abstract. Whereas 'art ignores the real world altogether' and 'religion contents itself with a cosmos outside the world', 'science alone tries to bring the concrete world into the unity, but destroys its concreteness in the attempt'. Here history succeeds. 'It actually achieves the idea of an object beyond which there is nothing and within which every part truly represents the whole.'[5]

Even so, history does not come away with the prize. Its trouble is that it is fragmentary. 'History is the knowledge of an infinite whole whose parts, repeating the plan of the whole in their structure, are only known by reference to their context. But since this context is always incomplete, we can never know a single part as it actually is.'[6]

[1] *An Autobiography*, p. 56, fn.
[2] *Speculum Mentis*, p. 88.
[3] ibid., p. 116.
[4] ibid., p. 130.
[5] ibid., p. 220.
[6] ibid., p. 231.

This leaves philosophy in possession of the field. But it remains rather as a judge than as a victorious competitor, and a judge in a race like the caucus-race in *Alice in Wonderland*, in which every competitor wins a prize. For what philosophy discovers is that Truth lies in the mirror of the mind and that it is only through the medium of an external world, which it constructs, that the mind can know itself. The competitors earn their prizes by contributing in their variously inadequate ways to the self-knowledge at which the mind perpetually aims.

We find ourselves here among the debris of Absolute Idealism: the synthesis of opposites, the dogma of internal relations, the doctrine that there is no truth short of the whole, so that even a proposition like 'this is a table' is 'false just as far as it is abstract'.[1] If Collingwood's philosophy had not progressed beyond this stage, there would be little point in exhuming it. Even so, it would be a mistake to condemn *Speculum Mentis* wholly without reservation. In so far as it makes fact a function of symbol systems, rather than the other way around, it anticipates much that was to follow.

An Essay on Philosophical Method is a contribution to *belles-lettres* rather than philosophy. The style is uniformly elegant, the matter mostly obscure. The thesis which emerges is that philosophy aims at systematizing what in a sense we know already, and that philosophical concepts form an overlapping hierarchy. No examples are given in detail, though there are occasional allusions to moral philosophy. For instance, it is said that there is no 'margin of expedient actions that are not dutiful and dutiful actions that are not expedient. All dutiful actions are expedient, for duty as the higher specification always and necessarily reaffirms the lower; and the lower not sometimes but always partially and incompletely affirms the higher.'[2] If this is taken literally, it is false.

An odd feature of the book, which moved Gilbert Ryle to indignant protest,[3] is Collingwood's bland acceptance of the ontological argument as proving not the existence of any particular God but that of a metaphysical reality, the essence of which implies existence. No attempt is made to show how the argument escapes Kant's or anybody else's criticism and, except for the inference that 'unlike

[1] ibid., p. 257.
[2] *An Essay on Philosophical Method*, p. 91.
[3] 'Mr Collingwood and the Ontological Argument' in *Mind* (1937), XLVI, reprinted in Ryle's *Collected Papers*, I.

mathematics or empirical science, philosophy stands committed to maintaining that its subject-matter is no mere hypothesis, but something actually existing',[1] no further use of it is made in the book.

The Principles of Art, which was published in 1937, is an altogether more impressive work. It can hardly be said to present a full-blooded aesthetic theory, since its conclusion that art is to be identified with language and that both consist in the expression of emotion stands obviously in need of further refinement, but it makes a number of interesting points by the way. Collingwood is at pains to distinguish what he calls art proper from what, translating the Greek word Techne, he calls craft. It is characteristic of craft that it fits into the pattern of means and ends, usually through the transformation of some pre-existing material, but this is not true of art proper. When Plato wished to banish poets among other artists from his ideal city, he was not, in Collingwood's view, renouncing art as such but only representative art, the purpose of which might be either to amuse the audience or else exert what Collingwood calls a magical effect upon them. Magic is here treated as a form of ritual which helps to put those who are subjected to it into a mood that is deemed appropriate to the occasion. Art proper, whether it is representative or not, is to be distinguished both from art as magic and from art as amusement. This does not mean that a work of art is incapable of producing these effects, but it does not do so *qua* work of art. So all aesthetic theories in which the crucial emphasis is laid upon the reactions of the customer are ruled out of court. Beauty may lie in the eye of the beholder, but that is only because the word is properly used just to express an attitude of admiration. Some aestheticians have tried to 'make it stand for that quality in things in virtue of which when we contemplate them we enjoy what we recognize as an aesthetic experience'.[2] But there is no such quality and 'the words "beauty", "beautiful", as actually used, have no aesthetic implication'.

I think that Collingwood may be mistaken here about actual usage, but I agree with him on the much more important point of there being no quality which is uniformly correlated to what is properly described as an aesthetic experience. On the other hand I am not inclined to follow him in identifying art proper with the expression of emotion, or to accept his treatment of works of art as imaginary entities. Thus,

[1] op. cit., p. 127.
[2] *The Principles of Art*, p. 38.

he says that it is only 'in the pseudo-aesthetic sense for which art is a kind of craft' that 'a piece of music is a series of audible noises'. 'If,' he continues, ' "work of art" means work of art proper, a piece of music is not something audible, but something which may exist solely in the musician's head. To some extent it must exist solely in the musician's head (including of course the audience as well as the composer under that name) for his imagination is always supplementing, correcting, and expurgating what he actually hears. The music which he actually enjoys as a work of art is thus never sensuously or "actually" heard at all. It is something imagined. But it is not imagined sound (in the case of painting it is not imagined colour-patterns, etc.). It is an imagined experience of total activity. Thus, a work of art proper is a total activity which the person enjoying it apprehends, or is conscious of, by the use of his imagination.'[1]

This is not quite so fantastic as it sounds, since Collingwood does not contrast imagination with perception. On the contrary, he takes imagination to be an essential ingredient in the process of acquiring, identifying and inter-relating 'sensa', in which he takes perception to consist. He refers to Hume's distinction between impressions and ideas and equates it, I fear without historical accuracy, with a distinction between real and imaginary sensa, which he thinks may be understood in two contrasting ways: either as the distinction 'between sensa interpreted by thought and sensa not so interpreted' or as 'the distinction between sheer feeling and feeling as modified by consciousness with the double result of dominating it and perpetuating it'.[2] It is the second of these interpretations that Collingwood adopts. He distinguishes three stages in what he calls 'the life of a feeling', one where it is below the level of consciousness, the second where one has become conscious of it, a process which requires us also to be conscious of ourselves, and a third where we place it in its relation to other feelings. It is with the second of these stages that Collingwood identifies what he thinks Hume meant by an idea, and he accuses Hume of leading subsequent philosophers astray by using the term 'impression' indifferently for the first and the third.[3] It is clear from the context that the word 'feeling' is here doing duty for any item of sense-experience and it is implied that the three stages in

[1] ibid., p. 151.
[2] ibid., p. 212.
[3] ibid.; see p. 213.

the life of a feeling can yield a phenomenalistic theory of perception. No attempt, however, is made to develop such a theory in detail and there is no discussion of the objections to which it might be exposed.

In the case of works of art, there is indeed no question but that the material in which they are embodied is modified by the consciousness of those who create or appreciate them. In this sense, we need not scruple to agree that a work of art is at least partly the product of the imagination. This hardly commits us, however, to locating a piece of music solely in the musician's head, still less to taking a similar step in the case of the other arts. It is in any case a mistake to try to treat them all alike. Whatever else they may be besides, a picture, a piece of sculpture, and a work of architecture are all physical objects, a work of literature is a series of words, considered not as physical tokens but as types, a piece of music a series of notes, again in the form of types rather than tokens. It is indeed true of such types that there can be a stage at which they are 'inscribed' only in the composer's head, though this is unlikely to be true of works of any considerable length, such as a symphony or a novel. I do not suggest that these distinctions are anything more than a preliminary to the development of an aesthetic theory.

I regret that I have no such theory to offer. My objection to saying that a work of art proper expresses emotion is not that it is untrue but that it is uninformative. Presumably, what is meant is that the emotion is expressed by the work itself, in the sense in which the tragedy of *Othello* expresses jealousy, rather than felt by the author or the audience. But that is hardly an adequate description of the tragedy and it is by no means obvious that such descriptions will always be ascribable. What emotions, for example, are expressed by Gray's 'Elegy' or by Cézanne's 'Card Players'? Collingwood's own examples that 'Dante has fused the Thomistic philosophy into a poem expressing what it feels like to be a Thomist' and that 'Shelley, when he made the earth say "I spin beneath my pyramid of night", expressed what it feels like to be a Copernican'[1] are not encouraging. Neither do the facts, on which Collingwood, no doubt rightly, insists, that the initial use of language is probably emotional and that even at a later stage the emotive and descriptive functions of language are not always easy to separate, throw very

[1] ibid., p. 295.

much light on the difficult questions of the ways in which art is symbolic or the manner and degree of its connection with truth.

The Theory of Absolute Presuppositions

I believe that I carry some responsibility for the appearance and content of Collingwood's *Metaphysics*. It contains several references to my *Language, Truth and Logic* and repeated condemnations of 'Logical Positivists' for basing their attacks on metaphysics upon a misunderstanding of the subject, and for serving the cause of irrationality. There was, indeed, an interval of slightly more than three years between the publication of the two books, but Collingwood had replied to me in his lectures at Oxford during that time, and in any case I am not suggesting that his *Metaphysics* is nothing more than a rebuttal of my *Language, Truth and Logic*.

Collingwood begins with the etymological reminder that the term 'metaphysics' goes back to Aristotle, not as being directly ascribable to him but inasmuch as its Greek equivalent was used by ancient editors to refer to a group of treatises which they placed after the Physics in their arrangement of his works. These treatises are said to deal with the science of metaphysics under three names. Sometimes Aristotle called it 'First Philosophy' or, as Collingwood prefers to put it, First Science, thereby ascribing logical priority to it. Sometimes he called it 'Wisdom', as that which it was supposed to achieve, and sometimes he called it 'Theology', the Greek word 'Theos', which we translate by 'God', being their 'ordinary name for that which is the logical ground for anything else'.[1]

From what Aristotle wrote under these three headings, Collingwood derives two propositions, each of which might pass for a definition of metaphysics. The first is that 'Metaphysics is the science of pure being' and the second that 'Metaphysics is the science which deals with the presuppositions underlying ordinary science'.[2] It is explained that the word 'science', in what Collingwood regards as its original and still proper sense, 'means a body of systematic or orderly thinking about a determinate subject-matter'[3]

[1] *Metaphysics*, p. 10.
[2] ibid., p. 11.
[3] ibid., p. 4.

and that the word 'ordinary' in this context simply serves to exclude metaphysics itself.

Collingwood rejects the first of these definitions as emptying metaphysics of all content. 'The universal of pure being represents the limiting case of the abstractive process.'[1] But this is just a way of saying that everything has been taken out, and if everything has been taken out nothing remains to be investigated. Consequently, if science has to have some subject-matter, a 'science of pure being' would be a contradiction in terms.

If, then, as Collingwood intends, we are to uphold Aristotle, we must turn to the second option. Metaphysics is the science which deals with the presuppositions underlying ordinary science. But this needs further explanation, which Collingwood sets about providing.

His first step is to advance the proposition that 'Every statement that anybody ever makes is made in answer to a question'.[2] As stated, this is plainly false if it implies that a question has been posed in every case. We may perhaps assume that Collingwood was thinking of scientific statements, and that he was adopting Bacon's thesis that science proceeds by torturing nature for answers, in legal language, putting her to the question.

Collingwood's second proposition is that every question involves a presupposition. I doubt whether this is true either, if it is understood to apply universally, but it may be true of the sort of scientific questions that Collingwood has in mind. He in fact assumes that there is always something that causes a question to arise and so exhibits what he calls its 'logical efficacy'. For a supposition to possess logical efficacy it need not be true or even thought true: it need only be supposed.

A presupposition, we are next told, is either relative or absolute. A relative presupposition is said to be 'one which stands relatively to one question as its presupposition and relatively to another question as its answer'.[3] The example which Collingwood gives is that of a measuring instrument which is presumed to be accurate when it is being used but can be found either to be or not to be so when the question of its accuracy is raised. An absolute presupposition, on the other hand, 'is one which stands, relatively to all questions to which it

[1] ibid., p. 14.
[2] ibid., p. 23.
[3] ibid., p. 29.

is related, as a presupposition, never as an answer'.[1] Collingwood's example is the assumption, no longer made in all branches of science, but still, he thinks, in medicine, that every event has a cause.

Since absolute presuppositions are never answers to questions, it follows, in Collingwood's view, that they are not propositions, from which in turn it follows that the distinction between truth and falsehood does not apply to them. This goes beyond their not having truth-values. Their being absolutely presupposed is taken to imply their not being asserted. Consequently, it is nonsensical to ask whether they are true, whether they can be demonstrated, or even what evidence there is in their favour. In so far as the utterances which the logical positivists pejoratively denounced as metaphysical were in fact formulations of such absolute presuppositions, they were quite right to bar them from the domain of truth and falsehood. Where they and many other philosophers have been at fault is in assuming that they claimed access to it. This is an error which philosophers who have themselves usurped the title of metaphysicians have not avoided. A metaphysician who deserves the name will not make the senseless attempt to validate or invalidate absolute presuppositions. He will content himself with trying to answer the historical question what absolute presuppositions in the various branches of science and at the successive stages of their development have actually been made.

As a historical science, metaphysics has its own presuppositions. They appear to consist in the principles which govern the assessment of historical evidence. In particular, metaphysicians are required to answer questions of the form 'Why did such and such people at such and such a time make such and such absolute presuppositions?' and their answer must take the form 'Because they or the predecessors from whom they inherited their civilization had previously made such and such a different set of absolute presuppositions, and because such and such a process of change converted the one set into the other'.[2] The presuppositions form a constellation, but not a hierarchy, so that metaphysics is not a deductive science.

It might be suggested that the question what presuppositions a group of scientists was making was a question for psychology, but Collingwood dismisses this idea with scorn, not on the ground that

[1] ibid., p. 31.
[2] ibid., p. 74.

psychology would be trespassing on the province of philosophy but that psychology, while it had proved its worth as 'a science of feeling', had no legitimate pretension to be taken seriously as a science of thought. In view of its concern with truth, thought must be left to the 'criteriological' sciences of ethics and logic. Collingwood offers no proof of the incapacity of psychologists to deal with thought beyond citing three works by well-known contemporary psychologists, selecting a passage from each, and condemning one as an example of red herrings, another as an example of self-contradiction and the third as an example of plagiarism. Even then, this contemptuous treatment did not do justice to the psychologists concerned, and a great deal of experimental work on the processes of thinking has been done since that time. All the same, a case can still be made for withholding the study of metaphysics, as Collingwood envisaged it, from psychology. It is that the presuppositions of a given branch of science at a particular period are to be elicited not by studying the thought-processes of the scientists in question but by detailing the structure of the theories which they accepted. Obviously, these two lines of enquiry are not entirely separate, since, except in the Platonic tradition which Sir Karl Popper has lately attempted to revive,[1] theories do not exist apart from those who hold them, but there is a difference in the manner of approach.

Collingwood's prime example of a metaphysical proposition is the proposition 'God exists'. Or rather, it is only in moments of carelessness that he calls this a proposition, since he has already admitted that he agrees with his enemies, the logical positivists, that if it is construed as a proposition, it is senseless, or at least devoid of truth-value. What he means to assert is that people have in different ages held the belief, which can fairly be described as the belief that God exists, though the content of this belief has varied with a change in the presuppositions which it represents. Accordingly, he modifies his earlier endorsement of the ontological argument. 'What it proves,' he says, 'is not that because our idea of God is an idea of *id quo maius cogitari nequit* [that than which nothing greater can be thought] therefore God exists, but that because our idea of God is an idea of *id quo maius cogitari nequit* we stand committed to belief in God's existence.'[2] Even with this emendation it seems to me that the

[1] See his *Objective Knowledge* (1972).
[2] op. cit., p. 190.

proof remains fallacious. There is no need to press the question whether the idea of there being something than which nothing greater can be thought has any meaning. Let the concept be allowed to pass. The mere fact that someone entertains it is not in the least inconsistent with his denying that there is anything to which it applies.

There would appear to be some difficulty also in the notion of someone's believing a presupposition and yet not thinking it true. Perhaps the use of the term 'belief' is misleading in this context. Absolute presuppositions are taken for granted. While they hold sway, the question of their truth or falsehood does not arise. This may shift the difficulty, but I do not see that it removes it. After all, it is not being suggested that absolute presuppositions are unintelligible. They take the form of propositions, although they are not so treated by those who adopt them. But what about those who do not adopt them? Why should they be limited to expounding them? If they can understand them at all, why can they not judge them to be false?

However that may be, Collingwood confines himself to the question what Christians mean when they say that they believe in God, and approaches it through what he calls the historical background. He suggests that the relation between religion and natural science in primitive society depended on two factors; first that primitive peoples distinguished between things which were and things which were not under their control, a distinction which he summarizes as one drawn between art and nature; and secondly that they took a polymorphic view of nature which was reflected in a plurality of religious cults. Surprisingly, these cults are not credited with any purpose. Passing to the Greeks, he notes that their polytheistic religion was at odds with the monotheism of their philosophers. A detailed and very persuasive account of the religious and philosophical attitudes of the Pre-Socratics, Plato and Aristotle, is to be found in *The Idea of Nature*, which is greatly to be recommended to students of Greek philosophy. The account given in *Metaphysics* is much more summary. It culminates in the attribution to Aristotle of the view that there is only one God, who did not create the world of nature, discovered by one's senses, which is a world of movements happening by themselves, but is the perfect being whom all the things in nature are trying to imitate; that God being mind, the only way that natural movements can imitate him is by taking place according to laws; that there are various realms of nature of which only one, the sphere of the fixed stars, directly imitates God, because it alone moves with a perpetual uniform rotation; and that the movements characteristic of other natural realms are imitations of the mental activities of intelligence which are neither divine nor human but something between the two.[1] I leave it to others to decide whether these were the presuppositions that Aristotle made. If they were, I have argued that they should at least be intelligible to those who do not share them, but I have to confess that I do not find them so.

That Collingwood did not regard absolute presuppositions as immune from criticism, at least by historians, is shown by his saying that Aristotle failed in his metaphysics. Aristotle's mistake allegedly lay in thinking that we obtain the idea of motion through the use of our senses, instead of treating it as 'an idea which we bring with us in the shape of an absolute presupposition to the work of interpreting what we get by using our senses',[2] and in supposing that motion happened of itself instead of arising out of something in God's nature. These metaphysical errors, which pervaded Greek thought, are said to have implied a breakdown of Greek science.

We come now to the presuppositions of Christianity which, according to Collingwood, 'have as a matter of historical fact been the main or fundamental presuppositions of natural science'[3] ever since they were formulated in the fifth century AD by the 'Patristic Writers'. These are, first, that there is one God, secondly, that God created the world, an article of faith which is rather surprisingly taken by Collingwood to have meant that 'the idea of a world of nature is an absolute presupposition of natural science', thirdly, that the activity of God is a self-differentiating activity, which is why there are diverse realms in nature, and fourthly that the creative activity of God is the source of motion in the world of nature.[4] When converted into the presuppositions of natural science, these doctrines, if one may so call them, undergo a rather startling transformation. According to Collingwood, writing in 1939, 'When a Christian theologian today says that God exists, or (to be precise by making explicit the metaphysical rubric) that we believe in God' or even 'when an

[1] op. cit., pp. 211–12.
[2] ibid., p. 217.
[3] ibid., p. 227.
[4] ibid., pp. 219–22.

uneducated Christian makes the same statement' and is not meaning the words in some 'private and heretical' sense of his own, what the words mean in 'their application to the absolute presuppositions of natural science' is first 'That there is a world of nature, i.e. that there are things which happen of themselves and cannot be produced or prevented by anybody's art', secondly 'That this world of nature is a world of events, i.e. that the things of which it is composed are things to which events happen or things which move', thirdly 'That throughout this world there is one set of laws according to which all movements or events, in spite of all differences, agree in happening; and that consequently there is one science of this world', and fourthly 'that nevertheless there are in this world many different realms' with events governed by peculiar laws which are modifications of the universal laws and catered for by special sciences which are modifications of the universal science.[1]

The Christian doctrine of the Trinity receives a similar interpretation. 'By believing in the Father' the devisers of the 'Catholic Faith' 'meant (always with reference solely to the procedure of natural science) absolutely presupposing that there is a world of nature which is always and indivisibly one world. By believing in the Son they meant absolutely presupposing that this one natural world is nevertheless a multiplicity of natural realms. By believing in the Holy Ghost they meant absolutely presupposing that the world of nature, throughout its entire fabric, is a world not merely of things but of events or movements.'[2]

In fairness to Collingwood, it should be repeated that the adoption of these scientific presuppositions is not regarded as exhausting the Christian faith. Even so, I think it would come as a surprise to most professing Christians to learn that they had automatically made such progress in science and no less a surprise to many scientists, who may well have supposed themselves to be agnostics or atheists, to learn that they were so far committed to Christianity. This is not to say that the heritage of Christianity had no influence upon the scientific thought of the sixteenth and seventeenth centuries, but the exact correspondences suggested by Collingwood do not carry conviction. This comes out most strongly in his manipulation of the Trinity. I am not, or do not suppose myself to be, a believer in the Holy Ghost, but

[1] ibid., pp. 222–3.
[2] ibid., pp. 225–6.

203

the equation of such a belief, even partially, with the hardly questionable belief that there are natural events and movements seems to me quite arbitrary.

Kant's *Critique of Pure Reason* is commonly seen as a threat to metaphysics, since it seeks to show that our understanding entangles itself in contradictions when it ventures beyond the bounds of possible experience. Collingwood, however, argues that the *Critique* is itself a work of metaphysics in so far as it sets out the absolute presuppositions of Newtonian physics. These are extracted from the passages where Kant describes the order which we impose on the raw material of experience to transform it into a possible object of knowledge. The first two presuppositions are that natural science is essentially an applied mathematics, and that in view of what Kant calls the principle of continuity, that is to say, the principle that between any two terms there is always a third, a science of nature must consist of differential equations. There follows a set of principles which are based on the idea of necessary connection. The first is described by Collingwood as a belief in the permanence and indestructibility of substance. It is seen at work 'where two percept- ible things are considered by a person thinking about them to be two possible appearances of the same thing'.[1] The second is concerned with necessary sequence and involves Kant's theory of causation, which Collingwood reserves for later criticism. Thirdly, there is the principle of reciprocal action, which is said to have been required by Newton for his theory of gravitation. It has become redundant, since the conception of force is obsolete. Indeed, all these principles except the very first, that natural science is applied mathematics, are thought by Collingwood to have been discarded by the physicists of the first third of this century.

This does not apply to Kant's further assumption that the 'categories of modality', that is, 'the notions of possibility, actuality and necessity are applicable to the perceptible or natural world'.[2] In Collingwood's view, these categories, as understood by scientists, do no more than distinguish three stages of research. 'When a scientist describes something as actual he means that it has been observed. When he describes it as necessary he means that its connexions with other things have been discovered. When he describes it as possible

[1] ibid., p. 262.
[2] ibid., p. 273.

he means that it is being looked for; that is, the question whether it is actual is a question that is being asked.'[1] I have some doubt whether this is the way that scientists do employ these modal terms, but it may be that they once did so and that they have not since been corrupted. One may hope that it is only philosophers who conjure with possible worlds and make heavy weather of necessity. Collingwood is not guilty in these ways, but he did have the strange idea that logical positivists were debarred from applying the notion of empirical possibility to this world. We have already seen that in adopting their principle of verifiability they were not restricting the class of admissible propositions to those that had actually been verified.

Causality and the Idea of Nature

The final section of Collingwood's *Metaphysics* consists in a very interesting study of the concept of causation. He distinguishes three senses of the term 'cause'. The first and original sense is the one where 'that which is "caused" is the free and deliberate act of a conscious and responsible agent, and "causing" him to do it means affording him a motive for doing it'. The second is the one where 'that which is "caused" is an event in nature, and its "cause" is an event or state of things by producing or preventing which we can produce or prevent that whose cause it is said to be'. In the third sense, 'that which is "caused" is an event or state of things, and its "cause" is another event or state of things standing to it in a one-one relation of causal priority: i.e. a relation of such a kind that (a) if the cause happens or exists the effect also must happen or exist, even if no further conditions are fulfilled, (b) the effect cannot happen or exist unless the cause happens or exists, (c) in some sense which remains to be defined, the cause is prior to the effect'.[2]

In fact, Collingwood allowed the notion of causal priority which is involved in his third sense of 'cause' to remain undefined, no doubt because he believed that this third sense was anyhow the mark of a confusion which we owe to Kant. In ruling that every event has a cause, Kant may have supposed that he was supporting Newton, but

[1] ibid., p. 274.
[2] ibid., pp. 285–6.

in fact Newton distinguished between events which were due to the operation of causes and those that were due to the operation of laws. Newton's principle was not that every event but that every change has a cause, understanding by change an event which cannot be accounted for by the laws of motion. Nevertheless, Kant's decision to include the force of inertia among causes does not constitute any serious break with Newton's theory.

Where Kant went astray, in Collingwood's view, was in trying to combine the concept of a cause as a uniquely sufficient condition with Hume's proposition that causes precede their effects. For it is only where a cause is used in the second of Collingwood's senses that Hume's proposition holds good. When I cause something, in the sense of producing it, I do no more than contribute what is at most a necessary element in a set of sufficient conditions, so that there is room for a time-interval between my action and the effect. But if the cause is a uniquely sufficient condition there is no room for any time-interval. It has to be simultaneous with its effect.

Collingwood's reasoning here depends on his taking a sufficient condition to be such that its effect would ensue, no matter what other conditions were or were not to obtain. If he cannot countenance a time-interval, it is because something might occur during that time which would prevent the effect from occurring. This difficulty could be avoided by our weakening the requirement for a sufficient condition. If we allow c to be sufficient for e if c never occurs without e in fact, we can allow c to precede e in time. We do not have to consider whether anything might happen within the interval which would prevent e from occurring; we are committed only to the hypothesis that nothing ever actually has or will. Admittedly, we are then left with the task of distinguishing accidental from lawful generalizations but, as I have tried to show elsewhere,[1] this problem is not insurmountable.

I have no grounds for disputing Collingwood's claim that his first sense of cause was the original one, or that the second sense was an anthropomorphic offshoot of the first. I find it a pity, however, that he wrote as if neither the concept of 'supplying a motive' nor that of 'the ability to produce or prevent' needed any further explanation. In both cases, I believe, there is a tacit appeal to an underlying generalization, though it need not be stronger than a statement of

[1] See 'What is a Law of Nature?' reprinted in *The Concept of a Person*.

tendency. This again is a point that I have tried to establish elsewhere.[1]

Though *The Idea of Nature* was not published in Collingwood's lifetime there is evidence that most of it was written in the early 1930s, before the publication of *Metaphysics*. It is a more overtly historical study of cosmological presuppositions, and it frankly treats them as subject to criticism. Thus, having said that the problems of the relation between dead and living matter and that of the relation between mind and matter did not exist for the Greeks, since they conceived of nature as a 'vast living organism', and having shown how this conception had given way by the seventeenth century to the idea of 'a world of dead matter, infinite in extent and permeated by movement throughout, but utterly devoid of ultimate qualitative differences and moved by uniform and purely quantitative forces',[2] he remarks that this left philosophers with the unsolved problem 'of discovering some intrinsic connexion between matter and mind'.[3] Materialism was ruled out of court because knowledge 'simply cannot be described' in terms of 'movements mathematically determined in time and space', and the 'two-substance doctrine', permeating both the monism of Spinoza and the pluralism of Leibniz, breaks down because it makes matter unknowable. If the conceptions of mind and matter are defined as they were defined by the cosmology of the seventeenth century, there is no way, says Collingwood, of escaping the admission that 'the problem of discovering an essential link between them can only be solved as Berkeley solved it'.[4] But Berkeley's notion of the material world as something which God creates by his activity of thinking leaves us with 'the problem of the relation between God's infinite mind and the various finite human minds'.[5] Berkeley's answer is that God's mind is active, creating what it thinks, and man's mind passive, taking its orders from God. But this, Collingwood points out, is at variance with Berkeley's own starting-point. For Berkeley inherited from Locke 'the doctrine that the mind creates one part of nature, the secondary qualities',[6] and this has to be the human mind. 'Deny that,'

---

[1] See *Probability and Evidence*.
[2] *The Idea of Nature*, p. 112.
[3] ibid., p. 113.
[4] ibid., p. 115.
[5] ibid.
[6] ibid., p. 116.

says Collingwood, 'and the whole structure of Berkeleian idealism falls to the ground.'[1]

The Kantian form of idealism is accurately described by Collingwood as representing nature, that is to say, the material world of Galileo and Newton, as a 'rational and necessary product of the human way of looking at things';[2] what it omits and is condemned by Collingwood for omitting is a consistent account of what things are in themselves. Hegel made an attempt to make good this omission but failed to achieve an acceptable synthesis 'between the conception of nature as a machine and the conception of all reality as permeated by process'.[3] The idea of process dominates the thought of the remaining three philosophers whose work Collingwood briefly expounds: Henri Louis Bergson (1859–1941), Samuel Alexander (1859–1938) and Alfred North Whitehead (1861–1947). He praises Bergson for his vitalism, but finds that 'the inanimate world of the physicist is a dead weight on [his] metaphysics'.[4] He criticizes Alexander for the strain of empiricism in his philosophy. Taking space-time as his starting-point, Alexander shows with great brilliance how space-time generates matter, how matter generates life, and how life generates mind, and he boldly conjectures that mind will generate God. He fails, however, to explain why any of these things should happen. The emergence of mind out of life, of life out of matter and of matter out of space-time are simply to be accepted as contingent matters of fact. As for Whitehead, 'no one has more vividly realized and described the resemblances, the fundamental continuity, running all through the world of nature, from its most rudimentary forms in the electron and proton and the rest of them to its highest development known to us in the mental life of man';[5] he more than anyone has succeeded in convincing Collingwood that 'since modern science is now committed to a view of the physical universe as finite, certainly in space and probably in time, the activity which this same science identifies with matter cannot be a self-created or ultimately self-dependent activity',[6] thus satisfying Collingwood's desire to find a role for God. All the same, Whitehead seems uncertain whether the development

[1] ibid.
[2] ibid.
[3] ibid., p. 132.
[4] ibid., p. 141.
[5] ibid., p. 174.
[6] ibid., p. 155.

of his series of forms from material particles to human minds is a temporal series, nor does he explain how one form is connected with the next. He can only speak vaguely of a creative process.

So where does this leave us? Collingwood's answer is that the defects which he has found in the works of even the foremost contemporary metaphysicians, like Alexander and Whitehead, who have the competence to evaluate natural science, are due to a fault in their starting-point, and this fault consists in its containing a relic of positivism. As Collingwood puts it, 'It involves the assumption that the sole task of a cosmological philosophy is to reflect upon what natural science can tell us about nature, as if natural science were, I will not say the only valid form of thought, but the only form of thought which a philosopher should take into account when he tries to answer the question what nature is'.[1] But this, he argues, is a mistake. Just as nature is a thing that depends for its existence on something else, so 'natural science is a form of thought that depends for its existence on some other form of thought'.[2] And what is this other form of thought? One fears for a moment that the answer is going to be 'Theology', but it is not. The answer is 'History'.

The Idea of History

Why 'History'? One might expect the answer to be linked with Collingwood's theory of absolute presuppositions, but one would again be mistaken. The reasons given are much more simple. They are first, that since an event is accepted as a scientific fact only if the claim of one or more persons to have observed it is generally accepted as reliable, a scientific fact is a class of historical facts; and, secondly, that the same applies to scientific theories. In Collingwood's own words, 'A scientific theory not only rests on certain historical facts and is verified or disproved by other historical facts; it is itself a historical fact, namely, the fact that someone has propounded or accepted, verified or disproved, that theory'.[3] The most that this seems to me to show is that we should have no good reason for

[1] ibid., p. 176.
[2] ibid.
[3] ibid., p. 177.

accepting any scientific theories unless we had good reasons for accepting a number of propositions about the past. To this extent it is a truism that natural science depends upon history. As it stands, however, this proves no more than that both natural science and history are exposed to philosophical scepticism. It does not prove that natural science and history are radically different branches of thought, in the sense that they pursue quite different aims or are governed by different canons of evidence. Collingwood clearly believed that there was such a difference, but he needed to justify the belief.

I do not think that he succeeded. In *The Idea of History*, which he did not live to complete, he proceeds in much the same fashion as in *The Idea of Nature*, giving a historical account of the different conceptions of history that philosophers and historians have held at different times, starting with theocratic history and myth, proceeding to Herodotus, 'the first scientific historian', passing in review Thucydides, Livy and Tacitus, Polybius, the influence of Christianity, Descartes and his opponent Vico, the British Empiricists, Herder, Kant, Schiller, and Fichte, Hegel and Marx, nineteenth-century positivism, the modern French and German historians who fell into the error of modelling history upon natural science, regarding the subjective and objective as two different things, 'whereas the process of historical thought is homogeneous with the process of history itself',[1] and ending with 'the only philosophical movement which has grasped the peculiarity of historical thought firmly and used it as a systematic principle', namely 'that which was initiated by Croce in Italy'.[2]

From this there emerges a view of history as having four essential characteristics; first 'that it is scientific, or begins by asking questions, whereas the writer of legends begins by knowing something and tells what he knows'; secondly, 'that it is humanistic or asks questions about things done by determinate men at determinate times in the past'; thirdly, 'that it is rational or bases the answers which it gives to its questions on grounds making appeal to evidence'; and, finally, 'that it is self-revelatory, or exists to tell man what he is by telling him what man has done'.[3]

[1] *The Idea of History*, p. 19.
[2] ibid.
[3] ibid., p. 18.

These reasonable requirements hardly prepare one for Collingwood's startling conclusion that there can be no history of anything other than thought, and then only of such thought as 'can be re-enacted in the historical mind'.[1] An explanation of his meaning is to be found in his *Autobiography*, a well-written book published in 1939 and primarily an attack on the destructive 'realism' of Cook Wilson and his school at Oxford and some of their Cambridge counterparts, a realism issuing from their blind acceptance of what Collingwood regarded as the senseless doctrine that 'knowing makes no difference to what is known'. His historical example was his understanding of Nelson's refusal to take off his coat with all its medals in order to become a less conspicuous target for the French snipers at the Battle of Trafalgar, saying 'In honour I wore them, in honour I will die with them'. In 're-enacting' this episode Collingwood claims to be thinking the very same thought as Nelson's. Yet 'in some way', he admits, there is not one thought but two different thoughts. 'The difference is one of context. To Nelson, that thought was a present thought, to me it is a past thought living in the present.'[2] So far, there is nothing much to quarrel over, though one may wonder what criterion Collingwood is using for individuating thoughts. But then we are surprised to find him able 'to switch into another dimension. I plunge beneath the surface of my mind, and there live a life in which I not merely think about Nelson but am Nelson and thus in thinking about Nelson think about myself.'[3]

This might be no more than a picturesque way of saying that a good historian needs to be able to imagine himself in the situation of the characters with whom he is concerned and at that point to identify with them, but the passage which I have quoted is not the only one from which it appears that Collingwood meant to be taken much more literally. This comes out quite clearly a little later in *An Autobiography*. The passage is decisive enough to be quoted in full. 'If what a historian knows is past thoughts, and if he knows them by rethinking them himself, it follows that the knowledge he achieves by historical inquiry is not knowledge of his situation as opposed to knowledge of himself, it is a knowledge of his situation which is at the same time knowledge of himself. In re-thinking what somebody else

[1] ibid., p. 302.
[2] *An Autobiography*, p. 113.
[3] ibid.

thought, he thinks it himself. In knowing that somebody else thought it, he knows that he himself is able to think it. And finding out what he is able to do is finding out what kind of a man he is. If he is able to understand, by re-thinking them, the thoughts of a great many different kinds of people, it follows that he must be a great many kinds of man. He must be, in fact, a microcosm of all the history he can know. Thus his own self-knowledge is at the same time his knowledge of the world of human affairs.'[1]

It is difficult to know what comment to make. That the historian should literally incarnate a multitude of persons seems to me incredible. The novelist also tries, as it were, to get into the skin of his characters. In so doing he may learn something more about himself, but not through becoming a compendium of the cast that he creates. Neither is it clear why history should be limited to the history of thought. Presumably, the idea is that the historian is interested in natural events only in so far as they affect human beings, but these natural events, like the eruption of Vesuvius or the spread of the Black Death, themselves need to be described.

Collingwood's one other book of note, *The New Leviathan*, was published in 1942. As its title indicates, it is modelled very closely on Hobbes's *Leviathan* and is written in somewhat the same style. It draws various distinctions, such as that between utility, right and duty, makes the rules of civil intercourse depend upon something like a social contract, and announces as the three laws of politics, first 'that a body politic is divided into a ruling class and a ruled class', secondly 'that the barrier between the two classes is permeable in an upward sense', and thirdly 'that there is a correspondence between the ruler and the ruled',[2] the ruler setting the fashion and the ruled falling in with his lead. Philosophically, the most rewarding passages occur at the beginning of the book, where there is a discussion of the division between body and mind. One point of interest is that matter is defined as what is studied by physics and chemistry, rather than the other way around, and similarly that life is what physiology is trying to discover. Both psycho-physical parallelism and psycho-physical interactionism are dismissed as old wives' tales. They are rooted in the false assumption that man is partly body and partly mind. But, says Collingwood, 'man's body and man's mind are not two different

[1] ibid., p. 115.
[2] *The New Leviathan*, pp. 179–80.

things. They are one and the same thing, man himself, as known in two different ways. Not a part of man, but the whole of man, is body in so far as he approaches the problem of self-knowledge by the methods of natural science. Not a part of man, but the whole of man is mind in so far as he approaches the problem of self-knowledge by expanding and clarifying the data of reflection.'[1] These rather dark sayings are not elucidated by Collingwood but, as with his doctrine of absolute presuppositions, they strike a contemporary note.

[1] ibid., p. 11.

VIII   Phenomenology and Existentialism

The Foundation in Brentano and Husserl

Phenomenology, which, with the revival of Existentialism as its offshoot, was the dominant philosophy on the European continent during the first half of this century, owed its name to Edmund Husserl, who lived from 1859 to 1938 and held Chairs successively at the Universities of Göttingen and Freiburg. Husserl had studied in Vienna under Franz Brentano, whom we have already mentioned for his devising of the doctrine of intentionality, the view that what is distinctive of mental phenomena is their being directed towards an object which might or might not objectively exist. Brentano also divided mental phenomena into three fundamental classes: presentations, where some object is simply present to the mind allowing no room for the distinction between truth and error, judgements, where this distinction does arise and is settled by an appeal to self-evidence, and affective attitudes of acceptance or rejection which have an inwardly self-justifying character. These affective attitudes were made to serve as the basis of moral intuitions.

Brentano's 'psychognosy', as he called it, was intended to further the interests of empirical psychology, and it was under his influence that Husserl in 1893 published a book on the philosophy of arithmetic which gave an intentionalist but still psychological account of mathematical procedures. For this he was severely criticized by Gottlob Frege, whose own book on the foundations of arithmetic had made an inconspicuous appearance in 1884. Husserl accepted Frege's criticisms, and in his *Logical Investigations* (*Logische Untersuchungen*), which appeared in 1900, he combined analyses of knowledge, intentionality and meaning with a sharp rejection of any attempt to subordinate logic and mathematics to psychology. He went rather to the other extreme, treating all the objects of intentional acts as having some sort of reality. This brought him close to another distinguished pupil of Brentano's, Alexius Meinong (1853–1920), whose Platonic Realism had an influence on the early work of G. E. Moore and Bertrand Russell. We have seen how Russell came to think that this extreme form of Platonism was untenable.

Husserl also moved away from it, though not for the same reasons. His interest returned to the philosophy of psychology, the delineation of acts of consciousness and their objects, to which he gives priority over all other forms of enquiry, whether philosophical or scientific. It was his belief in the primacy of these 'phenomena' that led to his invention of the term 'Phenomenology' for what he took to be his discovery of the genuine First Philosophy. The investigation of phenomena was treated as a conceptual rather than an empirical proceeding. They were subjected to a process of reduction, which meant their being bracketed off from any question of their real status or their empirical attachments. In so far as they had a genuine character, as conscious acts or intentional objects of such and such a type, they could be infallibly scrutinized. Their essences lent themselves to intuition, and it was in this 'intuition of essences' that the essence of phenomenology itself was said to consist.

The language was strange, but the intuition of essences need not have amounted to anything very different from Moore's analysis of concepts. It all depended on the details of the performance and the assumptions that went with it. What separated Husserl from Moore was the belief which grew on Husserl after the publication of his *Logical Investigations* that entities of every sort are not only hospitable to consciousness but constituted by it. In the *Ideas for a Pure Phenomenology*, which appeared in 1913, the *Cartesian Meditations*, which appeared in 1931, as well as in various other works of which several have been posthumously published, there is an increasing trend towards idealism. Moreover, the emphasis on Descartes's *Cogito* makes it a subjective idealism. Solipsism is not espoused, but one is made to wonder how it can be avoided.

Phenomenology, particularly in its later forms, obtained a strong following in France as well as in Germany. A good illustration of its influence is to be found in two studies of the imagination, entitled respectively *L'Imagination* and *L'Imaginaire*, which Jean-Paul Sartre (1905–80) published before the war. Sartre's massive *L'être et*

215

le néant (*Being and Nothingness*), which appeared in 1943, was more existentialist in temper and indeed was rather closely modelled on a book called *Sein und Zeit* (*Being and Time*) which was published as early as 1927 by a pupil of Husserl's who acquired an independent reputation, Martin Heidegger. I shall have a little to say later on about Existentialism, as Heidegger and Sartre developed it, but first I propose to examine the development of Phenomenology in the work of its best French exponent, Maurice Merleau-Ponty, concentrating especially on his treatment of perception.

Maurice Merleau-Ponty

His Account of Perception

Maurice Merleau-Ponty was born in 1907 and died in 1961. His first philosophical book, *La Structure du Comportement* (*The Structure of Behaviour*), was published in 1942. *Phénoménologie de la Perception* followed in 1945 and was translated into English by Colin Smith under the title of *Phenomenology of Perception* and published in 1962 as a volume in Routledge and Kegan Paul's *International Library of Philosophy and Scientific Method*. My quotations from the book will be taken from this translation.

Merleau-Ponty begins his account of perception with what can fairly be described as an attack on the sense-datum theory. Accepting the pronouncement of the Gestalt school of psychology that we can see nothing simpler than a figure against a different coloured background, he maintains that the notion of a 'pure sensation' or 'atoms of feeling' corresponds to nothing in our experience.[1] Neither are we justified, in his view, in adopting a theory which would authorize us to distinguish a layer of impressions within experiences. His reasons for this prohibition appear to be first that 'sensory processes are not immune to central influences',[2] so that, for example, our visual data do not simply correspond to the images cast by external stimuli upon our retinae, secondly, that the objects of perceptual consciousness do not have determinate qualities, as in the illusion where two perceived lines which really are of equal length

[1] *Phenomenology of Perception*, p. 3.
[2] ibid., p. 8.

appear neither equal nor unequal, and thirdly because of the meanings which are implanted in the 'elementary perceptions', so that each part of a coloured patch, seen against its background, 'arouses the expectation of more than it contains'.[1] The mistake made by empiricists is to introduce sense-data as objects, whereas it is a 'pre-objective realm that we have to explore in ourselves if we wish to understand sense experience'.[2]

I do not find these arguments decisive. They may tell against the primacy of Locke's 'simple ideas', but there is no reason why an upholder of some form of sense-datum theory should be obliged to deny that his primitive data are elements of sense-fields, or that even the simplest sense-field has a structure. Neither need he object to admitting that some sensory qualities are indeterminate. He might indeed demur to the claim that each part of a coloured patch 'announces the expectation of more than it contains', if this is supposed to happen independently of any previous experiences. His objection might be that he did not understand what could be meant by saying that a sensory element was intrinsically meaningful.

This is, however, the view that Merleau-Ponty appears to hold. Thus, he reproaches empiricists for '*deducing* the datum from what happens to be furnished by the sense organs'. In this way 'Perception is built up with states of consciousness as a house is built with bricks, and a mental chemistry is invoked which fuses these materials into a compact whole. Like all empiricist theories,' he continues, 'this one describes only blind processes which could never be the equivalent of knowledge, because there is, in this mass of sensations and memories, *nobody who sees*, nobody who can appreciate the falling into line of datum and recollection, and, on the other hand, no solid object protected by a meaning against the teeming horde of memories. We must then discard this postulate which obscures the whole question. The cleavage between given and remembered, arrived at by way of objective causes, is arbitrary. When we come back to phenomena we find, as a basic layer of experience, a whole already pregnant with an irreducible meaning: not sensations with gaps between them, into which memories may be supposed to slip, but the features, the layout of a landscape or a word, spontaneously in accord with the intentions of the moment, as with earlier experience.'[3]

[1] ibid., p. 4.
[2] ibid., p. 12.
[3] ibid., pp. 21–2.

The last clause does something to nullify the general tenor of the argument. Whatever he may have thought about sensory phenomena, Merleau-Ponty can hardly have supposed that words have meaning independently of the meaning that they had been given, so that in their case at least the pregnancy of the sense which was attributed to them could result only from the association of a present object of reference with some previous accompaniment. But if that is granted, the same would surely apply to the phenomena in question; for Merleau-Ponty himself insists that thought does not exist independently of words,[1] and it is hard to see how a phenomenon can have meaning without being conceptualized. Nor does it greatly matt∴r exactly where the line is drawn between past and present experience. Any account of our awareness of the passage of time must invoke the concept of the specious present, and it is not paradoxical to hold that the boundaries of the specious present are indeterminate.

A more difficult objection to meet is that 'There is, in the mass of sensations and memories, nobody who sees'. It can be countered only by showing how an adequate theory of the perceptible world can be erected on a basis of neutral sense-experiences. Admittedly, the sensory elements are presented to an observer who develops the theory, and even re-appear within the theory as dependent on their observer,[2] but this is not to say that they are introduced as objects of consciousness. In the development of the theory, consciousness is a late-comer on the scene. It waits upon the positing of bodies, and the selection among bodies of those that resemble the 'central body' in certain crucial respects, the central body, though not originally assigned any owner, being in fact the observer's own. Merleau-Ponty raises the objection that 'the pure *quale* would be given to us only if the world were a spectacle and one's own body a mechanism with which some impartial mind made itself acquainted'.[3] This is partly elucidated by his saying, in a later context, where he is discussing the part played by our movements in the development of our concepts of space, 'Consciousness is in the first place not a matter of "I think that" but of "I can" '.[4] If this implies no more than that we enter the world as agents as well as observers, and that what we attend to may

[1] ibid., p. 183.
[2] cf. my *The Central Questions of Philosophy*, Chapter v.
[3] op. cit., p. 52.
[4] ibid., p. 137.

at the most primitive level be a function of what we desire, I see no call to disagree. What I would dispute is that the positing of the central and other bodies must either pre-suppose or even go *pari passu* with the attribution of consciousness.

Merleau-Ponty's strongest argument against this approach is that it leaves us with no solution to the problem of one's right to ascribe experiences to persons other than oneself. He argues that if sense-experience is 'detached from the affective and motor functions' and treated as 'the mere reception of a quality', one's body, rather than being 'the visible expression of a concrete Ego', becomes one object among others. 'Conversely,' he says, 'the body of another person could not appear to me as encasing another Ego. It was merely a machine, and the perception of the other could not really be *of the other*, since it resulted from an inference and therefore placed behind the automaton no more than a consciousness in general, a transcendent cause and not an inhabitant of his movements.'[1] The same point is made more clearly in a passage where Merleau-Ponty is detailing the limitation of what he calls 'objective thought'. 'Other men,' he says, 'and myself, seen as empirical beings, are merely pieces of mechanism worked by springs, but the true subject has no counterpart, for that consciousness which is hidden in so much flesh and blood is the least intelligible of occult qualities. My consciousness, being co-extensive with what can exist for me, and corresponding to the whole system of experience, cannot encounter, in that system, another consciousness capable of bringing immediately to light in the world the background, unknown to me, of its own phenomena.'[2]

This is, indeed, a genuine difficulty. I myself have found no better solution for it than to argue that the acceptance of a whole body of theory which enables me to account for the behaviour of others by crediting them with consciousness is justified by its explanatory power.[3] But this position can be taken only at a level of theory where physical objects, including one's own body and the bodies of other persons, have been cut loose from the qualia on the basis of which they have been posited. If one starts with qualia as given to oneself and continuing to preside over everything that is erected on their

---

[1] ibid., p. 55.
[2] ibid., p. 349.
[3] See *The Central Questions of Philosophy*, pp. 134–5.

basis, the barrier of solipsism becomes insurmountable, as Merleau-Ponty argues in a continuation of the passage which I have just quoted. 'There are,' he says, 'two modes of being, and two only: being in itself, which is that of objects arrayed in space, and being for itself, which is that of consciousness. Now another person would seem to stand before me as an *in-itself* and yet to exist *for himself*, thus requiring of me, in order to be perceived, a contradictory operation, since I ought both to distinguish him from myself, and therefore place him in the world of objects, and think of him as a consciousness, that is, the sort of being with no outside and no parts, to which I have access merely because that being is myself, and because the thinker and the thought about are amalgamated in him. There is thus no place for other people and a plurality of consciousnesses in objective thought. In so far as I constitute the world, I cannot conceive another consciousness, for it too would have to constitute the world, and, at least as regards this other view of the world, I should not be the constituting agent. Even if I succeeded in thinking of it as constituting the world, it would be I who would be constituting the consciousness as such, and once more I should be the sole constituting agent.'[1]

The reference to 'an in-itself', as opposed to a person existing 'for himself' harks back to Sartre's *Being and Nothingness* (*L'être et le néant*). Physical objects are there said to exist 'in themselves' because they have determinate properties and are subject to causal laws. Persons, on the other hand, exist 'for themselves' not only as being self-conscious but rather in the sense that they freely make projects, so that at no time are their characters definitely fixed. The depth of this distinction may be questioned, but the fact that he frames it in these terms does not diminish the force of Merleau-Ponty's argument.

His own way of escape is to argue that our awareness of our own bodies and of their having a place in a world which includes the bodies of other persons is founded in a condition which is prior to objective knowledge. 'To be a consciousness or rather *to be an experience* is to hold inner communication with the world, the body and other people, to be with them instead of being beside them.'[2] Again, 'It is through my body that I understand other people, just as it is through

[1] ibid., pp. 349–50.
[2] ibid., p. 96.

my body that I perceive "things" '.[1] And 'my body' is said to escape Sartre's dichotomy. It exists ambiguously, neither as a thing nor as consciousness. 'Whether it is a question of another's body or my own, I have no means of knowing the human body other than that of living it, which means taking up on my own account the drama which is being played out in it, and losing myself in it. I am my body, at least wholly to the extent that I possess experience, and yet at the same time my body is as it were a "natural" subject, a provisional sketch of my total being. Thus experience of one's own body runs counter to the reflective procedure which detaches subject and object from each other, and which gives us only the thought about the body, or the body as an idea, and not the experience of the body or the body in reality.'[2]

From what has so far been said, it may not be clear whether this is intended to be a description of what is merely a primitive state or of one that persists alongside the employment of objective thought. There is at least no doubt that it is meant to describe a primitive state. Thus, we are told that 'The perception of other people and the intersubjective world are problematical only for adults. The child lives in a world which he unhesitatingly believes accessible to all around him. He has no awareness of himself or of others as private subjectivities, nor does he suspect that all of us, himself included, are limited to one certain point of view of the world'.[3] One difficulty here is that what the child does not suspect is true. On the other hand the only adults for whom the perception of other people and the intersubjective world are problematical are either deranged or engaging in philosophy. In the normal way, therefore, adults, even when they are thinking objectively, must retain their childish innocence. And Merleau-Ponty maintains that they do. He argues that I could not prevail over my subjectivity 'if I had not, underlying my judgements, the primordial certainty of being in contact with being itself, if before any voluntary *adoption of a position* I were not already situated in an intersubjective world'.[4] Psychologically, this may well be true. Philosophically, it might be held to beg the question.

It is on psychological grounds that Merleau-Ponty distinguishes bodily space, that is the space of one's bodily image, from what he calls external space. He uses the image of the darkness needed to show up a

[1] ibid., p. 186.
[2] ibid., pp. 198–9.
[3] ibid., p. 355.
[4] ibid.

theatrical performance as an illustration of the part played by the body image as a point of spatial reference. My being in the world is said to be expressed by my bodily image, and it is alleged that 'every figure stands out against the double horizon of external and bodily space'.[1] I do not pretend that this distinction is entirely clear to me, though I admit that one's concept of space is partly derived from one's experience of movement. Merleau-Ponty goes so far as to say that there would be no space at all for me if I had no body,[2] in a context where my having a body can be taken to imply my having a body image. Here I am not prepared to follow him. I see no good reason why someone who was unaware of the situation of his own body and also deprived of kinaesthetic sensations should not only perceive spatial relations between physical objects but also distinguish different places in his visual field.

When it comes to the visual field Merleau-Ponty maintains, I think rightly, that it is given as three-dimensional. The widely held view that it is initially two-dimensional, with the third dimension added through the correlation of visual with tactual kinaesthetic data, is based on inferences from the science of optics. The point is not that those inferences are incorrect but that in making use of them one is employing a physiological criterion for deciding what is given. If one is concerned only, as Merleau-Ponty is, with describing the phenomena, that is the appearances of which we are conscious, then experience shows that depth is as much an intrinsic property of the visual field as length and breadth.

Rather surprisingly, Merleau-Ponty includes a chapter on 'The Body in its Sexual Being' ('Le Corps Comme Etre Sexué'). One motive for this is that it gives him an opportunity to recur, as Sartre also does in *L'être et le néant*, to the Hegelian dialectic of the master and the slave. Man is said to have 'the impression that the alien gaze which runs over his body is stealing it from him, or else, on the other hand, that the display of his body will deliver the other person up to him, defenceless, and that in this case the other will be reduced to servitude. Shame and immodesty, then, take their place in a dialectic of the self and the other which is that of master and slave; in so far as I have a body, I may be reduced to the status of an object beneath the gaze of another person, and no longer count as a person

---

[1] ibid., p. 101.
[2] ibid., p. 102.

for him, or else I may become his master and, in my turn, look at *him*. But this mastery is self-defeating, since, precisely when my value is recognized through the other's desire, he is no longer the person by whom I wished to be recognized, but a being fascinated, deprived of his freedom, and who therefore no longer counts in my eyes.'[1]

Undeniably this is a good psychological description of a form of frustration that is sometimes experienced. There is, however, no reason to suppose that it occurs only in sexual relations or in all of them. Still less are we entitled to conclude, as it would appear that Sartre would have us do, though not, I think, Merleau-Ponty, that it applies to every human relation whatsoever.

On the World as Perceived

Passing from the analysis of perception to an account of the world as perceived, Merleau-Ponty says that what needs to be elucidated is what he calls our 'primary conception of the world'. He believes that there is 'a logic of the world to which my body in its entirety conforms' and that one is thereby supplied in advance with a setting for one's sensory experiences. He infers from this that 'a thing is, therefore, not actually *given* in perception, it is internally taken up by us, reconstituted and experienced by us in so far as it is bound up with a world, the basic structures of which we carry with us, and of which it is merely one of many possible concrete forms'.[2] There is an echo of Kant in this passage, and Merleau-Ponty is willing to describe the natural world as 'the schema of inter-sensory type-relations'. He dissociates himself, however, from Kant by adding that he does not take this to be 'a system of invariable relations to which every existent thing is subject in so far as it can be known'.[3] The unity of the world is compared with the unity of style which a person may display in his various activities. But this style may change. In the case of the world, according to Merleau-Ponty, the change is confined to the growth or decline of one's knowledge. 'The world remains the same world throughout my life, because it is that permanent being within which I make all corrections to my knowledge, a world which in its unity remains unaffected by those corrections, and the self-evidence of

[1] ibid., pp. 166–7.
[2] ibid., p. 326.
[3] ibid., p. 327.

which attracts my activity towards the truth through appearance and error.'[1] Presumably, this is not meant to deny that the permanent being may possess different properties at different times.

Time itself is said to be 'a setting to which one can gain access and which one can understand only by occupying a situation in it, and by grasping it in its entirety through the horizons of that situation'.[2] This need not be true if it is possible to conceive of time as the domain of the relation which holds between events when one is earlier than another. On the other hand, if the concepts of past, present and future are taken as fundamental then, since the present is captured in this schema only by the use of the demonstrative 'now', all siting of events in time will contain at least a tacit indication of the temporal position of the speakers. Merleau-Ponty takes the second course, but pursues it in such a way that he is led into a thicket of idealism. His difficulty is to accommodate the past and future, in spite of his also putting forward the view, which he does not elucidate, that the past is directly accessible to memory. Perhaps he holds that this brings it into the present, since, as he sees it, the trouble with the past and future is just that they do exist in the present, from which they have to escape if there is to be such a thing as time. 'Past and future' are said to 'withdraw of their own accord from being and move over into subjectivity in search, not of some real support, but, on the contrary, of a possibility of not-being which accords with their nature'.[3] The underlying idea, I think, is that a set of actual events, each instantiating a 'now', could not constitute the passage of time. Nor would the trouble be met by transferring the events from 'the objective world' to consciousness. 'Ultimate subjectivity', we are told, 'is not temporal in the empirical sense of the term: if consciousness of time were made up of successive states of consciousness, there would be needed a new consciousness to be conscious of that succession and so on to infinity. We are forced to recognize the existence of "a consciousness having behind it no consciousness to be conscious of it" which, consequently, is not arrayed out in time, and in which its "being coincides with its being for itself".'[4] It appears that Husserl came to the same conclusion.

[1] ibid., pp. 327–8.
[2] ibid., p. 332.
[3] ibid., p. 412.
[4] ibid., p. 422.

I confess that I can see no good reason for our being driven to such straits. Why should not the relation of temporal priority be taken as sensibly given and then projected indefinitely on either side of the specious present? It may be objected that we are not entitled to 'spatialize' time in this fashion, but even if we subordinate any series of this kind to the series which is based on the concepts of past, present and future, there is no reason why events which are earlier or later than the present should all be targets of contemporary demonstratives. On the contrary, if we make them so, we put ourselves in the awkward position of seeming to contradict the well-established scientific hypotheses that there have been and will be times which are not contemporaneous with any manifestations of human consciousness.

Merleau-Ponty is aware of this difficulty but leaves it unclear how he would dispose of it. Once more I am reduced simply to quoting what he says. 'It is,' he says, 'only intellectualist, abstract reflection which is incompatible with misconceived "facts". For what precisely is meant by saying that the world existed before any human consciousness? An example of what is meant is that the earth originally issued from a primitive nebula from which the combination of conditions necessary to life was absent. But every one of these words, like every equation in physics, pre-supposes *our* pre-scientific experience of the world, and this reference to the world in which we *live* goes to make up the proposition's valid meaning. Nothing will ever bring home to my comprehension what a nebula that no one sees could possibly be. Laplace's nebula is not behind us, at our remote beginnings, but in front of us in the cultural world. What, in fact, do we mean when we say that there is no world without a being in the world? Not indeed that the world is constituted by consciousness, but on the contrary that consciousness always finds itself already at work in the world. What is true, taking one thing with another, is that there is a nature, which is not that of the sciences, but that which perception presents to me, and that even the light of consciousness is, as Heidegger says, *lumen naturale*, given to itself.'[1]

It is very difficult to know what to make of this. It is not exactly a return either to absolute or to subjective idealism. Thus, in the next paragraph, Merleau-Ponty allows the possibility of things existing outside one's own experience. He speaks of 'my living present' as

[1] ibid., p. 432.

opening on to temporalities outside my living experience and acquiring a social horizon 'with the result that my world is expanded to the dimensions of that collective history which my private existence takes up and carries forward'.[1] But while solipsism is avoided, the outlook remains anthropocentric. Indeed, the most plausible conclusion on this evidence is that one of the more surprising outcomes of phenomenology is a conjunction with pragmatism.

The Early Work of Heidegger and Sartre

How then does it also lead to Existentialism? Mainly through Martin Heidegger, who was a pupil of Husserl's, and by an opportune adherence to the Nazi party supplanted him in his Chair at Freiburg and indeed became Rector of the University. Heidegger, who lived from 1889 to 1976, wrote numerous pamphlets, and had also arranged for the publication of many volumes of his lectures and seminar papers, but his only considerable book was *Sein und Zeit* (*Being and Time*) which was published in 1927, and the pamphlet in which his existentialism is most uncompromisingly stated was *Was ist Metaphysik?* (*What is Metaphysics?*), which was published in 1929. *Sein und Zeit* takes its inspiration from Husserl in that it too is a search for a philosophy without presuppositions, thereby digging deeper than any of the natural or social sciences. It assumes that the most fundamental presuppositions are presuppositions about what there is, and consequently that the basic problem of phenomenology, as the first philosophy, is the search for the meaning of Being. What is sought is not a definition of Being but an insight into its essence. Though Existentialism acquired its name from the tenet that existence is prior to essence, a proposition not easy to interpret but one that might amount to no more than the innocent claim that a thing cannot have properties unless it exists, the tables here appear to be turned. Heidegger is concerned not with what things there are, but with what it is for anything to be.

The first step that Heidegger takes is to query Husserl's assumption that Being is correlative to Consciousness. He thinks that what calls for examination is the more primitive level of experience at which we

[1] ibid., p. 433.

make the distinction between them. This undercuts not only the philosophical standpoints of Descartes and Kant, but even the approaches of Plato and Aristotle to the question of Being. We have to recover the naïveté of the Pre-Socratics. With this end in view, Heidegger makes some dubious excursions into the etymology of Ancient Greek words, but in the main he devises his own terminology, relying on the hospitality to neologisms of the German language. This makes what argument he proffers even harder than it might otherwise have been to follow.

Heidegger does not entirely forsake Descartes. He decides that before attempting the examination of being in general, a task which he reserved for a second volume which never in fact appeared, one must obtain an insight into the being of the Ego for whom the question of being arises. He calls the Ego 'Dasein', 'being-there', probably to underline the point that it is supposed to be situated in the world and not a detached spectator. Like Descartes, Heidegger palters with solipsism. His *Dasein*, like Descartes' Ego, is rather a variable than a constant; what is said to be true of it is intended to apply to us all, not just to the speaker. Nevertheless, Heidegger credits *Dasein* with the property of *Jemeinigheit*, always being mine. There is a tension here which he does not relax.

The distinction between things existing in-themselves and things existing for-themselves, which we have seen to be prominent in the work of Merleau-Ponty and Sartre, has its counterpart in Heidegger's conception of a *Dasein*. It is in the world, but not in the way that physical objects are in the world. What puts it in the world is the complex of its interests and attitudes. The possession of this complex underlies the distinction between thought and action. The distinction between subject and object is not so much superficial as misguided, since it represents the *Dasein* as just another thing. For Heidegger, things make a relatively late appearance in the web that the *Dasein* spins. They are subordinate to the notion of an instrument, something of which the *Dasein* is able to make use. It is indeed allowed by Heidegger that there are things of which one cannot in fact make use, but they are lumped together with the things of which one can. It does not appear to strike him that this is hardly a sufficient characterization. With a similar insufficiency he analyses space in terms of what a *Dasein* does or does not have ready to hand.

Since all the activities of a *Dasein*, including the adoption of propositional attitudes, like wondering, believing or knowing, display concern for something or other, either concern for what can be done with it or concern with what it is, the essence of *Dasein*, its peculiar mode of Being is eventually said to be Care (*Sorge*). Moreover, since *Dasein* is something that exists for itself, and consequently has potentialities that may or may not be realized, the mode of being of the *Dasein*, and so derivatively of all existence, is being in the form of Time. Heidegger therefore concentrates on the nature of Temporality.

At this point one is in for a shock. For it turns out that the Time in which we deploy our existence is not time at all in the common acceptance of the term. According to Heidegger, the time which is kept by clocks, the time in which events succeed one another, is derivative, if it exists at all. The reason why it may not exist is that the pure 'now' is a myth. Time is, indeed, fundamentally constituted out of the past, present and future, but the present consists in the presence of something that we care about; the past, which at one point the *Dasein* is mysteriously said to be, is what cannot be altered; the future is the open domain of our possibilities. We have found an echo of this treatment of time in Merleau-Ponty, but it is obvious that any such attempt to extract temporal predicates out of psychological or metaphysical ones must be circular at best if it is not wholly beside the mark. Thus, the object of care by which the present is supposed to be defined has to be tacitly understood as a temporal presence. It is not only past events that it is beyond our power to alter. Not all future events afford us opportunities for choice.

Displaying a surprising ignorance, or engaging in an unscrupulous distortion, of Greek etymology, Heidegger takes the term 'metaphysics' to refer not, as we have seen that it actually does, to the works following the books on physics in the Aristotelian canon but to what lies beyond nature, that is beyond everything that exists.[1] After a display of what can fairly be described as charlatanism, making such statements as 'What interests us in our relation with the world is the existent itself and apart from that – nothing, what all action takes its direction from is the existent itself and besides that – nothing' and then asking what about this Nothing ('Wie steht es um dieses Nichts?'),[2] he concludes that if the task of metaphysics is to transcend

---

[1] See *Was ist Metaphysik?*, p. 24.
[2] ibid., p. 11.

everything that there is, its proper object must be the exploration of Nothing. This is not the analysis of negation, since negation is subordinate to the Nothing, not the other way around. The nothing does not negate anything. Its activity just consists in being nothing. At least, this is the only semblance of sense that I can give to 'Das Nichts selbst nichtet',[1] mistranslated by Sartre in *L'être et le néant* as *'le néant se néantise'* ('the nothing negates itself').

Heidegger sees that to talk of nothing as if it were something of a unique sort is to set logic at defiance, but the moral which he draws is 'so much the worse for logic'. Both logic and science are subservient to metaphysics, which sets the boundaries within which truth and knowledge, while confined to the existent, can function. This is achieved not by reasoning but by the operation of various affective attitudes of which the most important is *Angst*, usually rendered in French as 'l'angoisse', in English perhaps better by 'anxiety' than 'anguish', though anxiety on a cosmic scale with no specific object. Very strange things are said about *Angst* and the nullity that it unmasks for us but their burden is that it fixes *Dasein* in existence. This implies that we are all continuously beset by *Angst*, though Heidegger does allow that it may be dormant.

For Heidegger there remains one metaphysical question: Why is there anything at all and not rather nothing? Perhaps this should be treated in Collingwood's way as the senseless querying of an absolute presupposition. At least, if it is treated as a question, there is no way of answering it. If the 'Why' is construed as a request for a cause, then even if an answer is forthcoming, it merely relates one existent item to all the others, or leaves us with a theory for which we have no more general explanation. If it is construed as a request for a reason, then not only are we making the unwarranted assumption that the totality of what there is has been designed, but we are still committed to the being of the designer. Perhaps the question is deliberately drafted in order to be unanswerable. There are those who bracket Heidegger with Wittgenstein. There seems no justification for this except for the implication in the *Tractatus* that there are things of importance that cannot be said. One can only reply, once again, with Neurath: 'One must indeed be silent but not *about* anything.'

Just as the existent as a whole is bounded and indeed penetrated by nullity, so the existence of every human being is bounded and indeed penetrated by death. Bounded, because one's death is inescapable;

[1] ibid., p. 19.

penetrated, because one's attitude towards death is charged by Heidegger with special moral significance. It is said to be the most personal of our possibilities, though the ground for this is not clear. It is true, as Heidegger remarks, that no one else can die my death, though someone may die in my place, but this is a logical platitude. It is equally true that no one else can smile my smile or cry my tears. A more serious point is that death inevitably restricts the number of choices that I can actually make. If I keep this in mind, then I have a motive for taking life seriously. If certain courses of action express my individuality, as opposed to those that I pursue merely out of social conformity, then the thought of death as leaving me little room for manoeuvre may lead me to behave authentically in a way I otherwise might not.

Unfortunately, this is not all that Heidegger has to say about authenticity. To live authentically we have to recognize not only the inevitability of death but also its negativity. The *Dasein* has to understand itself as nothingness, whatever that may mean, and freely accept the burden that this imposes. It has to consent to finitude, which entails that it is infected with guilt. Why a consenting to finitude, which is something unavoidable, should be a source of guilt is utterly unclear. The idea is found also in the work of Søren Kierkegaard (1813–55), who has claims to be regarded as the originator of existentialism, and is probably of religious provenance, but this does not make it any the more acceptable.

This alleged source of guilt is also the source of freedom, indeed the only source of freedom that Heidegger allows there to be. But whereas the guilt is inescapable, the freedom has to be earned through an authentic mode of living, which implies the proper concentration upon death. In Heidegger's view, only a few men achieve it, the rest being members of the herd, accepting the values and opinions of their society, not making the prospect of death a spur to their self-realization.

The treatment of this question of freedom by existentialist writers is generally puzzling. Sartre's very long and intricate discussion of it in *L'être et le néant*[1] is governed both by his distinction between things that exist in-themselves ('en-soi') and things that exist for-themselves ('pour-soi') and by his notion, derived at least in part from Heidegger, of the nullity ('le néant') which lies at the heart of

---

[1] Part II, Chapter I.

man's consciousness and by inserting itself between the past, present and future secures his continuity in time. Freedom is held to be an inalienable attribute of 'le pour-soi'. It cannot be captured in a definition, but an account can be given of the function it performs. Its intrusion into time, made possible by its alliance with 'le néant' which links and separates successive instants, cuts off a man from his past and releases him to choose how he will act. This action will not be determined and not even motivated by any existent matter of fact, because an action is a projection of a conscious being towards what is not, and what is cannot on its own determine what is not. It will hardly escape notice that this is a very bad argument. If, as is generally the case, an effect succeeds its cause then there must be a time at which the cause exists and the effect is still to come, yet this does not in the least prevent the two events from being linked by a causal law. It is equally obvious that a past or present state of affairs can be a motive for an action which has yet to be performed, whether or not we assimilate motives to causes. Sartre does make a point of claiming that freedom is not subject to any logical necessity,[1] but whatever he means by this it does not withdraw the discussion of freedom from the grasp of logic; it does not entitle him to make simple logical blunders.

To be fair to Sartre, we must observe that he does not go on to conclude that our actions are all entirely gratuitous, or that we are always free to do or to become whatever suits our fancy. He recognizes that we are always placed in a situation, which encompasses not only the surrounding circumstances but our own mental and physical capacities and dispositions and that it is from this situation that our motives are drawn, if only because of its lack of something that we wish to bring into existence. At the same time he insists that it is not the situation itself that provides us with our motives, but rather our interpretation of it, the meaning with which we choose to endow it. But how does it come about that we choose to endow it with this meaning rather than with that? Sartre makes it depend upon a fundamental choice that each one of us makes of the kind of life that he wishes to lead and the kind of man he wishes to be. This is not a very clear concept since the fundamental choice is said to be liable to change, to admit various courses of action on any given occasion which are consonant with it, and not even to exclude actions which

[1] ibid., p. 133.

run counter to it. Nor is any empirical evidence provided for the assumption of its universal existence. Moreover, even if it were shown to exist, the question could still be raised why a person makes the fundamental choice that he does rather than some other; so that the fatal objection to libertarianism that to the extent that our actions are not causally explicable they are haphazard is not finally met.

Merleau-Ponty's treatment of freedom adds nothing to Sartre's. It is summarized by his saying that there is 'ultimately nothing that can set limits to freedom, except those limits that freedom itself has set in the form of its various initiatives, so that the subject has simply the external world that he gives himself'.[1] Taken literally, this last clause is simply false, but perhaps Merleau-Ponty meant no more than to make the Sartrean point that the way in which the external world is treated as a field for action is at least partly dependent upon the agent's interest in it.

As befits so good an imaginative writer, Sartre has more to say of psychological interest, including his celebrated account of insincerity ('mauvaise-foi'). Philosophically, it is also worth noticing his moral theory that we have to assume the responsibility of choosing how to live, and that in legislating for ourselves we legislate also for others. We posit a set of moral standards as holding universally. My only disagreement with him in this connection is that he seems to take it ill that there are no absolute values, existing independently of our valuations. He sometimes seems to imply that if the world had been different, if there had been a God, for example, we should have had our proper caucus of actions laid down for us and so have been relieved of our responsibility to choose them. But here he overlooks the logical fact that morals cannot be founded on authority, whether the authority be supposed human or divine. One has to make the independent assumption that the authority in question is good and that what it enjoins is right. Similarly, if there are no absolute values, it is not just a contingent matter of fact. It is rather that the term 'absolute value' is being used in such a way that nothing could possibly answer to it: and for this there is no reason to repine.

In retrospect, the popularity of Existentialism in the years immediately following the war appears to have been mainly due to the mistaken belief that it prescribed a concrete way of life. Its vogue was largely superseded by that of a neo-Marxism in which the concept of

[1] op. cit., p. 436.

alienation, the being at odds with one's conditions of life or work, played a dominant role. Now there are reports that neo-Marxism is yielding to structuralism. Structuralism has a sense in anthropology, linguistic and literary criticism. In literary criticism it is a matter of dissociating the text from any intention that might plausibly be ascribed to its author. In linguistics it is the mistaken view that a language can be adequately characterized in terms of the frequency with which certain groups of sounds or marks are produced by its speakers. In anthropology it denotes the sensible practice of inter-preting particular observances in the light of the whole culture of the tribe which is under investigation. When the term is extended to philosophy, it may remain attached to its anthropological origin and so amount to nothing more sinister than the insistence that a person's utterances, beliefs and desires are to be taken together in the interpretation of his behaviour. At the worst, with its emphasis on internal relations, it may mark a return to Absolute Idealism.

IX Later Developments

Linguistic Philosophy

J. L. Austin

There is a widespread belief that in the years following the Second
World War the English philosophical scene was dominated by
something called Linguistic Philosophy. This was thought to be an
offshoot of Logical Positivism, and the term was applied indiscrimi-
nately by unprofessional commentators to work as diverse as that of
Wittgenstein and his Cambridge pupils, Gilbert Ryle and his
followers at Oxford, and my own. In the interest of clarity, however,
I think that the term should be reserved for a distinctive approach to
philosophy which was centred in Oxford and flourished mainly in the
1950s under the direction of John Langshaw Austin.

Austin was born in 1911, and after distinguishing himself as a
classical scholar at school and at Oxford was elected to a Fellowship
at All Souls in 1933. Subsequently he became a Tutorial Fellow of
Magdalen College, Oxford. He served in Military Intelligence at the
War Office during the war and rose to the rank of lieutenant-colonel.
In 1952 he succeeded H. J. Paton, the Kantian scholar, as Professor
of Moral Philosophy at Oxford. His visits to Harvard as William
James Lecturer in 1955 and to the University of California in 1958
procured him a following in the United States. He died after a short
illness in 1960.

Like G. E. Moore and H. A. Prichard, both of whom he admired
for their philosophical persistence and attention to detail, Austin
owed his reputation mainly to his teaching. Apart from a translation
from the German of Frege's *Foundations of Arithmetic* and a few
reviews, Austin published only seven articles in his lifetime. These
were collected by his literary executors J. O. Urmson and G. J.
Warnock and, with the addition of three further pieces, published

under the title *Philosophical Papers* in 1961. Austin had been in the habit of delivering a series of lectures at Oxford on the topic of perception under the title *Sense and Sensibilia*, and Warnock worked up the notes for these lectures into a book which he published under the same title in 1962. Urmson did the same with the manuscript of Austin's William James lectures, publishing them also in 1962 under the title *How to do Things with Words*. A *Symposium on J. L. Austin*, containing biographical sketches and both favourable and unfavourable appraisals of his work, was edited by K. T. Fann and published in 1969 as a volume in Routledge and Kegan Paul's *International Library of Philosophy and Scientific Method*.

Austin took seriously the view put forward by Wittgenstein and the Vienna Circle that philosophers had been gratuitously puzzled and in some cases led into talking nonsense by their failure to understand the workings of the language they were employing, and consequent abuses of it. Unlike Wittgenstein, however, Austin did not aim merely at a dissolution of philosophical problems through the correction of these linguistic errors. He believed that a painstaking investigation of the ways in which some set of expressions of a natural language, like English, were ordinarily used would have a positive value. It might, indeed, show that philosophers had simply entangled themselves in a pseudo-problem, but it might also uncover a genuine problem, or set of problems, of which it would point the way to a solution, and apart from their philosophical bearings its results might be of interest in themselves. Austin, drawing on his war experiences, conceived of this investigation as a collective enterprise. The field for linguistic study would be parcelled out among different investigators, their results would be pooled and their implications discussed. It was hoped that agreement would then be reached as to what was and what was not legitimate usage, and important distinctions thereby brought to light.

I do not know how much, if any, of Austin's published work was the result of such cooperative effort. His two most interesting papers are 'A Plea for Excuses' and 'Ifs and Cans', both of which were composed in 1956. In the first of them he examines the concept of doing an action, and with the help of subtle and amusing examples brings out the different shades of meaning that are to be found in the use of such adverbs as voluntarily, deliberately, inadvertently, carelessly or by mistake. In the second he argues both against the

assumption that a conditional is always implied in the statement that
someone could do or could have done something or other, and also
against the assumption that when a conditional is used as in the
sentence 'I can if I choose' the conditional is always causal. Here I
think that he is right on both counts. In both papers he includes a
defence of his procedure, in the first of them pointing out among
other things that 'when we examine what we should say when, what
words we should use in what situations, we are looking again not
merely at words (or "meanings", whatever they may be) but also at
the realities we use the words to talk about',[1] and in the second both
that he was taking preliminary steps towards making important
linguistic distinctions[2] and that he was making a flank attack on the
problem of free will and determinism. This is an issue in which there
are many difficult questions to be unravelled, but it would undeniably
be a help if we understood clearly what we mean by saying of an agent
that he could have acted otherwise.

In the earliest papers that are included in the posthumous
collection Austin was content to speak of sensa as the immediate
objects of perception. Later, he came to think this a mistake, and his
Sense and Sensibilia was a savage attack on the sense-datum theory,
especially as exemplified in the opening chapter of my book *The
Foundations of Empirical Knowledge*, which had been published in
1940. His lectures were witty and made a few good debating points
but as I think I succeeded in showing in a rebuttal, which I published
first in the journal *Synthèse* in 1967 and then reprinted both in my
book *Metaphysics and Common Sense* and in the *Symposium on J. L.
Austin*, they did not contain much serious argument. Among other
things they entirely ignored the causal considerations which have
probably furnished philosophers with their strongest inducement to
anchor their theories of perception on something of the order of
sense-data.

Austin took his main steps towards developing a science of
language first in his contribution to a symposium on *Other Minds* in
1946 and finally in his lectures *How to do Things with Words*. In
considering the question how one can know what goes on in the mind
of another he dealt with the evaluation of claims to knowledge, and in
considering this question he commented on the existence of a class of

[1] *Philosophical Papers*, p. 130.
[2] ibid., p. 179.

utterances which did not function as true or false reports but constituted or helped to constitute the performance of some act. For instance, saying 'I promise', in the appropriate circumstances, is to make a promise, rather than to report that a promise is being made, saying 'I bet' is to make a bet, saying 'I will' at the appropriate moment is part of the process of getting married and so forth. Such statements could be sincere or insincere, or felicitous or infelicitous in various other ways, but they could not on the face of it be characterized as either true or false. Austin came to call them performative statements, coining the name 'constative' for narrative statements which do have a truth-value. He implied that he consider-ed 'I know' to be a performative statement, but here he was at least partly at fault. 'I know' does indeed have the force of offering a guarantee, but it also makes a true or false statement about the speaker. If what I claim to know is not the case, or I am not in a position to guarantee its truth, then my saying that I knew was not merely insincere or infelicitous, it was false.

Later, Austin became convinced that the distinction between performative and constative utterances was not so sharp as he had at first thought. He was worried by the use of expressions like 'I state' or 'I admit'. To say 'I state that whales are mammals' is to make a statement: to say 'I admit that whales are mammals' is to make an admission. It would, however, be perverse to insist that the prefixing of the words 'I state that' or 'I admit that' to the sentence 'whales are mammals' robs the resulting statement of the truth-value that 'whales are mammals' undoubtedly possesses. Conversely, though this is not I think, a point that Austin himself conceded, I see no very good reason why even an exemplary performative should not have a truth-value. What is the objection to saying that the statement 'I promise to come as soon as I can', expressed by a speaker A at a time t is true if and only if A promises to come as soon as he can after the time in question? It may be objected that that blurs a useful distinction, but the difference in the responsibility incurred by saying 'I promise to do such and such' rather than just 'I will do such and such', or in saying 'I assure you that p' rather than just asserting p, is only a difference of degree. The fact is that, in terms of the speaker's commitment and their informative function, there is no putting per-formative and constative statements into different compartments: most statements are both.

For the reason given, Austin in the course of his Harvard lectures introduced a new set of distinctions in the nature of what he liked to call 'speech-acts'. He distinguished the *locutionary act* which was said to be 'roughly equivalent to uttering a certain sentence with a certain sense and reference'[1] from *illocutionary acts* 'such as informing, ordering, warning, undertaking, &c, i.e. utterances which have a certain (conventional) force',[2] which we perform *in* performing a locutionary act, and both these from *perlocutionary* acts: 'What we bring about or achieve *by* saying something, such as convincing, persuading, deterring, and even, say, surprising or misleading.'[3] The illocutionary act must be intended, though it may not be successfully performed; what is intended as an entreaty may, for example, not be so understood. The perlocutionary act may or may not be intended, and its intention may or may not be fulfilled. I may mean to offend you by something that I say, and either succeed or fail, but I may also offend you without meaning to.

Austin was especially interested in the ways verbs differed in their illocutionary forces, and he divided them into five general classes, namely *verdictives* like 'acquit' or 'grade', where some appraisal is given, *exercitives* like 'appoint' or 'warn', where some power, right, or influence is exercised, *commissives* like 'promise' or 'intend', whereby one commits oneself, *behavitives* like 'apologize' or 'congratulate', which have to do with attitudes and social behaviour, and, fifthly, *expositives* like 'describe' or 'mention' or 'testify', which 'make plain how our utterances fit into the course of an argument or conversation'.[4] He does not claim that these distinctions are more than rough and ready but claims that they do 'play Old Harry' with what he calls 'the true/false fetish' and 'the value/fact fetish'.[5] I agree that they show estimations of fact and value to be frequently commingled but I do not think either distinction is seriously menaced. I also wish that Austin had paid more attention to the notion of *locutionary* acts. 'Uttering a certain sentence with a certain sense and reference' is hardly an adequate account of meaning.

There are those who wonder what work of this kind has to do with philosophy. Since I share their doubts to some extent, I think it fair to return to the defence of his procedure that Austin gives at the

---

[1] *How to do Things with Words*, p. 108.
[2] ibid.
[3] ibid.
[4] ibid., pp. 150–51.
[5] ibid.

conclusion of his paper 'Ifs and Cans' and this time to cite it in his own words. 'There are,' he says, 'constant references in contemporary philosophy, which notoriously is much concerned with language, to a "logical grammar" and "a logical syntax" as though these were things distinct from ordinary grammarian's grammar and syntax: and certainly they do seem, whatever exactly they may be, different from traditional grammar. But grammar to-day is itself in a state of flux; for fifty years or more it has been questioned on all hands and counts whether what Dionysius Thrax once thought was the truth about Greek is the truth and the whole truth about all language and all languages. Do we know, then, that there will prove to be any ultimate boundary between "logical grammar" and a revised and enlarged *Grammar*? In the history of human inquiry, philosophy has the place of the initial central sun, seminal and tumultuous: from time to time it throws off some portion of itself to take station as a science, a planet, cool and well regulated, progressing steadily towards a distant final state. This happened long ago at the birth of mathematics, and again at the birth of physics: only in the last century we have witnessed the same process once again, slow and at the time almost imperceptible, in the birth of the science of mathematical logic, through the joint labours of philosophers and mathematicians. Is it not possible that the next century may see the birth, through the joint labours of philosophers, grammarians, and numerous other students of language, of a true and comprehensive *science of language*? Then we shall have rid ourselves of one more part of philosophy (there will still be plenty left) in the only way we ever can get rid of philosophy, by kicking it upstairs.'[1]

Noam Chomsky

The man who has done most, if not to develop a true and comprehensive science of language, at least to supply linguistics with a philosophical foundation is Noam Chomsky, whose first book *Syntactic Structures* was published in 1957, three years before Austin's death. Chomsky, who became celebrated not only for his innovations in linguistics, but for his outspoken opposition to the United States government on account of its intervention in the Vietnam War, was born in 1928 and educated at the University of

[1] *Philosophical Papers*, pp. 179–80.

Pennsylvania, where he numbered among his teachers the structural linguist Zellig Harris and the philosopher Nelson Goodman, against both of whom he can be said to have reacted. He holds a Professorship at the Massachusetts Institute of Technology.

Chomsky's early view of the nature of his subject is clearly stated towards the outset of *Syntactic Structures*. 'Syntax,' he says, 'is the study of the principles and processes by which sentences are constructed in particular languages. Syntactic investigation of a given language has as its goal the construction of a grammar that can be viewed as a device of some sort for producing the sentences of the language under analysis. More generally, linguists must be concerned with the problem of determining the fundamental underlying properties of successful grammars. The ultimate outcome of these investigations should be a theory of linguistic structure in which the descriptive devices utilized in particular grammars are presented and studied abstractly, with no specific reference to particular languages. One function of this theory is to provide a general method for selecting a grammar for each language, given a corpus of sentences of this language.'[1]

It is not immediately obvious that there must be one general method for deriving the grammar of a language from a limited corpus of its sentences, irrespective of what the language may be, but Chomsky came to accept the even stronger hypothesis that there is a universal grammar which underlies the syntax of all human languages, however great their more superficial diversity. This conclusion is not the outcome of a close examination of a wide variety of languages actually in use, but is part of a theory which accounts, in Chomsky's view, for what would otherwise be a mysterious set of facts. These facts are that a natural language consists of an infinite number of sentences; that normal children master natural languages in a relatively short period of time; that the number of sentences of the language in question that have been pronounced in their hearing during that period is quite small; and that they very soon manifest the ability both to decide whether sentences which they have not previously heard are grammatically correct and to formulate correct grammatical sentences of their own origination. That children possess these abilities is not in dispute. What can and has been disputed is Chomsky's contention that their acquisition of them

[1] *Syntactic Structures*, p. 11.

cannot be accounted for by a behavioural theory concerning their responses to stimuli, or by any other theory which would involve nothing more than their power to extrapolate from the data presented to them. Believing that empiricism in this domain can thus be ruled out of court, Chomsky turns to rationalism. He argues that children could not display the linguistic capacity that they do unless they were antecedently programmed to adopt a certain form of grammar. For technical reasons, this grammar is held to consist not simply in the choice of certain structures but in the use of certain rules of transformation. The propensity to employ these rules of trans- formation so as to generate the sentences of whatever language we are brought up to employ is regarded as part of the constitution of the human mind. As a declaration of adhesion to what he takes to have been the view of Descartes, Chomsky equates it with our possession of innate ideas.

That we possess such innate ideas is advanced as an empirical hypothesis, but it is not clear what positive evidence could be adduced in its favour. Since it is not suggested that anyone, except perhaps a few grammarians, is actually conscious of having these ideas, it is hard to see how Chomsky escapes John Locke's objection to Descartes that the failure of a great part of mankind to have any notion of these principles 'is enough to destroy that universal assent which must needs be the necessary concomitant of all innate truths: it seeming to me near a contradiction to say that there are truths imprinted on the soul, which it perceives or understands not; imprinting, if it signify anything, being nothing else but the making of certain truths to be perceived. For to imprint anything on the mind without the mind's perceiving it, seems to me hardly intelligible.'[1]

Sympathizing as I do with Locke, I find that the strength of Chomsky's position consists less in what he asserts than in what he denies. He is at his most convincing when he argues that a purely behavioural account of the acquisition of language in terms of conditioned reflexes does not do justice to the complexity of the facts.[2] His case, however, may be thought to gain an unmerited support from the assumption, accepted at least tacitly by both parties, that a natural language is the first symbolic system that children acquire, and that the process of acquisition begins with the

[1] John Locke, *Essay Concerning Human Understanding*, i, Chapter i, Section 5.
[2] cf. N. Chomsky's review of B. F. Skinner's 'Verbal Behaviour' in *Language* (1959), 35.

241

first overt use of words. If we agree rather with Nelson Goodman that 'before anyone acquires a language, he has had an abundance of practice in developing and using rudimentary prelinguistic symbolic systems in which gestures and sensory and perceptual occurrences of all sorts function as signs',[1] we may be more ready to concede that the search for an empirical theory of learning is not a hopeless undertaking. Such a theory need not be wedded to behaviourism, nor would it set *a priori* limits to the mind's flexibility and inventiveness. If it could be developed, it might have the explanatory power that the recourse to innate ideas so far appears to lack. To say this is naturally not to detract from the interest and acuteness of Chomsky's grammatical analyses.

W. V. Quine

Since the death of Wittgenstein and the transference of Russell's principal interests from philosophy to politics, the living philosopher who has commanded the greatest influence among his colleagues, at least in the English-speaking world, is the American Willard Van Orman Quine. Quine, who was born in Ohio in 1908, was educated at Oberlin College, where he read mathematics and philosophy, and at Harvard, where he worked under Whitehead, Lewis and H. M. Sheffer and obtained a doctorate with a thesis on 'The Logic of Sequences'. After an excursion to Europe, on which he made contact with the philosophers in Vienna, Prague and Warsaw, he returned to Harvard in 1934 as a Junior Fellow of the Society of Fellows, becoming a professor there in 1946 after four years' service in the United States Navy. He has been a full professor and Senior Fellow at Harvard since 1948.

Quine has been a very productive writer. He has published at least fourteen books and many articles and reviews. Most of his early work, especially, has been devoted to the more technical problems of mathematical logic, but he has always been concerned with its philosophical implications and he has ventured freely into other areas of philosophy. At the outset he stood close to the Vienna Circle, accepting its use of the verification principle of meaning to exclude

[1] N. Goodman, *Problems and Projects*, p. 71.

metaphysics and, in spite of his admiration for Carnap's powers of logical construction, as displayed in *Der logische Aufbau der Welt*, rejecting its phenomenalist basis in favour of the physicalism to which we have seen that Neurath later converted Carnap, in opposition to Schlick. This physicalism is something that Quine has never abandoned, and he has remained faithful also to Neurath's ideal of the unity of science, refusing indeed to make any clear-cut distinction between science and philosophy.

There was, however, one central thesis of the logical positivists that he was soon to question. This was the thesis that the true propositions of logic and pure mathematics are true by convention. As held by the logical positivists, this thesis included acceptance of the claim made by Russell and Whitehead that mathematics is reducible to logic. Quine has been disposed to accept this claim in so far as he allows that mathematics is reducible to set-theory, though in his later work, for example in his *Philosophy of Logic*, which was published in 1970, he has objected to including set-theory within logic on the ground that this would be 'overestimating the kinship between membership and predication'.[1] In a much earlier work, an article 'Truth by Convention' which he contributed in 1936 to a volume of *Philosophical Essays for A. N. Whitehead*, and republished in his own collection of essays *The Ways of Paradox* in 1966, he had questioned the possibility of reducing geometry to logic, but allowed that it might be feasible if geometry were identified with algebra, through the correlations of analytic geometry and algebraic expressions which could be defined on the basis of logical expressions as in *Principia Mathematica*.[2] What he objected to, among other things, was the suggestion that the reduction could be effected by framing some set of geometrical postulates and then relying on the hypothetical proposition that if the postulates were true the theorems of geometry were true; for if the postulates are appropriately chosen, a similar reduction can be carried out for any subject whatsoever which can be cast in a deductive form.

What Quine has to say about geometry in 'Truth by Convention' is of interest in itself, but the chief purport of his essay is to query the point of saying that the propositions of logic are true by convention, whether they include the propositions of mathematics or not. He

---

[1] *Philosophy of Logic*, p. 66.
[2] cf. *The Ways of Paradox*, p. 80.

grants that we can reduce all our logical devices to a limited set of primitives, such as the not-idiom, the if-idiom and the every-idiom, and that conventions of finite length involving these idioms, such as the convention 'Let any expression be true which yields a truth when put for "q" in the result of putting a truth for "p" in "If p then q" ', will generate an infinite number of consequences, including all the logical truths of the propositional calculus. He objects, however, that 'If logic is to proceed *mediately* from conventions, logic is needed for inferring logic from the conventions'.[1] The same objection can be raised with regard to the logical primitives. 'It is supposed that the *if*-idiom, the *not*-idiom, the every-idiom, and so on, mean nothing to us initially, and that we adopt [certain] conventions by way of circumscribing their meaning; and the difficulty is that communication of [these conventions] themselves depends upon free use of those very idioms which we are attempting to circumscribe, and can succeed only if we are already conversant with the idioms.'[2] Quine allows that one might attempt to meet this difficulty by arguing that the requisite conventions are observed from the start without being explicitly formulated, but argues that once the notion of linguistic convention is no longer conceived of as explicit, it ceases to have any explanatory force. 'We may wonder,' he says, 'what one adds to the bare statement that the truths of logic and mathematics are a priori, or the still barer behaviouristic statement that they are firmly accepted, when he characterizes them as true by convention in such a sense.'[3]

It is to the still barer behaviouristic statement that Quine reverts in what is perhaps the most famous of all his essays, 'Two Dogmas of Empiricism', which first appeared in the *Philosophical Review* in January 1951 and was reprinted in 1953 in a collection of his essays entitled *From a Logical Point of View*. The two dogmas, both of which Quine rejects, are first that there is a fundamental distinction between analytic and synthetic propositions and secondly the dogma of reductionism, 'the belief,' as he puts it, 'that each meaningful statement is equivalent to some logical construct upon terms which refer to immediate experience'.[4] An analytic proposition, as we have seen, is one that is supposed to be true solely in virtue of the meaning

[1] ibid., p. 97.
[2] ibid.
[3] ibid, p. 99.
[4] *From a Logical Point of View*, p. 20.

of the signs which express it. This applies to the propositions of logic and mathematics, according to the linguistic account of their validity which we have just been discussing, but not to them only. It also applies to semantic propositions like 'All bachelors are unmarried men', which are thought to be convertible into logical truths by an interchange of synonyms. If 'bachelor' just means 'unmarried man', 'All bachelors are unmarried men' can be rewritten as a statement of logical identity. Quine's objection is that we lack any criterion for synonymity. We can say that the expressions 'bachelors' and 'unmarried men' are synonymous if the statement 'All bachelors are unmarried men' is analytic, but then we are going round in a circle. We can say that the two expressions are synonymous if the statement that all bachelors are unmarried men is necessarily true, but again we are caught in a circle, for the function of the word 'necessarily' here is just to imply that the statement which it governs is analytic.

No doubt such procedures are circular. Yet one wants to protest that there is a difference, worth remarking, between statements like 'oculists are eye doctors', which we know to be true as soon as we understand the words, and statements like 'oculists are prosperous', which depend on empirical evidence. Quine admits the difference up to a point, since he allows that 'taken collectively, science has its double dependence upon language and experience'[1] but denies that the distinction can be made in any individual case. This goes with his rejection of the second dogma. Here he wants not only to deny the feasibility of Carnap's original project of translating every item of significant discourse into a language which, in addition to its logical apparatus, contained only references to sense-data, but also to take the much more radical and more questionable step of denying that any statement, taken in isolation, can be confirmed or discredited by the occurrence of sensory events that fall within some special range. The dogmas are connected by the fact that if we could accept the second of them even in its weaker form, we could conceive of an analytic statement as one 'which is vacuously confirmed, *ipso facto*, come what may'.[2]

The alternative which Quine favours is, in his owns words, that 'the totality of our so-called knowledge or beliefs, from the most casual matters of geography and history to the profoundest laws of atomic

[1] ibid., p. 42.
[2] ibid., p. 41.

physics or even of pure mathematics and logic, is a man-made fabric which impinges on experience only along the edges'.[1] This totality is underdetermined by its boundary conditions, so that if it runs counter to experience we have considerable latitude as to the alterations that we should make to bring it back into line. Statements near to the edge, that is, those expressing beliefs which are directly evoked by external stimuli, in yet other words, reports of observation, are relatively secure. They are not sacrosanct; by making adjustments in other areas we can dismiss them as deceptive, reports of hallucinations; but we are unlikely to take this course if the statements in question also command the assent of other observers. For a different reason, the statements that may be said to form the central core of our beliefs, the truths of logic and mathematics, or what we take to be such, perhaps also some very general scientific principles, are unlikely to be disturbed, but they too are not sacrosanct. They can be abandoned or modified, if in face of the breakdown of accepted theories this seems the most economical or reliable way of restoring overall harmony.

But, even on this view, can we not distinguish changes in belief concerning matters of fact and changes in linguistic usage? Is not there a difference between abandoning the statement 'All swans are white' because of our discovery of black swans, and abandoning the statement 'A part is never equal to the whole' because our criterion of equality changes when it applies to infinite numbers? Quine would not, I think, dispute that there is a difference in the two cases but would not contrast them in the same way. He would treat the examples as showing that there are various reasons for which one might come to dissent from a sentence to which one had previously assented. In general, Quine prefers to talk of linguistic behaviour, interpreted by evidences of assent or dissent to various formulations, than to talk of meaning. In his most considerable book, *Word and Object*, which appeared in 1960, he does allow himself to talk of stimulus-meaning, but defines it in terms of the class of stimulations that would prompt a speaker's assent to or dissent from a given sentence at a given date.[2] He is even willing to speak of terms as 'stimulous-synomous' for a given speaker on the basis of their having the same stimulus-meaning for him when treated as sentences,[3] and

[1] ibid., p. 42.
[2] *Word and Object*, pp. 32–3.
[3] ibid., pp. 54–5.

to countenance the usage of 'stimulus-analytic' for sentences to which every speaker of the language in question is disposed to assent. In a later work, *The Roots of Reference*, published in 1974, he relents further to the point of allowing a sentence to be called analytic if everybody to whose mother tongue it belongs 'learns that it is true by learning its words'.[1] He is also willing to 'allow for chains of proof; we would want a recondite sentence to count still as analytic if obtainable by a chain of inferences each of which is individually assured by the learning of the words'.[2] This is a strong criterion which should perhaps be relativized to persons, since not *everybody* can follow even the simplest chain of proof. On a liberal interpretation it would put some logic back into the grasp of analyticity; some, but not all, for as Quine himself points out, disputed propositions, such as the law of excluded middle, would have to count as synthetic.

In another well-known essay, 'On What There Is', which appeared in the *Review of Metaphysics* in 1948 and is also reprinted in *From a Logical Point of View*, Quine coined what has become a well-known slogan that to be is to be the value of a variable. This may sound mysterious, but it is no more than a development of Russell's theory of descriptions. It will be remembered that this theory supplied a method of transmuting nominative phrases into predicates. Quine simply extended it to the point of eliminating all singular terms. Proper names succumb to the device of treating 'being identical with so and so' as a unique descriptive predicate, and pronouns and other demonstratives are replaced by individuating descriptions, selected in accordance with the context. It is not claimed that this regimentation, as Quine puts it, of our ordinary way of speaking yields perfect translations of the sentences to which it is applied, but it is said to yield paraphrases, which are adequate in the sense that they comport no loss of information. The result is that we obtain a language in which the only way of referring to objects is indefinitely, through the use of signs which stand for quantified variables. It follows that the things over which the variables of such regimented discourse range are the only ones that it allows any title to existence, and the question what particular things there are is turned into the question what things actually satisfy the predicates with which the signs for quantified variables are coupled. This explains Quine's saying that to be is to be the value of a variable.

[1] *The Roots of Reference*, p. 79.
[2] ibid., pp. 79–80.

As Quine himself recognizes, this is an account of what there is, only if there is what there is said to be. What he claims to have provided is, as he puts it, a criterion of ontological commitment. A theory, in the broad sense, used by Quine, in which any set of assertions and their logical consequences is said to constitute a theory, is ontologically committed to the sorts of entities over which its variables range, and this will be determined by the predicates which it contains. It follows that the range of entities to which a theory is committed will depend upon the way in which the theory is formulated. In some cases the avoidance of commitments which one finds undesirable will be a more or less simple matter of reparsing, but in others, the more interesting cases, it will turn on the question whether one can find a means of reducing one type of entity to another. Thus, if someone wishes to renounce abstract entities, as Quine once said he did, in a paper called 'Steps Toward a Constructive Nominalism' which he and Nelson Goodman published in the *Journal of Symbolic Logic* in 1947, he will have to avoid quantifying over properties or classes, and then, as this paper showed, he will need considerable ingenuity in order to be able to devise the rough equivalent of even so humdrum a statement as that there are more dogs than cats. In his more recent writings, Quine has given up this austere nominalism, on the ground that it does not allow for the amount of classical mathematics which one is obliged to accept if one wishes to do justice to contemporary science, and he now admits a hierarchy of classes into his ontology. He believes that classes can do all the respectable work for which properties might be thought to be needed, and he thinks that classes are to be preferred to properties because, unlike properties, they are provided with a clear criterion of identity, a class A being identical with a class B if and only if A and B have the same members.

Since Quine conceives of quantification as ranging over objects rather than linguistic expressions, except in the cases where linguistic expressions are themselves treated as objects, it is important for his purpose that the functions which take these objects as values should be well behaved, in the sense that they do not allow anything to be true of an object under one designation which is not true of it under another. But, notoriously, there are areas, both of ordinary and of philosophical discourse, in which this condition is not satisfied. One conspicuous class of cases results from the use of modal operators like 'necessarily'. To take one of Quine's own examples, the number nine is identical with the number of the planets, but while '9 is necessarily greater than 7' would commonly pass for a true statement, 'The number of the planets is necessarily greater than 7' would commonly be thought to be false. More familiar instances are supplied by indirect discourse and by the use of words which stand for what Russell called propositional attitudes. Thus, to adapt another of Quine's examples, I may believe that the man who stole such and such documents is a spy, and yet not believe that my respectable neighbour is a spy, though in fact it was my respectable neighbour who stole the documents. Consequently, 'being believed by me to be a spy' is true of this man under one description and false under another.

The difficulty about modal operators is not serious for Quine, since his rejection of the analytic-synthetic distinction enables him to do without them. He does indeed countenance talk about possibilities, in that we can speak significantly not only about what does happen but also about what would happen if the appropriate conditions were realized; but he holds that such conditional statements can be resolved into statements about dispositions and, less plausibly in my view, that statements about dispositions can be resolved into statements about the structure of the objects to which the dispositions are ascribed, these attributions of structure being themselves derived, in many cases, from theories about the constitution of 'natural kinds' to which the objects belong. As for propositional attitudes, he shows that we can deal with the example concerning the spy by having me believe *of* the thief of the documents that he is a spy, rather than believe *that* the thief of the documents is one. For in the first case, if the thief is in fact my neighbour, my ignorance of this fact will not prevent its being true *of* my neighbour that I believe him to be a spy, while it will remain false that I believe *that* my neighbour is a spy if this is taken, as it naturally would be, as a description of the content of my belief. In the case which allows the substitution I am said to be construing belief transparently; in the other more normal case I am said to be construing it opaquely. It would suit Quine for belief always to be construed transparently, but he does not think this feasible.[1] What would please him most of all would be to resolve all talk about propositional attitudes into talk about the constitution and

[1] cf. *Word and Object*, p. 149.

behaviour of the persons who have them, where the references to behaviour should be taken as implying no more than that the persons in question make, or are disposed to make, certain physical movements. But neither he nor anyone else has found a way of overcoming all the obvious difficulties to which such a programme is exposed.

A fact which emerges in *Word and Object* and also in Quine's more recent work, especially his *Ontological Relativity and Other Essays*, which appeared in 1969, is that his distaste for the concept of synonymity reflects a wider philosophical standpoint. He holds that there is bound to be a radical indeterminacy in any translation from one language to another, or even from one sentence to another within the same natural language. The argument for this view was first set out in the opening chapter of *Word and Object*. A linguist, studying a native language, notes that a native says 'Gavagai' when a rabbit runs past. After making further experiments, he forms the hypothesis that 'Gavagai' is the native word for a rabbit. But this hypothesis can never be fully confirmed. For any evidence that went to show that 'Gavagai' referred to a rabbit would be equally consistent with its referring to rabbithood, or to rabbit, where 'rabbit' is construed as a bulk term, or to a rabbit-stage, that is to say a temporal slice of a rabbit, or to an undetached rabbit part. The linguist would, indeed, try to remove these uncertainties by asking questions about number and identity, but in order to interpret the answers to these questions he has to form what Quine calls analytical hypotheses about the semantical structure of the language which he is investigating; and a different chain of such hypotheses would still lead to a different interpretation of his subject's meaning, which would be equally in accordance with all his data.

It might be suggested that the linguist's difficulties were simply due to his having to penetrate the native language from the outside. If he were bilingual there would be no problem. But Quine will not accept this easy way out. He argues that the same problem arises in interpreting the utterances of those who speak the same language as oneself. We assume a community of meaning, because we assent to the same sentences in the same observable situations as in the case of the native's 'Gavagai'. At least, it may be said, one knows what one means oneself, but Quine seems unwilling to concede this, since he speaks of semantics as being 'vitiated by a pernicious mentalism so long as we regard a man's semantics as somehow determinate in his mind beyond what might be implicit in his dispositions to overt behaviour'.[1] I feel bound to remark that this surrender to behaviourism does not appear to be the outcome of any decisive argument.

The indeterminacy of translation goes together, in Quine's view, with what he calls 'Ontological Relativity'. Let us assume, what may indeed be questioned, that we can make out a good case for accepting all the predicates, which delimit our ontological commitments. We may still be mistaken on particular occasions in judging whether they are satisfied, and further predicates may be added to them. There may be kinds of objects that have not yet come within our ken. It remains true, however, that whatever does come within our ken must be covered by our stock of concepts, for the question of its existence or non-existence to have any significance. But then the considerations which dictate the indeterminacy of translation come into play. Since our theories are under-determined by the experiences which give rise to them, quite different accounts of what there is, each with its own way of interpreting the evidence, may be equally in accord with the evidence. It would, indeed, seem that theories which were alike in provoking assent or dissent in all conceivable circumstances would have to be regarded as equivalent, according to Quine's behavioural criteria of meaning, but this still leaves him free to hold that there can be a radical difference between physical theories, each of which accommodates all the relevant observations that actually have been or will be recorded. In that case, he argues, there is no sense in asking which theory represents the world as it really is. We cannot even compare them except in terms of a common background theory, and to this theory also there will be alternatives, though to see them as alternatives we have to set them against a further background. The relativity is inescapable.

But surely physical objects must figure in all our theories in one guise or another, if we are to do justice to our experience? Quine's answer is yes, in practice, though he represents it as a matter of convenience. 'As an empiricist,' he says towards the end of 'Two Dogmas of Empiricism', 'I continue to think of the conceptual scheme of science as a tool, ultimately, for predicting future experience in the light of past experience. Physical objects are conceptually imported into the situation as convenient interme-

[1] *Ontological Relativity*, p. 27.

diaries – not by definition in terms of experience, but simply as irreducible posits comparable, epistemologically, to the gods of Homer. For my part I do, *qua* lay physicist, believe in physical objects and not in Homer's gods; and I consider it a scientific error to believe otherwise. But in point of epistemological footing the physical objects and the gods differ only in degree and not in kind. Both sorts of entities enter our conception only as cultural posits. The myth of physical objects is epistemologically superior to most in that it has proved more efficacious than other myths as a device for working a manageable structure into the flux of experience.'[1]

We must not be misled by this remarkable passage into supposing that Quine considers us able to describe the flux of experience independently of making any cultural posits, or even that he allows us any genuine alternative to throwing in our lot with the physicists. Thus, he declines to start out with sense-data on the ground that they do not cohere as an autonomous domain, and goes so far as to maintain that it is only by positing physical objects that we obtain any data to systematize.

This opting for physicalism divides Quine from James and Lewis, but does not sever his attachment to pragmatism. In fact, the chief interest of his thesis of Ontological Relativity is that it is pragmatic. It brings ontology into prominence, but then takes away its importance. If, in the last resort, I cannot find out whether my neighbour is referring to rabbits, or to rabbit-stages, or to rabbit parts, or to regions of space-time with rabbity properties, and if my observations are equally well catered for under each of these interpretations, then the fact that I am theoretically able to differentiate between them is not of much consequence. This would be even more obvious, if it could be convincingly established that my uncertainty covered not only my neighbour's utterances but my own. The moral, which Quine himself does not explicitly draw, is that once we have laid down constraints on what there can be, we are left only with the technical question whether, and if so how, one type of entity is reducible to another. The difficulty for the pragmatist, and indeed for any philosopher, is to make out a case for the constraints.

---

[1] *From A Logical Point of View*, p. 44.

Nelson Goodman

A philosopher who has collaborated on equal terms with Quine, resembling him in his command of logic and readiness to make it serve philosophy, but having a style and method, opinions and interests, of his own, is Nelson Goodman, to whose work we have already had occasion to refer. Goodman, who was born in 1906, was an undergraduate and a graduate at Harvard and taught at Tufts, the University of Pennsylvania and Brandeis before returning to Harvard as a professor. His doctoral thesis at Harvard, completed in 1940 and entitled *A Study of Qualities*, began as a critical study of Carnap's *Der Logische Aufbau der Welt*. It was very extensively revised and expanded before being published in 1951 under the more appropriate title of *The Structure of Appearance*. A second edition, containing various corrections and improvements, appeared in 1966. In the meantime he had published *Fact, Fiction and Forecast*, which mainly consisted in a series of three Shearman Lectures delivered in 1953 at University College, London. The book appeared in 1955, and a second edition, with few alterations, in 1965. The acceptance of an invitation to give the John Locke Lectures at Oxford in 1962 led to the publication six years later of Goodman's *Languages of Art*. A collection of his papers entitled *Problems and Projects* appeared in 1972 and his latest work, *Ways of Worldmaking*, in 1978.

Goodman's approach to philosophy is admirably illustrated in the exordium to his London lectures, which now appears as the second chapter of *Fact, Fiction and Forecast*. Having made a plea for clarity, he remarks that 'in the absence of any convenient and reliable criterion of what is clear, the individual thinker can only search his philosophic conscience'.[1] Goodman's own philosophical conscience is exceptionally strict. Among the things that seem to him 'inacceptable without explanation are powers or dispositions, counterfactual assertions, entities or experiences that are possible but not actual, neutrinos, angels, devils and classes'. His rejection of classes constitutes the nominalism which runs throughout his work. I shall have more to say about it presently. Such particles as neutrinos he considers to be 'as yet beyond our philosophical reach'. It is 'the problems of dispositions, counterfactuals and possibles' that he will be attacking in the lectures. But here again his conscience comes into

[1] *Fact, Fiction and Forecast*, 2nd edn, p. 32.

play by limiting his armoury with which these problems can legitimately be attacked. 'For example,' he says, 'I shall not rely on the distinction between causal connections and accidental correlations, or on the distinction between essential and artificial kinds, or on the distinction between analytic and synthetic statements. You may decry some of these scruples and protest that there are more things in heaven and earth than are dreamt of in my philosophy. I am concerned, rather, that there should not be more things dreamt of in my philosophy than there are in heaven or earth.'[1]

Preceding the Shearman Lectures in *Fact, Fiction and Forecast* is an earlier paper of Goodman's on 'Counterfactual Conditionals'. We have seen that conditionals of this sort play a prominent part in the philosophy of C. I. Lewis and also that they are not truth-functional. The conditional is not to be held true just in case its antecedent is false. In cases where the consequent is an observation-statement, the antecedent may be required only for putting a hypothetical observer in a position where the observation can be made, and in that event the case can be treated as a 'projection' of actual cases in which such observations actually are made, though we shall see that this procedure is not without difficulties of its own. More frequently what makes the conditional acceptable is that there is a suitable connection between the antecedent and the consequent. But how is this connection to be specified? Goodman's strategy was to construe the conditional as asserting the truth of a set of conditions which are such that when the statements affirming them are conjoined with the antecedent, the consequent logically follows. He failed, however, to discover any watertight procedure of selecting the relevant conditions. Clearly the formula cannot be 'all true statements' or even 'some true statements', for in the second case it might and in the first it would have to include the negation of the antecedent, which would make the premiss contradictory. We have therefore to stipulate that the conditions chosen be logically compatible with the antecedent. But Goodman had no difficulty in showing that this was insufficient. The formula at which he eventually arrived, after running through an ingenious array of counter-examples to every suggestion that he had previously considered, was one of daunting complexity but still failed to accomplish its purpose. One obstacle was the need to exclude true statements which although logically compatible with the antecedent

---

[1] ibid., p. 34.

were such that the truth of the antecedent would have cost them their truth. To put it more positively, it is required of the statements which are to join the antecedent in entailing the consequent that they be 'co-tenable' with the antecedent. But now we fall into a circle for, as Goodman puts it, 'cotenability is defined in terms of counterfactuals, yet the meaning of counterfactuals is defined in terms of cotenability'.[1] Another obstacle lay in the need to speak of one statement as leading by law to another, for this is a notion that calls for explanation. The best that Goodman was able to offer was that 'A general statement is lawlike if and only if it is acceptable prior to the determination of all its instances'.[2] This is not objectionable in itself but again calls for further explanation. We need to have some principle for discriminating between the predicates which can legitimately be projected from known to unknown cases and those which cannot. In short, as Goodman sees, we have made our way into the heart of the problem of induction.

Goodman entitled the second of his London lectures 'The New Riddle of Induction' in the belief that he had shifted the problem from 'Why does a positive instance of a hypothesis give any ground for predicting further instances?', which was the question raised by Hume, to 'What is a positive instance of a hypothesis?' and thence to the question 'What hypotheses are confirmed by their positive instances?'[3] In fact, the shift was mainly a matter of form. Hume had already shown that there was no sort of necessity which would safeguard any passage from past to future experience. He thought that our ventures into the unknown from the known were the outcome of habit, but he did not think that one habit was as good as another, or that conflicting procedures could not be equally consistent with our past experience. What Goodman did was to dramatize this last fact by devising a means of representing the point at which a universal and so far unviolated hypothesis fails as one at which two universal hypotheses diverge. He achieved this by taking the example 'All emeralds are green' and introducing the predicate 'grue', which applies to anything just in case it is examined before a time t and found to be green, or not so examined and blue. Then evidently the fact that all emeralds examined before t have turned out to be green is

[1] ibid., p. 16.
[2] ibid., p. 22.
[3] ibid., p. 81.

255

equally consistent with the mutually incompatible hypotheses that all emeralds are green and that all emeralds are grue. To the objection that 'grue' is not a genuinely qualitative predicate like 'green' because it was introduced by reference to a specific time, Goodman had the perfectly good answer that it depends on what you start with. If 'grue' and its converse 'bleen' are taken as primitive, 'blue' and 'green' become positional. Clearly this is a device that could take various other forms. One may be less inclined to find fault with it when one realizes that it merely highlights the fact that qualitative and quantitative predicates are equally vulnerable. No one wishes to deny that a curve which fits a finite number of points can be prolonged in any number of ways.

Goodman's merit is to have shown, in his own words, first 'that a whole cluster of troublesome problems concerning dispositions and possibility can be reduced to this problem of projection' and secondly that 'lawlike or projective hypotheses cannot be distinguished on any merely syntactical grounds or even on the ground that these hypotheses are somehow purely general in meaning'.[1] His own proposal for distinguishing them is to give preference among unviolated but rival hypotheses to those that are the more firmly 'entrenched', where the degree of their entrenchment is made to depend on the extent to which their antecedents and consequents have been projected in the past. The introduction of new predicates is legitimized by their kinship with those that are already established. With the difference that conformity with past experience is tied in an original way to our linguistic habits, this is just a modernization of the position taken by Hume. I am not implying that it is any the worse for that.

There is a fainter echo of Hume in Goodman's *The Structure of Appearance*, which is a formidable attempt to construct a phenomenalist system on a basis which is both nominalist and as economical as possible. What Goodman understands by nominalism is most clearly explained in an essay called 'A World of Individuals' which is reprinted in his *Problems and Projects*. It amounts, in fact, to the exclusion of classes. What is objectionable about the notion of a class is that it allows a distinction of entities without a distinction of content. For instance, the departments of France and the provinces of France would be reckoned as two different classes, yet they are

[1] ibid., p. 83.

made up of the same territory. According to the nominalist, there is just one entity here which is the sum of whatever pieces of land are taken as the basic individuals. As Goodman construes the term, any sum of individuals is itself an individual, whether or not its parts are cohesive in time or space, and anything counts as an individual which can figure as an element in a world that can be described as 'made up of entities no two of which break down into exactly the same entities'.[1] In their earlier paper, 'Steps Toward a Constructive Nominalism', Goodman and Quine had begun with the statement 'We do not believe in abstract entities',[2] but at a later stage Goodman could no longer detect any clear distinction between the abstract and the concrete. All he required, at whatever mathematical cost, was the substitution of individuals for classes, with the relation of overlapping between individuals replacing that of class membership.

Another distinction which is made in *The Structure of Appearance* is that between a particularistic and a realistic system. A particularistic system is one like that of Carnap's *Aufbau*, which starts from undifferentiated elements of experience and proceeds to construct sensory qualities; a realistic system is one that starts with qualia which it combines into what Goodman calls 'concreta'. Goodman regards either starting-point as legitimate, but after criticizing the details of Carnap's constructions, himself develops a realistic system with colours, places and times as primitive qualia. He admits the qualia of other sense-modalities, such as sounds and smells, as primitive also, but the sensory world which he takes the trouble to develop is purely visual. Besides the relation of overlapping he makes use of a relation of togetherness which combines one quale with the sum of two others, say a colour-spot with a time or a colour with a place-time. A mere togetherness of the three qualia would not suffice to form a concretum, for the colour might be together with the place, and separately with the time, without being at the place at the time. Because they are not additive in the way that colour is, visual sizes and shapes are not treated as basic qualia but defined with the help of the primitive predicate of being of equal aggregate size. The ways in which qualia match are then ingeniously ordered into a topology of quality.

[1] *Problems and Projects*, pp. 159–60.
[2] ibid., p. 173.

It is noteworthy that Goodman, unlike Carnap in the *Aufbau*, and indeed unlike the usual run of phenomenalists, does not claim any priority for his system in the order of knowledge. On the contrary, he argues[1] that the question whether there is any difference in this respect between the choice of a phenomenalistic or a physicalistic basis is thoroughly confused. Here I am not in agreement. I have tried to make a case for the priority of a phenomenalistic basis in the fourth and fifth chapters of my book *The Central Questions of Philosophy*. On the other hand, while I think that a physical world could not be logically constructed on this basis, but only justifiably posited, Goodman sees this as an open question. He thinks it unclear what the criteria of reduction are, and also whether 'the physical world that we are to explain is the somewhat inconsistent world of common sense and stale science or the very abstruse and continually revised world of the latest physical theory'.[2] In any event, his purpose in writing the book was not to pave the way for any such endeavour but simply to analyse phenomena. It bears out his view of philosophy as 'having the function of clearing away perplexity and confusion'.[3]

Languages of Art is concerned, as its title might suggest, with forms of symbolization. One of its principal aims is to stress the analogy, rather than make out the distinctions, between pictorial representation and verbal description. Exemplification and expression are intimately related, as modes of symbolization, to representation and description, though they run in opposite directions, representation and description relating a symbol to things it applies to, exemplification relating the symbol to a label that denotes it literally, and expression relating the symbol to a label that denotes it metaphorically.[4] Thus, a picture may exemplify what 'grey' denotes and express what is labelled 'sad'. When it comes to distinguishing between descriptions and depictions, Goodman insists that nothing depends on the internal structure of a symbol. He argues convincingly against making resemblance a criterion of representation or imposing structural similarity as a requirement upon language.[5] He thinks that a too facile distinction between the cognitive and the emotive has prevented us from seeing that 'in aesthetic experience

[1] See *The Structure of Appearance*, 2nd ed., pp. 136–40.
[2] ibid., p. 379.
[3] ibid., p. xvii.
[4] *Languages of Art*, p. 92.
[5] ibid., p. 231.

the emotions function cognitively'.[1] He lists four 'symptoms of the aesthetic', of which the most important is the feature which distinguishes systems that exemplify from those that denote. These symptoms are not meant to be marks of merit. When it comes to aesthetic values, Goodman effects a 'subsumption of aesthetic under cognitive excellence'.[2]

Much of *Languages of Art* is difficult reading, especially the long chapter in which Goodman develops his 'Theory of Notation', but an appreciation of its general trend may make one more receptive to Goodman's most recent book, *Ways of Worldmaking*, of which he claims in the preface that it 'is at odds with rationalism and empiricism alike, with materialism and idealism and dualism, with essentialism and existentialism, with mechanism and vitalism, with mysticism and scientism, and with most other ardent doctrines'.[3] In fact, it is not so much at odds with these doctrines as unconcerned with them, though it may reject some of them by implication. What it is, as the author fairly describes it, is 'a radical relativism under rigorous restraints, that eventuates in something akin to irrealism'.[4]

The book is short, amounting with the foreword to 142 pages, and consisting of seven chapters composed over a period of seven years. The argument flows from a paragraph in the first chapter, an essay written in honour of Ernst Cassirer (1874–1945).[5] 'Frames of reference, though,' it runs, 'seem to belong less to what is described than to systems of description: and each of the two statements [namely, "The Sun always moves" and "The Sun never moves"] relates what is described to such a system. If I ask about the world, you can offer to tell me how it is under one or more frames of reference, but if I insist that you tell me how it is apart from all frames, what can you say? We are confined to ways of describing whatever is described. Our universe, so to speak, consists of these ways rather than of a world or of worlds.'[6]

Goodman makes it clear that he is not speaking of possible worlds. He wants to say that there are many actual worlds or rather, as he would prefer to see it put, that there are many world-versions, which

[1] ibid., p. 248.
[2] ibid., p. 259.
[3] *Ways of Worldmaking*, p. x.
[4] ibid.
[5] His principal works included *Philosophy of Symbolic Forms* and *Language and Myth*.
[6] op. cit., pp. 2–3.

cannot be combined or reduced into one. World-versions are made not out of nothing but out of one another by processes of taking things apart and putting them differently together, by elimination or addition of entities, by the shifts of emphasis that occur most conspicuously in the arts, by reordering and reshaping. Psychological experiments amply prove that what we might suppose to be given in perception is very much the fruit of our own construction. Neither does truth provide the straightforward constraint that one might naïvely suppose. 'Truth,' in Goodman's view, 'far from being a solemn and severe master, is a docile and obedient servant. The scientist who supposes that he is single-mindedly dedicated to the search for truth deceives himself. He is unconcerned with the trivial truths he could grind out endlessly: and he looks to the multifaceted and irregular results of observations for little more than suggestions of overall structures and significant generalizations. He seeks system, simplicity, scope; and when satisfied on these scores he tailors truth to fit. He as much decrees as discovers the laws he sets forth, as much designs as discerns the patterns he delineates.'[1]

Moreover, Goodman conceives of truth, or rather of literal truth, as belonging only to what is literally said. But a world, in his view, can also be made by what is said metaphorically or by what is not said at all but, as in the case of works of art, exemplified or expressed. To avoid the risk of confusion, Goodman prefers not to attribute truth to pictures or other 'non verbal versions'. Nevertheless, he maintains that 'much the same considerations count for pictures as for the concepts or predicates of a theory: their relevance and their revelations, their force and their fit – in sum their *rightness*'.[2] Rightness is what generally matters. We should do better to speak of theories as right or wrong than of pictures as true or false.[3]

We need then to know in what rightness is deemed to consist. Goodman remarks, what is anyhow obvious, that he is not using the term in its moral sense, but when it comes to telling us how he is using it he is more epigrammatic than explicit. One point that is made clearly is that rightness covers both deductive and inductive validity. Inductive validity is explained as in *Fact, Fiction and Forecast* and deductive validity in much the same fashion as consisting of

[1] ibid., p. 18.
[2] ibid., p. 19.
[3] ibid.

'conformity with rules of inference – rules that codify deductive practice in accepting or rejecting particular inferences'.[1] It is required both of deductive and inductive rightness that the premisses be true, but only of deductive rightness and indeed deductive validity that it proceeds to true conclusions. Credibility and coherence are tentatively commended as tests for truth. Right representation is referred to sampling and non-verbal sampling made to comply with something like the canons of induction. So 'rightness of design, colour, harmonics – fairness of a work as a sample of such features – is tested by our success in discovering and applying what is exemplified. What counts as success in achieving accord depends upon what our habits, progressively modified in the face of new encounters and new proposals, adopt as projectible kinds.'[2] From this we may infer, correctly, that Goodman does not wish to align the distinction between truth in the sciences and rightness in the arts with that between the objective and the subjective. We are still left wondering what constitutes a single world-version, whether it be a particular picture, or an artist's entire output, or the works belonging to some 'period' of his painting, or the work of some whole school, but perhaps these are questions to which it would be wrong to look for a determinate answer.

No realist in his right mind would claim that the world is objective in a sense that implied that it was truly describable in a way that was independent of all methods of describing it. The most he would claim is that some descriptions were objectively true, in the sense that they were made true by states of affairs which obtained independently of our having any cognizance of them. What would most shock him in Goodman's position, and perhaps some irrealists also, is the contention that there are incompatible truths. Among the examples that Goodman gives are the statements 1. 'The earth always stands still' and 2. 'The earth dances the role of Petrouchka'.[3] He acknowledges that these statements would generally be construed as elliptical and that when they are expanded, say, into 1. 'In the Ptolemaic system, the earth stands always still' and 2. 'In a certain Stravinsky-Fokine-like system, the earth dances the role of Petrouchka', the conflict disappears. He argues, however, that this method effects too much,

[1] ibid., p. 125.
[2] ibid., p. 137.
[3] ibid., p. 111.

adducing as illustrations the two statements 'The kings of Sparta had two votes' and 'The kings of Sparta had only one vote' and expanding them into 'According to Herodotus, the kings of Sparta had two votes' and 'According to Thucydides, the kings of Sparta had only one vote'. The question is whether this is a fair analogy. For my own part, I am strongly inclined to say that whereas there is no fact of the matter in the first pair of cases, independently of relativization to a system, there is in the second. Either Herodotus or Thucydides was mistaken and it is the ancient historian's business to try to find further evidence which will favour one version or the other, or perhaps suggest that both were wrong. What it cannot indicate, surely, is that both were right, albeit in different actual worlds.

An example of which Goodman makes frequent use is the definition of a geometrical point. In *Ways of Worldmaking* he cites the two statements 'Every point is made up of a vertical and a horizontal line' and 'No points are made up of lines or anything else'.[1] Elsewhere he refers to the conception of a point as a pair of diagonals and to Whitehead's definition of it as a class of series of volumes.[2] These characterizations of points are not only not synonymous; they do not even have the same extensions, though the systems to which they severally belong can be shown to be isomorphic. Does this show that there are incompatible truths? The standard answer would be that we are presented here not with conflicting statements of fact but with a choice of different conventions. Goodman's riposte to this is if 'we strip off all layers of convention – all differences – among ways of describing'[3] a space, nothing will be left. My own views about the role of conventions in mathematics are no longer firm enough for me to venture to adjudicate this dispute. It should, however, be remarked that the method that led to Whitehead's definition, his so-called 'Principle of Extensive Abstraction', was at least designed to give such terms as geometrical points and lines an empirical meaning.[4]

Michael Dummett

A philosopher who is inclined to share Goodman's hostility to

[1] ibid., p. 114.
[2] cf. A. N. Whitehead, *The Principles of Natural Knowledge*, Part III.
[3] op. cit., p. 118.
[4] cf. C. D. Broad, *Scientific Thought*, Chapter I.

realism, without appearing to have any sympathy for other aspects of Goodman's philosophical thought, is Michael Dummett, who currently holds the Chair of Logic at Oxford. Dummett was born in 1925. He was educated at Winchester and Christ Church and was a Fellow of All Souls and Reader in the Philosophy of Mathematics at Oxford before his election to the professorship in 1978. His first published book, running to nearly 700 pages and appearing in 1973, was a study of Frege which was primarily concerned with Frege's philosophy of language. A second volume, dealing with Frege's philosophy of mathematics, is in preparation. In the meantime Dummett has published a volume in the series of *Oxford Logic Guides* entitled *Elements of Intuitionism* and a collection of essays and reviews entitled *Truth and Other Enigmas*. These works, each of more than 450 pages, appeared respectively in 1977 and 1978. Dummett has also since published a comprehensive history of the card-game of tarot and a separate volume setting out the rules of *Twelve Tarot Games*.

Truth and Other Enigmas contains the review of Goodman's *The Structure of Appearance* which Dummett published in *Mind* in 1955, together with two articles on 'Nominalism' and 'Constructionalism', earlier versions of which were included in the review but excised for reasons of space. While he pays tribute to Goodman's mastery of logic, he is severely critical not only of many details of Goodman's system but of the value of the whole enterprise. He believes, in spite of Goodman's disclaimer and his choice of a realistic basis for his construction, that Goodman continues to renounce abstract entities, and he suggests that the different treatment accorded to the concepts of colour and shape is due to the fact that whereas a colour like 'red' can be construed in Quine's materialistic system as a sum total of molecule-moments,[1] and in Goodman's particularistic system as a sum total of presentations, a shape like 'square' cannot. Dummett thinks that the mistake that both Quine and Goodman have made is to look for the sense of such terms in isolation rather than discover it, as Frege suggested, in an account of the sense of the sentences in which they occur.

Dummett also objects to what he regards as Goodman's failure to harmonize his axiom of matching, employed as a criterion for the identity of colour qualia, with his declaration that attributions of

[1] *Truth and Other Enigmas*, p. 46.

predicates to qualia are settled by revocable decrees, and he finds it a blemish in the system both that the ordering of qualia depends in certain cases on contingent features of experience and that Goodman's phenomenalistic language is not one that anyone could learn to use, unless he were already in possession of concepts which are not primitive in the system but only introducible, if at all, at a later stage. His chief objection, however, is more general and is set out as follows in the last paragraph of the essay on 'Constructionalism'.

'The constructionalist's desire to turn philosophy into an exact science leads him at every point to substitute tasks whose criteria for success are precise for those in which success is impossible to assess with complete objectivity: while it is true that if philosophy consisted wholly in tasks of the kind the constructionalist sets himself, it would be an exact science, he forgets to ask at each point what value or interest lies in performing those tasks at all. When I know, for instance, that, provided the facts are sufficiently accommodating (e.g. that each category will have a describable peculiarity enabling me to pick it out), I should be able to define by means of a certain logical vocabulary the expression "is a colour" in terms of a relation which has not been at all precisely described but is something like the union of such relations as looking the same colour as, seeming to be simultaneous, and so on, then I certainly do not understand the term "colour" any better; for it is, to say the least, no more obscure to me than "matches". What then have I learned? What, for example, do I understand about the world that I did not understand before?'[1] And Dummett goes on to reject the analogy with mathematics, which has a different interest and where such ways of solving its problems would anyhow not be tolerated.

At the same time, Dummett's own approach to philosophy proceeds from his study of a fundamental division in the philosophy of mathematics: that between the Platonist, who holds that every mathematical statement has a determinate truth-value, whether or not we are in a position to say what it is, and the intuitionist, who holds that we are not entitled to count a mathematical statement as true or false unless we have some evidence counting for or against it. Dummett, for whom the chief purpose of philosophy is to arrive at a satisfactory theory of meaning, sees that this dispute within the philosophy of mathematics derives from different conceptions of

[1] ibid., p. 64.

meaning, which have a more general application. The Platonist represents the realist, for whom to understand a statement is simply to know its truth-conditions. 'For the anti-realist,' as Dummett puts it, 'an understanding of a statement [belonging to some disputed class] consists in knowing what counts as evidence adequate for the assertion of the statement, and the truth of the statement can consist only in the existence of such evidence.'[1] The attractions and drawbacks of anti-realism are very much the same as those that we have seen to be attendant on the adoption of the principle of verifiability as a criterion of meaning. Dummett does not come out decisively on either side, though his sympathies, especially in the area of mathematics, appear to incline towards the anti-realists.

Whatever his estimation of Frege's realistic view of the truths of mathematics, Dummett's verdict on Frege's philosophy of language is almost wholly favourable. The one serious mistake that he attributes to him is that of treating sentences as complex proper names, with the result that the truth-values, to which it was reasonable, in Dummett's view, for Frege to construe sentences as referring, are counted as two mysterious objects, The True and The False. No doubt this was part of what Ryle had in mind when he referred, as we have seen, to Frege's truth-values as queer contraptions. This blemish in Frege's theory is, however, taken by Dummett to be more than counterbalanced by the emphasis placed by Frege on sentences as the vehicles of meaning and by the importance of his distinction between sense and reference.

One controversial point on which Dummett supports Frege, in my view rightly, against some contemporary critics is that of Frege's treatment of proper names. Frege's theory is, in Dummett's words, 'that a proper name, if it is to be considered as having a determinate sense, must have associated with it a specific criterion for recognizing a given object as the referent of the name; the referent of the name, if any, is whatever object satisfies that criterion'.[2] Very often, though not invariably, the sense is introduced by means of a definite description. Among those who contest this view is the American philosopher Saul Kripke (*b.* 1941), notably in his article entitled 'Naming and Necessity', which appeared in 1972 in a collection of papers by various authors entitled *Semantics of Natural Language*.

[1] ibid., p. 155.
[2] *Frege, Philosophy of Language*, p. 110.

Kripke distinguishes proper names from definite descriptions by saying that they, unlike descriptions, are what he calls 'rigid designators', and he explains that a rigid designator is one that refers to the same object in every possible world in which that object exists at all. On the other hand there are possible worlds in which a definite description is satisfied by different objects. Thus, to take one of Dummett's examples, while it is true in every possible world that the tutor of Alexander taught Alexander, there are possible worlds in which this tutor is not the philosopher Aristotle. On the other hand the name 'Aristotle', employed in this usage, must refer to the same man in every possible world in which that philosopher exists. This doctrine has what seems to me the clearly false consequence that empirical statements of identity like 'George Eliot was Mary Ann Evans' are necessary truths.

But how are such conclusions reached? How are we to cash this metaphor of possible worlds? What Kripke does, as Dummett succeeds in making clear, is to treat the satisfaction of definite descriptions as a possible property which can then significantly be attributed to any object that one pleases, whether it be real or imaginary. Proper names, on the other hand, are always given the reference, if any, that they have in the actual world and then become credited with properties that they may or may not actually have. Dummett shows that this distinction is quite unwarranted. There is no reason why the reference of definite descriptions should not be construed in the way that Kripke construes the reference of proper names, or indeed the other way round.

It is true that one can attach a sense to saying that Mary Ann Evans might not have written *Middlemarch* but not to saying that she might not have been Mary Ann Evans. The point here, as Dummett sees, is that, with some obvious exceptions, such as 'George Eliot' or 'Giorgione', proper names do not replace antecedently standard designations of the objects that bear them. From this, since every object could be assigned a proper name, Kripke draws the absurd conclusion that the details of its origin furnish every object with a set of necessary properties; as if it were not legitimate to suppose that Mary Ann Evans was born in 1820 rather than in 1819, or to assert that this table might have been made by a different carpenter from the one who actually made it. The reason why 'Mary Ann Evans might not have been Mary Ann Evans' makes no sense is not that we are envisaging the possibility of denying a necessary truth, but precisely that we are not furnished with any criteria for fixing the reference of either occurrence of the proper name.

Essentialism

The conception of rigid designators has impinged upon that of natural kinds. The theory is that objects which are originally grouped under a single heading because they appear to manifest some high degree of similarity are subsequently found to share a common underlying structure. Not only that, but it is their common possession of this structure that serves to explain the phenomena which initially led to their being sorted into different kinds. The inference is then drawn that the meaning of the term by which objects of the kind in question are characterized is such that throughout its use it applies only to objects which possess the common structure. Correspondingly, the possession of this structure is regarded as an essential, or necessary, property of such objects.

One of the ablest exponents of this view is Hilary Putnam, an American philosopher who was born in 1926 and has been a professor of philosophy at Harvard since 1965. He expounds it in several of the essays included in the second volume of his Philosophical Papers, *Mind, Language and Reality*. It figures especially prominently in the long essay 'The Meaning of "Meaning" ', which Putnam first published in the seventh series of Minnesota Studies in the Philosophy of Science in 1975.

Putnam rejects the traditional view that 'to say that something belongs to a natural kind is just to ascribe to it a conjunction of properties'.[1] His first objection to it is that the set of objects which form a natural kind may have abnormal members. He takes the example of lemons, remarking that 'The supposed "defining characteristics" of lemons are: Yellow colour, tart taste, a certain kind of peel, etc',[2] and he then points out that it is not analytically true that all these characteristics belong to every specimen. A green

[1] 'Is Semantics Possible?' in *Mind, Language and Reality*, p. 140.
[2] ibid.

lemon, which failed to turn yellow, might be a rarity, but to speak of such a thing would not be a contradiction in terms.

The obvious answer to this objection, as Putnam sees, is that what the list of characteristics defines is a 'normal member' of the kind in question. If a particular object fails to possess one or more of these characteristics it may still be reckoned a member of the kind, so long as it possesses the others. How far an object may deviate from the norm without forfeiting its membership is a matter for decision. It would seem too that not all properties can be accorded equal weight. Lions are carnivorous quadrupeds, but whereas an object born with only three legs might still be included in the class in virtue of its other characteristics, just as we allow a one-legged man to be an exception to the rule that men are featherless bipeds, an animal that was not carnivorous would most probably not qualify as a lion.

Putnam rejects this rejoinder. He argues first that 'the normal members of the natural kind in question may not really be the ones we *think* are normal'[1] and secondly that 'the characteristics of the natural kind may change with time, possibly due to a change in the conditions without the "essence" changing so much that we want to stop using the same word'.[2] And here, when Putnam speaks of our using the same word, what we must presume him to have in mind is not the use of a word which retains the same spelling but one to which we attach the same meaning.

These two answers have a common source. It is assumed that the meaning of a word which applies to members of a natural kind is uniquely associated with their 'essence', and this allows both for the possibility that at a given time the specimens of the kind that we regard as normal form an untypical sub-class of all those that have this essence, and for the possibility that the manifest properties of the genuinely typical members of the class change in the course of time. The meaning of the word stays constant in either case because of its constant attachment to the essence.

But how is this essence supposed to be determined? Putnam addresses himself to the problem in his essay 'The Meaning of "Meaning" '. The example he takes is that of water. The everyday use of the English word 'water' and its counterparts in other natural languages is said to be fixed extensionally. There are common ways of

---

[1] ibid., p. 142.
[2] 'The Meaning of "Meaning" ', op. cit., pp. 232–3.

268

identifying the stuff, including that of pointing to what are taken to be specimens of it, which Putnam summarizes as constituting the operational definition of the word 'water' and its counterparts. At some time the scientific discovery is made that the chemical composition of the stuff which is regarded as belonging to the extension of these words is H_2O. Then water is to be defined as anything that possesses this chemical composition, which constitutes its essence, and we are asked to believe that this is not only what the words that stand for water must now be understood to mean but that it is what they have always meant, whether those who used them knew it or not.

To enforce his conclusion, Putnam conjures up an imaginary world called 'Twin-Earth' which differs from the actual earth in that the stuff which there satisfies the operational definition of water has a different chemical composition from what it has here, and he uses the expression 'same$_L$' as short for 'same liquid as'. Then his argument runs as follows: 'The operational definition, like the ostensive one, is simply a way of pointing out a standard – pointing out the stuff *in the actual world* such that for *x* to be water, in *any* world, is for *x* to bear the relation same$_L$ to the *normal* members of the class of *local* entities that satisfy the operational definition. "Water" on Twin-Earth is not water, even if it satisfies the operational definition, because it doesn't bear *same*$_L$ to the *local* stuff that satisfies the operational definition, and local stuff that satisfies the operational definition but has a microstructure different from the rest of the local stuff that satisfies the operational definition isn't water either, because it doesn't bear *same*$_L$ to the *normal* examples of the local water.'[1] So 'Once we have discovered that water (in the actual world) is H_2O, *nothing counts as a possible world in which water isn't H_2O*. In particular, if a "logically possible" statement is one that holds in some "logically possible world", *it isn't logically possible that water isn't H_2O*.'[2]

Putnam is himself prepared to extend this argument not only to the instances of all natural kinds but also to instances of artefacts. This may raise special difficulties, but I shall not try to explore them, since I already find the argument which is embodied in his example quite unacceptable. Let me summarize it succinctly. It consists in the following four propositions: 1. *x* is to be counted the same liquid as *y*

[1] ibid., pp. 232–3.
[2] ibid., p. 233.

if and only if specimens of x have the same microstructure as quantities of stuff which are operationally identified as specimens of y: 2. If y is water its specimens have the microstructure H_2O: 3. What is and always has been meant by the English word 'water', and its counterparts in other languages, is anything that has this microstructure, whatever its manifest properties may be: 4. Nothing that has a different microstructure, whatever its manifest properties may be, is such that the word 'water', or its counterparts in other languages, is properly applicable to it.

Of these propositions I believe only the second to be true. I am convinced that the third is false and think it likely that the fourth is also false. There is no need to have recourse to possible worlds. Suppose that in some part of this world we came upon stuff which had the chemical composition H_2O but did not have the properties of falling as rain, allaying thirst, quenching fire and so forth, perhaps even failed to appear in liquid form. I certainly should not call it 'water' and should be surprised if the majority of English speakers did so either. Conversely, I believe that most English speakers would still apply the term 'water' to stuff that had such manifest properties as I have listed, even if it had a different chemical composition. And the same would apply *mutatis mutandis* to speakers of other natural languages.

I take the first of Putnam's propositions to be a proposal, which he is indeed free to make. But if his third and fourth propositions are false it has little to recommend it. My own proposal is that we stick to the facts, which are that we are presented with a set of properties which are habitually found in combination and that so far as we know the stuff in which they are combined invariably has the chemical composition H_2O. It is not necessary, in any sense which I can understand, that these properties should occur together, or that all the specimens of the stuff in which they are combined should have the same chemical composition, or that this composition should satisfy the formula H_2O rather than some other. It is enough for any reasonable purpose that these generalizations should actually hold, and I judge there to be more loss than profit in any attendant talk of essence or necessity or possible worlds. In my opinion, such talk is retrogressive, though currently in vogue. I should be more proud than otherwise if my opposition to it led to my being taken for an old-fashioned empiricist.

Index

ABOUT THE AUTHOR

A. J. AYER was Grote Professor of the Philosophy of Mind and Logic at the University of London from 1946 to 1959 and Wykeham Professor of Logic at the University of Oxford from 1959 to 1978. He has been a fellow of the British Academy since 1952 and holds honorary doctorates from many universities. He is an honorary member of the American Academy of Arts and Sciences and Chevalier of the Légion d'Honneur. He was knighted in 1970. His many published works include *Language, Truth and Logic; The Foundations of Empirical Knowledge; The Problem of Knowledge; The Origins of Pragmatism; Metaphysics and Common Sense; Probability and Evidence; The Central Questions of Philosophy;* and an autobiographical volume, *Part of My Life.*